Commercial Data Mining

Commercial Data Mining

Processing, Analysis and Modeling for Predictive Analytics Projects

David Nettleton

AMSTERDAM • BOSTON • HEIDELBERG • LONDON
NEW YORK • OXFORD • PARIS • SAN DIEGO
SAN FRANCISCO • SINGAPORE • SYDNEY • TOKYO

Morgan Kaufmann is an imprint of Elsevier

Acquiring Editor: Andrea Dierna
Editorial Project Manager: Kaitlin Herbert
Project Manager: Punithavathy Govindaradjane
Designer: Matthew Limbert

Morgan Kaufmann is an imprint of Elsevier
225 Wyman Street, Waltham, MA 02451, USA

Library of Congress Cataloging-in-Publication Data
Nettleton, David, 1963-
    Commercial data mining : processing, analysis and modeling for predictive analytics projects / David Nettleton.
        pages cm
    Includes bibliographical references and index.
    ISBN 978-0-12-416602-8 (paperback)
1. Data mining. 2. Management–Mathematical models. 3. Management–Data processing. I. Title.
    HD30.25.N48 2014
    658′.056312–dc23

                            2013045341

British Library Cataloguing-in-Publication Data
A catalogue record for this book is available from the British Library

ISBN: 978-0-12-416602-8

Printed and bound in the United States of America
14   15   16   17   18   10 9 8 7 6 5 4 3 2 1

For information on all Morgan Kaufmann publications
Visit our Website at www.mkp.com

Contents

Dr. David Nettleton is a contract researcher at the Pompeu Fabra University, Barcelona, Catalonia, Spain, and at the IIIA-CSIC, Bellaterra, Catalonia, Spain.

I would first like to thank the reviewers of the book proposal: Xavier Navarro Arnal, Dr. Anton Dries (KU Leuven, Belgium), Tim Holden (Imagination Technologies, United Kingdom) and Colin Shearer (Advanced Analytic Solutions, IBM). Second, I would like to thank the reviewers of the book manuscript: Dr. Vicenç Torra (IIIA-CSIC, Catalonia, Spain), Tim Holden, Dr. Anton Dries, Joan Gómez Escofet (Autonomous University of Barcelona, Catalonia, Spain), and the anonymous reviewers for their suggestions, corrections, and constructive criticisms, which have helped enhance the content.

Third, I would like to thank the following people and companies for their permission to adapt and include material for the book: IBM, Newprosoft, Professor Ian Witten, Dr. Ricardo Baeza-Yates (Yahoo! Research and Pompeu Fabra University, Catalonia, Spain), Dr. Joan Codina-Filba (Pompeu Fabra University, Catalonia, Spain), Dra. Liliana Calderón Benavides (Autonomous University of Bucaramanga, Columbia), and Néstor Martinez.

I would also like to thank Kaitlin Herbert and Andrea Dierna of Morgan Kaufmann Publishers for their belief in this project and their support throughout the preparation of the book.

Finally, I would like to thank my supporting institutions: Pompeu Fabra University, Catalonia, Spain, and the IIIA-CSIC, Catalonia, Spain.

Chapter 1

Introduction

This book is intended to benefit a wide audience, from those who have limited experience in commercial data analysis to those who already analyze commercial data, offering a vision of the whole process and its related topics. The author includes material from over 20 years of professional business experience as well as a diversity of research projects he was involved in, in order to enrich the content and give an original approach to commercial data analysis. In the appendix, practical case studies derived from real-world projects are used to illustrate the concepts and techniques that are explained throughout the book. Numerous references are included for those readers who wish to go into greater depth about a given topic.

Many of the methods, techniques, and ideas presented, such as data quality, data mart, customer relationship management, data sources, and Internet searches, can be applied by small business owners, freelance professionals, or medium to large-sized companies. The reader will see that it is not a prerequisite to have large volumes of data, and many tools used for data analysis are available for a nominal cost.

Although the steps in Chapters 2 through 10 can be carried out sequentially, note that, in practice, aspects such as data sources, data representation, and data quality are often carried out in parallel and reiteratively. This also applies to the variable/factor selection, analysis, and modeling steps. However, note that the better each step is performed, the fewer iterations will be necessary.

In order to obtain meaningful results, data analysis requires an attention to detail, an adequate project definition, meticulous preparation of the data, investigative capacity, patience, rigor, and objectives that are well defined from the beginning. If these requirements are taken together as a starting point, then a basis can be built from which a data warehouse is converted into a high-value asset. One of the motivators for data analysis is to realize a return on investment for the database infrastructures that many businesses have installed. Another is to gain competitive leverage and insight for products and services by better understanding the marketplace, including customer and competitor behavior.

The analysis and comprehension of business data are fundamental parts of all organizations. Monitoring national economies and retail sales tendencies depend on data analysis, as does measuring the profitability, costs, and competitiveness of commercial organizations and businesses. Analyzing customer data has become easier due to data management infrastructures that separate the operational data from the analytical data, and from Internet applications and cloud computing, which facilitate the gathering of large-volume historical data logs.

On the other hand, computer systems have swamped us with large volumes of data and information, much of which is irrelevant for a specific analysis objective. Also, customer behavior has become more complex due to the diversity of applications that compete in the marketplace, especially for mobile devices. Thus, the objective of data analysis should be that of discovering useful and meaningful knowledge and separating the relevant from the irrelevant.

Chapters 2 through 10 follow the sequential steps for a typical data mining project. A scheme of the organization of these chapters can be seen in Figure 1.1. Chapter 2, "Business Objectives," discusses the definition of a data mining project, including its initial concept, motivation, business objectives, viability, estimated costs, and expected benefit (returns). Key considerations are defined and a way of quantifying the cost and benefit is presented in terms of the factors that most influence the project. Finally, two case studies illustrate how the cost/benefit evaluation can be applied to real-world projects.

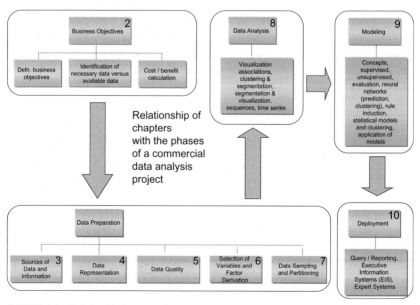

FIGURE 1.1   Relationship between chapters and the phases of a commercial data analysis project

Chapter 3, "Incorporating Various Sources of Data and Information," discusses possible sources of data and information that can be used for a commercial data mining project and how to establish which data sources are available and can be accessed for a commercial data analysis project. Data sources include a business's own internal data about its customers and its business activities, as well as external data that affects a business and its customers in different domains and in given sectors: competitive, demographic, and macro-economic.

Chapter 4 "Data Representation," looks at the different ways data can be conceptualized in order to facilitate its interpretation and visualization. Visualization methods include pie charts, histograms, graph plots, and radar diagrams. The topics covered in this chapter include representation, comparison, and processing of different types of variables; principal types of variables (numerical, categorical ordinal, categorical nominal, binary); normalization of the values of a variable; distribution of the values of a variable; and identification of atypical values or outliers. The chapter also discusses some of the more advanced types of data representation, such as semantic networks and graphs.

Chapter 5, "Data Quality," discusses data quality, which is a primary consideration for any commercial data analysis project. In this book the definition of "quality" includes the availability or accessibility of data. The chapter discusses typical problems that can occur with data, errors in the content of the data (especially textual data), and relevance and reliability of the data and addresses how to quantitatively evaluate data quality.

Chapter 6, "Selection of Variables and Factor Derivation," considers the topics of variable selection and factor derivation, which are used in a later chapter for analysis and modeling. Often, key factors must be selected from a large number of variables, and to do this two starting points are considered: (i) data mining projects that are defined by looking at the available data, and (ii) data mining projects that are driven by considering what the final desired result is. The chapter also discusses techniques such as correlation and factor analysis.

Chapter 7, "Data Sampling and Partitioning," discusses sampling and partitioning methods, which is often done when the volume of data is too great to process as a whole or when the analyst is interested in selecting data by specific criteria. The chapter considers different types of sampling, such as random sampling and sampling based on business criteria (age of client, length of time as client, etc.).

With Chapters 2 through 7 having laid the foundation for obtaining and defining a dataset for analysis, Chapter 8, "Data Analysis," describes a selection of the most common types of data analysis for data mining. Data visualization is discussed, followed by clustering and how it can be combined with visualization techniques. The reader is also introduced to transactional analysis and time series analysis. Finally, the chapter considers some common mistakes made when analyzing and interpreting data.

Chapter 9, "Modeling," begins with the definition of a data model and what its inputs and outputs are, then goes on to discuss concepts such as supervised and unsupervised learning, cross-validation, and how to evaluate the precision of modeling results. The chapter then considers various techniques for modeling data, from AI (artificial intelligence) approaches, such as neural networks and rule induction, to statistical techniques, such as regression. The chapter explains which techniques should be used for various modeling scenarios. It goes on to discuss how to apply models to real-world production data and how to evaluate and use the results. Finally, guidelines are given for how to perform and reiterate the modeling phase, especially when the initial results are not the desired or optimal ones.

Chapter 10, "Deployment Systems: From Query Reporting to EIS and Expert Systems," discusses ways that the results of data mining can be fed into the decision-making and operative processes of the business.

Chapters 11 through 19 address various background topics and specific data mining domains. A scheme of the organization of these chapters can be seen in Figure 1.2.

Chapter 11, "Text Analysis," discusses both simple and more advanced text processing and text analysis: basic processing takes into account format checking based on pattern identification, and more advanced techniques consider named entity recognition, concept identification based on synonyms and hyponyms, and information retrieval concepts.

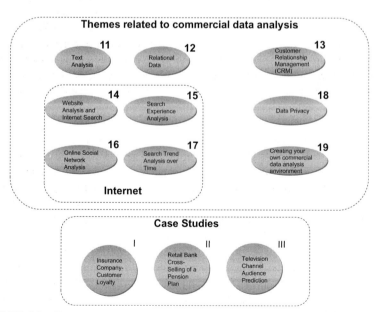

FIGURE 1.2 Chapter topics related to commercial data analysis and projects based on real-world cases

Chapter 12, "Data Mining from Relationally Structured Data, Marts, and Warehouses," deals with extracting a data mining file from relational data. The chapter reviews the concepts of "data mart" and "data warehouse" and discusses how the informational data is separated from the operational data, then describes the path of extracting data from an operational environment into a data mart and finally into a unique file that can then be used as the starting point for data mining.

Chapter 13, "CRM – Customer Relationship Management and Analysis," introduces the reader to the CRM approach in terms of recency, frequency, and latency of customer activity, and in terms of the client life cycle: capturing new clients, potentiating and retaining existing clients, and winning back ex-clients. The chapter goes on to discuss the characteristics of commercial CRM software products and provides examples and functionality from a simple CRM application.

Chapter 14, "Analysis of Data on the Internet I – Website Analysis and Internet Search," first discusses how to analyze transactional data from customer visits to a website and then discusses how Internet search can be used as a market research tool.

Chapter 15, "Analysis of Data on the Internet II – Search Experience Analysis," Chapter 16, "Analysis of Data on the Internet III – Online Social Network Analysis," and Chapter 17, "Analysis of Data on the Internet IV – Search Trend Analysis over Time," continue the discussion of data analysis on the Internet, going more in-depth on topics such as search experience analysis, online social network analysis, and search trend analysis over time.

Chapter 18, "Data Privacy and Privacy-Preserving Data Publishing," addresses data privacy issues, which are important when collecting and analyzing data about individuals and organizations. The chapter discusses how well-known Internet applications deal with data privacy, how they inform users about using customer data on websites, and how cookies are used. The chapter goes on to discuss techniques used for anonymizing data so the data can be used in the public domain.

Chapter 19, "Creating an Environment for Commercial Data Analysis," discusses how to create an environment for commercial data analysis in a company. The chapter begins with a discussion of powerful tools with high price tags, such as the IBM Intelligent Miner, the SAS Enterprise Miner, and the IBM SPSS Modeler, which are used by multinational companies, banks, insurance companies, large chain stores, and so on. It then addresses a low-cost and more artisanal approach, which consists of using ad hoc, or open source, software tools such as Weka and Spreadsheets.

Chapter 20, "Summary," provides a synopsis of the chapters.

The appendix details three case studies that illustrate how the techniques and methods discussed throughout the book are applied in real-world situations. The studies include: (i) a customer loyalty project in the insurance industry, (ii) cross-selling a pension plan in the retail banking sector, and (iii) an audience prediction for a television channel.

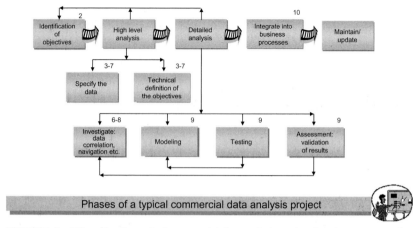

FIGURE 1.3 Life cycle of a typical commercial data analysis project (numbers correspond to chapters)

For readers who wish to focus on business aspects, the following reading plan is recommended: Chapters 2, 3, 6, 8 (specifically the sections titled "Visualization," "Associations," and "Segmentation and Visualization"), 9, 10, 11 (specifically the sections titled "Basic Analysis of Textual Information" and "Advanced Analysis of Textual Information"), 13, 14, 18, 19, and the case studies in the appendix. For readers who want more technical details, the following chapters are recommended: Chapters 4 through 9, 11, 12, 15 through 17, 19, and the case studies in the appendix.

The demographic data referred to in this book has been randomly anonymized and aggregated; that is, individual people cannot be identified by first and last names or by any unique or derivable identifier. Any resemblance to a real person or entity is purely coincidental.

Figure 1.3 illustrates the phases of a project. The cyclic nature of the phases of a detailed analysis is evident, including the modeling phase. The cyclic nature is evident when, for example, after obtaining the first results of a data analysis and modeling, different input factors are then chosen, or the business objective changes. (However, if the business objectives have been well chosen and the first phases have been performed correctly, there should be no need to go back and redefine the high-level analysis.)

Chapter 2

Business Objectives

INTRODUCTION

This chapter discusses the definition of a data mining project, including its initial concept, motivation, objective, viability, estimated costs, and expected benefit (returns). Key considerations are defined, and a way of quantifying the cost and benefit is presented in terms of the factors that most influence the project. Two case studies illustrate how the cost/benefit evaluation can be applied for real-world projects.

A commercial data analysis project that lives up to its expectations will probably do so because sufficient time was dedicated at the outset to defining the project's business objectives. What is meant by business objectives? The following are some examples:

- Reduce the loss of existing customers by 3 percent.
- Augment the contract signings of new customers by 2 percent.
- Augment the sales from cross-selling products to existing customers by 5 percent.
- Predict the television audience share with a probability of 70 percent.
- Predict, with a precision of 75 percent, which clients are most likely to contract a new product.
- Identify new categories of clients and products.
- Create a new customer segmentation model.

The first three examples define a specific percentage of precision and improvement as part of the objective.

> **Business Objective**
>
> *Assigning a Value for Percent Improvement*
>
> The percentage improvement should always be considered with regard to the current precision of an existing index as a baseline. Also, the new precision objective should not get lost in the error bars of the current precision. That is, if the current precision has an error margin of $\pm 3\%$ in its measurement or calculation, this should be taken into account.

In the fourth and fifth examples, an absolute value is specified for the desired precision for the data model. In the final two examples the desired improvement is not quantified; instead, the objective is expressed in qualitative terms.

CRITERIA FOR CHOOSING A VIABLE PROJECT

This section enumerates some main issues and poses some key questions relevant to evaluating the viability of a potential data mining project. The checklists of general and specific considerations provided here are the bases for the rest of the chapter, which enters into a more detailed specification of benefit and cost criteria and applies these definitions to two case studies.

Evaluation of Potential Commercial Data Analysis Projects – General Considerations

The following is a list of questions to ask when considering a data analysis project:

- Is data available that is consistent and correlated with the business objectives?
- What is the capacity for improvement with respect to the current methods? (The greater the capacity for improvement, the greater the economic benefit.)
- Is there an operational business need for the project results?
- Can the problem be solved by other techniques or methods? (If the answer is no, the profitability return on the project will be greater.)
- Does the project have a well-defined scope? (If this is the first instance of a project of this type, reducing the scale of the project is recommended.)

Evaluation of Viability in Terms of Available Data – Specific Considerations

The following list provides specific considerations for evaluating the viability of a data mining project in terms of the available data:

- Does the necessary data for the business objectives exist, and does the business have access to it?
- If part or all of the data does not exist, can processes be defined to capture or obtain it?
- What is the coverage of the data with respect to the business objectives?
- What is the availability of a sufficient volume of data over a required period of time, for all clients, product types, sales channels, and so on? (The data should cover all the business factors to be analyzed and modeled. The historical data should cover the current business cycle.)

- Is it necessary to evaluate the quality of the available data in terms of reliability? (The reliability depends on the percentage of erroneous data and incomplete or missing data. The ranges of values must be sufficiently wide to cover all cases of interest.)
- Are people available who are familiar with the relevant data and the operational processes that generate the data?

FACTORS THAT INFLUENCE PROJECT BENEFITS

There are several factors that influence the benefits of a project. A qualitative assessment of current functionality is first required: what is the current grade of satisfaction of how the task is being done? A value between 1 and 0 is assigned, where 1 is the highest grade of satisfaction and 0 is the lowest, where the lower the current grade of satisfaction, the greater the improvement and, consequently, the benefit, will be.

The potential quality of the result (the evaluation of future functionality) can be estimated by three aspects of the data: coverage, reliability, and correlation:

- The coverage or completeness of the data, assigned a value between 0 and 1, where 1 indicates total coverage.
- The quality or reliability of the data, assigned a value between 0 and 1, where 1 indicates the highest quality. (Both the coverage and the reliability are normally measured variable by variable, giving a total for the whole dataset. Good coverage and reliability for the data help to make the analysis a success, thus giving a greater benefit.)
- The correlation between the data and its grade of dependence with the business objective can be statistically measured. A correlation is typically measured as a value from −1 (total negative correlation) through 0 (no correlation) to 1 (total positive correlation). For example, if the business objective is that clients buy more products, the correlation would be calculated for each customer variable (age, time as a customer, zip code of postal address, etc.) with the customer's sales volume.

Once individual values for coverage, reliability, and correlation are acquired, an estimation of the future functionality can be obtained using the formula:

Future functionality = (correlation + reliability + coverage)/3

An estimation of the possible improvement is then determined by calculating the difference between the current and the future functionality, thus:

Estimated improvement = Future functionality − Current functionality

A fourth aspect, volatility, concerns the amount of time the results of the analysis or data modeling will remain valid.

Volatility of the environment of the business objective can be defined as a value of between 0 and 1, where 0 = minimum volatility and 1 = maximum volatility. A high volatility can cause models and conclusions to become quickly out of date with respect to the data; even the business objective can lose relevance. Volatility depends on whether the results are applicable over the long, medium, or short terms with respect to the business cycle.

Note that this *a priori* evaluation gives an idea for the viability of a data mining project. However, it is clear that the quality and precision of the end result will also depend on how well the project is executed: analysis, modeling, implementation, deployment, and so on. The next section, which deals with the estimation of the cost of the project, includes a factor (expertise) that evaluates the availability of the people and skills necessary to guarantee the *a posteriori* success of the project.

FACTORS THAT INFLUENCE PROJECT COSTS

There are numerous factors that influence how much a project costs. These include:

- Accessibility: The more data sources, the higher the cost. Typically, there are at least two different data sources.
- Complexity: The greater the number of variables in the data, the greater the cost. Categorical-type variables (zones, product types, etc.) must especially be taken into account, given that each variable may have many possible values (for example, 50). On the other hand, there could be just 10 other variables, each of which has only two possible values.
- Data volumes: The more records there are in the data, the higher the cost. A data sample extracted from the complete dataset can have a volume of about 25,000 records, whereas the complete database could contain between 250,000 and 10 million records.
- Expertise: The more expertise available with respect to the data, the lower the cost. Expertise includes knowledge about the business environment, customers, and so on that facilitates the interpretation of the data. It also includes technical know-how about the data sources and the company databases from which the data is extracted.

EXAMPLE 1: CUSTOMER CALL CENTER – OBJECTIVE: IT SUPPORT FOR CUSTOMER RECLAMATIONS

Mr. Strong is the operations manager of a customer call center that provides outsourced customer support for a diverse group of client companies. In the last quarter, he has detected an increase of reclamations by customers for erroneous billing by a specific company. By revising the bills and speaking with the client company, the telephone operators identified a defective batch software program in the batch billing process and reported the incident to Mr. Strong, who, together with the IT manager of the client company, located the defective process. He determined the origin of the problem, and the IT manager gave instructions to the IT department to make the necessary corrections to the billing software. The complete process, from identifying the incident to the corrective actions, was documented in the call center's audit trail and the client company. Given the concern for the increase in incidents, Mr. Strong and the IT manager decided to initiate a data mining project to efficiently investigate reclamations due to IT processing errors and other causes.

Hypothetical values can be assigned to the factors that influence the benefit of this project, as follows: The available data has a high grade of correlation (0.9) with the business objective. Sixty-two percent of the incidents (which are subsequently identified as IT processing issues) are solved by the primary corrective actions; thus, the current grade of precision is 0.62. The data captured represents 85 percent of the modifications made to the IT processes, together with the relevant information at the time of the incident. The incidents, the corrections, and the effect of applying the corrections are entered into a spreadsheet, with a margin of error or omission of 8 percent. Therefore, the degree of coverage is 0.85 and the grade of reliability is $(1 - 0.08) = 0.92$.

The client company's products and services that the call center supports have to be continually updated due to changes in their characteristics. This means that 10 percent of the products and services change completely over a one year period. Thus a degree of volatility of 0.10 is assigned. The project quality model, in terms of the factors related to benefit, is summarized as follows:

- Qualitative measure of the current functionality: 0.62 (medium)
- Evaluation of future functionality:
  - Coverage: 0.85 (high)
  - Reliability: 0.92 (high)
  - Correlation of available data with business objective: 0.9 (high)
- Volatility of the environment of the business objective: 0.10 (low)

Values can now be assigned for factors that influence the cost of the project.

Mr. Strong's operations department has an Oracle database that stores the statistical summaries of customer calls. Other historical records are kept in an Excel spreadsheet for the daily operations, diagnostics arising from reclamations, and corrective actions. Some of the records are used for operations monitoring. The IT manager of the client company has a DB2 database of software maintenance that the IT department has performed. Thus there are three data sources: the Oracle database, the data in the call center's Excel spreadsheets, and the DB2 database from the client IT department.

There are about 100 variables represented in the three data sources, 25 of which the operations manager and the IT manager consider relevant for the data model. Twenty of the variables are numerical and five are categorical (service type, customer type, reclamation type, software correction type, and priority level). Note that the correlation value used to estimate the benefit and the future functionality is calculated as an average for the subset of the 25 variables evaluated as being the most relevant, and not the 100 original variables.

The operations manager and the IT manager agree that, with three years' worth of historical data, the call center reclamations and IT processes can be modeled. It is clear that the business cycle does not have seasonal cycles; however, there is a temporal aspect due to peaks and troughs in the volume of customer calls at certain times of the year. Three years' worth of data implies about 25,000 records from all three data sources. Thus the data volume is 25,000.

The operations manager and the IT manager can make time for specific questions related to the data, the operations, and the IT processes. The IT manager may also dedicate time to technical interpretation of the data in order to extract the required data from the data sources. Thus there is a high level of available expertise in relation to the data.

Factors that influence the project costs include:

- Accessibility: three data sources, with easy accessibility
- Complexity: 25 variables
- Data volume: 25,000 records
- Expertise: high

Overall Evaluation of the Cost and Benefit of Mr. Strong's Project

In terms of benefit, the evaluation gives a quite favorable result, given that the current functionality (0.62) is medium, thus giving a good margin for improvement on the current precision. The available data for the model has a high level of coverage of the environment (0.85) and is very reliable (0.92); these two factors are favorable for the success of the project. The correlation of the data with the business objective is high (0.9), again favorable, and a low volatility (0.10) will prolong the useful life of the data model. Using the formula defined earlier (factors that influence the benefit of a project), the future functionality is estimated by taking the average of the correlation, reliability, and coverage (0.9 + 0.92 + 0.85)/3 = 0.89, and subtracting the current precision (0.62), which gives an estimated improvement of 0.27, or 27 percent. Mr. Strong can interpret this percentage in terms of improvement of the operations process or he can convert it into a monetary value.

In terms of cost, there is reasonable accessibility to the data, since there are only three data sources. However, as the Oracle and DB2 databases are located in different companies (the former in the call center and the latter in the client company), the possible costs of unifying any necessary data will have to be evaluated in more detail. The complexity of having 25 descriptive variables is considered as medium; however, the variables will have to be studied individually to see if there are many different categories and whether new factors need to be derived from the original variables. The data volume (25,000 records) is medium-high for this type of problem. In terms of expertise, the participating managers have good initial availability, although they will need to commit their time given that, in practice, the day-to-day workings of the call center and IT department may reduce their dedication. The project would have a medium level of costs.

As part of the economic cost of the project, two factors must be taken into account: the services of an external consultant specializing in data analysis, and the time dedicated by the call center's own employees (Mr. Strong, the operations manager; the IT manager; a call center operator; and a technician from the IT department). Also, for a project with the given characteristics and medium complexity, renting or purchasing a data analysis software tool is recommended. With a benefit of 27 percent and a medium cost level, it is recommended that Mr. Strong go ahead with his operations model project.

EXAMPLE 2: ONLINE MUSIC APP – OBJECTIVE: DETERMINE EFFECTIVENESS OF ADVERTISING FOR MOBILE DEVICE APPS

Melody-online is a new music streaming application for mobile devices (iPhone, iPad, Android, etc.). The commercial basis of the application is to have users pay for a premium account with no publicity, or have users connect for free but with publicity inserted before the selected music is played. The company's application was previously available only on non-mobile computers (desktop, laptop, etc.), and the company now wishes to evaluate the effectiveness of advertising in this new environment. There is typically a minimum time when non-paying users cannot deactivate the publicity, after which they can switch it off and the song they selected starts to play. Hence, Melody-online wishes to evaluate whether the listening time for users of the mobile device app is comparable to the listening time for users of the fixed computer applications. The company also wishes to study the behavior of mobile device app users in general by incorporating new types of information, such as geolocation data.

Values are assigned to the factors that influence the benefit of this project. The available data has a high grade of correlation (0.9) with the business objectives. Fifty percent of users are currently categorized in terms of the available data, thus the current grade of precision is 0.50.

The data available represents 100 percent of users, but only six months of data is available for the mobile app, whereas five years' worth of data has been accumulated for the non-mobile app. A minimum of two years' worth of data is needed to cover all user types and behaviors, hence only a quarter of the required data is available. User data is automatically registered by cookies and then sent to the database, with a margin of error or omission of 5 percent. Therefore, the degree of coverage is 0.25 and the grade of reliability is $(1 - 0.05) = 0.95$.

The music genres and artists that Melody-online has available have to be continually updated for changing music tendencies and new artists. This means 25 percent of the total music offering changes completely over a one-year period. Thus a degree of volatility of 0.25 is assigned. The project quality model, in terms of the factors related to benefit, are summarized as follows:

- Qualitative measure of the current functionality: 0.50 (medium-low)
- Evaluation of future functionality:
  - Coverage: 0.25 (low)
  - Reliability: 0.95 (high)
  - Correlation of available data with business objective: 0.9 (high)
- Volatility of the environment of the business objective: 0.25 (medium)

Values can now be assigned to factors that influence the cost of the project.

Melody-online maintains an Access database containing statistical summaries of user sessions and activities. Some records are transferred to an Excel spreadsheet and are used for management monitoring. Thus, there are two data sources: the Access database and the Excel spreadsheets.

There are about 40 variables represented in the two data sources, 15 of which the marketing manager considers relevant for the data model. Ten of the variables are numerical (average ad listening time, etc.) and five are categorical (user type, music type, ad type, etc.). As with the previous case study, note that the correlation value used to estimate the benefit and the future functionality is calculated as an average for the subset of 15 variables, not for the 40 original variables.

The IT manager and the marketing manager agree that user behavior can be modeled with two years' worth of historical data, taking into account the characteristics of the business cycle. This much data implies about 500 thousand user sessions with an average of 20 records per session, totaled from both data sources. Thus the data volume is 10 million data records for the 2 year time period considered.

The IT manager and the marketing director can make some time for specific questions related to the data and the production process, but the IT manager has very limited time available. (The marketing manager is the main driver behind the project.) Thus there is a medium level of available expertise in relationship to the data.

Factors that influence the project costs include:

- Accessibility: two data sources, with easy accessibility
- Complexity: 15 variables
- Data volume: 10 million records
- Expertise: medium

Overall Evaluation of the Cost and Benefit of Melody-online's Project

In terms of benefit, the evaluation gives a quite favorable result, given that the current functionality (0.50) is at a medium-low level, thus giving a good margin for improvement on the current precision. The available data is very reliable

(0.95); however, the low coverage of the environment (0.25) is a major draw-back. The values for these two factors are critical for the project's success. The correlation of the data with the business objective is high (0.9), which is favor-able, but a medium volatility (0.25) will reduce the useful life of the analysis results. The future functionality is estimated by taking the average of the cor-relation, reliability, and coverage $(0.9 + 0.95 + 0.25)/3 = 0.7)$, and subtracting the current precision (0.50) which gives an estimated improvement of 0.2, or 20 percent. Melody-online can interpret this percentage in terms of users having increased exposure times to advertising, or it can convert the percentage into a monetary value (e.g., advertising revenues).

In terms of cost, there is good accessibility to the data, given that there are only two data sources. However, there is a serious problem with low data cov-erage, with only 25 percent of the required business period covered. The com-plexity of having 15 descriptive variables is considered medium-low, but the variables will have to be studied individually to see if there are many different categories, and whether new factors must be derived from the original variables. The data volume, at 10 million records, is high for this type of problem. In terms of expertise, the IT manager stated up front that he will not have much time for the project, so there is a medium initial availability. The project would have a medium-high level of costs.

Renting or purchasing a data analysis software tool for a project with these characteristics is recommended. As part of the economic cost of the project, the services of an external consultant for the data analysis tool and the time dedi-cated by the company's employees (the IT manager and the marketing manager) must be taken into account.

With a benefit of 20 percent, a medium-high cost level, the lack of the IT manager's availability, and especially the lack of available data (only 25 per-cent), it is recommended that Melody-online postpone its data mining project until sufficient user behavior data for its mobile app has been captured. The IT manager should delegate his participation to another member of the IT department (for example, an analyst-programmer) who has more time available to dedicate to the project.

SUMMARY

In this chapter, some detailed guidelines and evaluation criteria have been discussed for choosing a commercial data mining business objective and eval-uating its viability in terms of benefit and cost. Two examples were examined that applied the evaluation criteria in order to quantify expected benefit and cost, and then the resulting information was used to decide whether to go ahead with the project. This method has been used by the author to successfully evaluate real-world data mining projects and is specifically designed for an evaluation based on the characteristics of the data and business objectives.

FURTHER READING

Boardman, A.E., Greenberg, D.H., Vining, A.R., Weimer, D.L., 2008. *Cost–Benefit Analysis*, fourth ed. Pearson Education, New Jersey, ISBN: 0132311488.

Zerbe, R.O., Bellas, A.S., 2006. *A Primer for Benefit–Cost Analysis*. Edward Elgar Publishing, Northampton, MA, ISBN: 1843768976.

Chapter 3

Incorporating Various Sources of Data and Information

INTRODUCTION

This chapter discusses data sources that can be accessed for a commercial data analysis project. One way of enriching the information available about a business's environment and activity is to fuse together various sources of information and data. The chapter begins with a discussion of internal data; that is, data about a business's products, services, and customers, together with feedback on business activities from surveys, questionnaires, and loyalty and customer cards. The chapter then considers external data—which affects a business and its customers in various ambits—such as demographic and census data, macro-economic data, data about competitors, and data relating to stocks, shares, and investments. Examples are given for each source and where and how the data could be obtained.

Although some readers may be familiar with one or more of these data sources, they may need help selecting which to use for a given data mining project. Table 3.1 gives examples of which data sources are relevant for which business objectives and commercial data mining activities. Columns two through eight show the seven data sources described in this chapter, and the column labeled "Business Objectives" lists generic business examples. Each cell indicates whether a specific data source would be required for the given business objective.

Data Sources

Primary Data Sources

The primary data sources include the data already in the basic data repository derived from a business's products, services, customers, and transactions. That is, a data mining project could be considered that uses only this elemental data and no other sources. The primary data sources are indicated in the columns labeled "Internal" in Table 3.1.

TABLE 3.1 Business objectives versus data sources

Business Objectives	Data Sources[1]						
	Internal				External		
	Own products and services	Surveys and questionnaires	Loyalty card	Demographic data[2]	Macro-economic data	Data about competitors	Stocks and shares
Data mining of customer data; transactional data analysis/modeling for new customer targeting: cross-selling, win-back	yes	possibly	yes	possibly	generally not	generally not[3]	generally not
Market surveys for new product/service launch; situation/market awareness	yes	yes	yes	yes	possibly[4]	yes	possibly[4]
What-if scenario modeling	yes	possibly	yes	possibly	possibly	possibly	possibly

[1] Multiple sources indicated as "yes" across a row implies that one or more are optional for the business objective.
[2] Demographic data refers to anonymous, general demographic data as opposed to demographic details of specific clients.
[3] Specific models for win-back may require data about competitors.
[4] Macro-economic data and stock/share data may be unnecessary, depending on the survey.

Each data mining project must evaluate and reach a consensus on which factors, and therefore which sources, are necessary for the business objective. For example, if the general business objective is to reduce customer attrition and churn (loss of clients to the competition), a factor related to customer satisfaction may be needed that is not currently in the database. Hence, in order to obtain this data, the business might design a questionnaire and launch a survey for its current customers. Defining the necessary data for a data mining project is a recurrent theme throughout Chapters 2 to 9, and the results of defining and identifying new factors may require a search for the corresponding data sources, if available, and/or obtain the data via surveys, questionnaires, new data capture processes, and so on. Demographic data about specific customers can be elicited from them by using the surveys, questionnaires and loyalty registration forms discussed in this chapter.

With reference to demographic data, we distinguish between the general anonymous type (such as that of the census) and specific data about identifiable customers (such as age, gender, marital status, and so on).

DATA ABOUT A BUSINESS'S PRODUCTS AND SERVICES

The data available about a business's products and services depends on the type of business activity and sector the business is in. However, there are some useful general rules and characteristics that can be applied to the data.

Typically, a business's products and services can be classified into categories such as paint, polymers, agriculture and nutrition, electronics, textile, and interior design. For each group of products, the characteristics of the products are defined by type of packaging, weight, color, quality, and so on. Paint, for example, can sell in pots weighing two, five, and 25 kilograms, in matte or glossy, and in 18 different colors.

Once a business begins to sell its products and services, it accumulates data about sales transactions: sales point (store, commercial center, zone), day, time, discount, and, sometimes, customer names. A significant history of sales transactions and data will be accumulated after just six months' worth of sales.

Internal Commercial Data

Business Reporting

Internal commercial data allows a business to create ongoing business reports with summaries of sales by period and geographical area. The report may have subsections divided by groups of products within period and zone. For example, a business can determine the total sales for paint products in the eastern region for the second quarter. It can also know the proportion of sales by region, for example: south, 35 percent; north, 8 percent; east, 20 percent; center, 25 percent; west, 12 percent; or by product group: paint, 27.7 percent; polymers, 20.9 percent; agriculture and nutrition, 15.2 percent; electronics, 12.8 percent; textile and interiors, 23.4 percent.

From this data the company can deduce, by simple inspection, that one product line of paint sells best in the central region, and that the sale of polymers has gone up 8 percent in the last quarter (with respect to the same quarter in the previous year), whereas in the same period the sales of electronic goods has gone down by 4.5 percent. The company can also identify commercial offices that sell above or below the average for a given period, which can indicate where corrective action is needed or success should be praised.

The company can also derive information about the production or running costs, including commissions to distributors and sales personnel. Each line of products will have its own cost profile: some will include the depreciation incurred by investment and machinery, infrastructure costs, supplies, and so on. The costs may vary in terms of production volume: in general, greater production implies an economy of scale and a greater margin of profit. If the gross income data by sales and the production or running costs are known, then the net income, or net profit, can be calculated. Thus profitability can be calculated by product, service, or groups of products or services.

When performing commercial data analysis, detailed calculations of production costs are not usually done. Instead, the interest lies in the qualitative or quantitative values for business indicators, such as those presented in Chapter 2. It is only through the measurement of these factors that a business can know whether its profitability is getting better or worse due to its own business practices or due to external factors.

Clearly, the data discussed in this section can be interrelated with other analytical data of interest. For example, customer profiles can be derived by region or specific sales data can be related to specific customer types. Other categorizations of services and products include: risk level (low, medium, high) for financial products; low-cost flights for airline services; basic/no frills lines for supermarket products; and professional, premium, and basic for software products or Internet services.

In practice, and in order to avoid getting lost in the sea of available data, a business needs a good classification system, with subgroupings where necessary, of its own products and services. An adequate classification for its commercial structure, by sales channels, regional offices, and so on, is also important. Classifications for products, services, and sales channels are useful variables for exploring and modeling the business data.

SURVEYS AND QUESTIONNAIRES

Surveys and questionnaires are mainstays of marketing; they allow for feedback from actual and potential customers and can give a company a feel for current trends and needs. Offering questionnaires online, rather than on paper, greatly facilitates data capture and controls the quality of the input and subsequent data processing. The style and content of a market survey or questionnaire depend on the type and the nature of the business.

Questionnaires

Objectives of Data Capture

The basic objective of capturing data is to create profiles of customers so that a business knows them better, can sell them more products and services, and can give greater customer satisfaction by providing more personalized attention—as if the business knows its customers personally. The company may be planning a new marketing campaign and the questionnaire it used in the past didn't elicit the appropriate responses, or the company needs to obtain variables that it doesn't currently have, ones that are highly relevant for the data mining business objective. A key aspect is to have a data mining business objective in mind when designing a questionnaire or survey.

Examples of Survey and Questionnaire Forms

This section examines three examples of survey and questionnaire forms, each one for a different business objective and business area. The form in Example 1 is designed to obtain market information in order to improve targeting potential clients. The general business objective is to augment the rate of conversion of potential clients to clients. The form in Example 2 is targeted at current clients to obtain additional information for the business objective of cross-selling a mortgage loan. The form in Example 3 is designed to obtain the reasons why some clients stop working with an insurance company. The business objective is to use this information to take *a priori* action to reduce customer attrition and churn.

Example 1 Automobile Survey – Evaluation of Potential Clients

1. Are you thinking of buying a new car?
   ○ Yes
   ○ No
2. If you answered yes to the first question, when are you thinking of buying?
   ○ Immediately
   ○ Within a month
   ○ Within a year
   ○ I haven't decided yet
3. What is the make and model of your current car?
   Make: _____
   Model: _____
4. Hold long have you had your current car?
   Years: _____
5. What do you principally use your car for?
   ○ Driving to/from work
   ○ Leisure

Continued

Example 1 —cont'd

6. Please indicate the characteristics you feel are most important for your car.
    - ○ABS brakes
    - ○Ecological
    - ○Economical
    - ○Power
    - ○Air conditioning
    - ○Security features (airbag, lateral protection)
7. What price would you pay for a car?
    - ○Less than $15,000
    - ○$15,000 to $25,000
    - ○$25,000 to $50,000
    - ○More than $50,000

Example 2 Bank Survey – Cross-Selling and Customer Retention

Questionnaire Form

Please help us to offer you a better service by participating in this survey.

How did you learn about our mortgage loan?
- ○A. Branch manager
- ○B. Customer service
- ○C. Internet
- ○D. Other

Did our bank give you the information you asked for?
- ○Yes
- ○No

Rate the utility of the information on a scale of 1 to 10:

```
|--+--|--+--|--+--|--+--|--+--|--+--|
0   1   2   3   4   5   6   7   8   9   10
```

How would you rate the readability of the information provided?
- ○Easy
- ○Difficult

How would you rate the speed of the bank's reply?
- ○Very fast
- ○Fast
- ○Normal
- ○Slow
- ○Very slow

Which characteristics did you like best about the mortgage loan?
- ○Interest rate
- ○Repayment period
- ○Flexibility
- ○Down-payment amount

Are you a customer of the bank?
- ○Yes
- ○No

Customer name: _____

Example 3 Insurance Company Cancellation Form – Customer Win-Back

We are very sorry to hear that you are thinking of canceling one of your financial products. If there's anything we can help with, please email our customer support team.
I am canceling my personal insurance policy because:
  ○Unhappy with premium rates
  ○Unhappy with conditions/coverage (please specify): _____
  ○Unhappy with customer service (please specify): _____
  ○Job related (insurance provided by employer)
  ○Financial considerations
  ○Moving residence/work, no convenient branch near new residence/office
Please give new address: _____
  ○Transferring policy
Please indicate which company you are transferring to: _____
  ○Other
Please explain: _____
Date: _____

There is a mixture of data types in these examples: categories, with several reply choices of binary type; that is, with two possible values (Yes, No); numerical values; date; and free text fields. Surveys of this kind can be done anonymously to obtain feedback about the level of acceptance for and quality of the products, services, sales channels, and customer support. Alternatively, the individuals could be asked to identify themselves, if they so wished, once the form has been completed. Question 3 in Example 1 could use a pull-down list of makes and models of cars in order to control data input and guarantee data consistency.

This last concept, controlling data input and capturing consistent data, is essential if the data is to be merged with individual demographic data (and customer data if the person is already a customer), thus allowing the replies to be interpreted in terms of the customer profile.

Designing Questionnaires

Merging Data for a Business Objective

Assume that the business objective for the developers of anti-spam software is to more accurately segment its customers in order to market an "Enterprise"-level anti-spam software. One of the items on the questionnaire asks for the number of spam email messages arriving in a person's inbox in the past month. One respondent chose to include his name. When this new information was cross-referenced with the respondent's demographic data, it was discovered that this person listed a financial services company as his address and he had already downloaded the company's free antivirus software. With some additional business intelligence gathering, the number of employees at the company he works at can be calculated, as well as the total amount of spam the financial services company's employees might receive. The sales opportunity for the anti-spam company can then be quantified. This is why merging with the customer's demographic data is important.

Surveys and Questionnaires: Data Table Population

This section examines data tables populated with the data captured from the registration forms discussed in the previous section. Table 3.2 shows four records collected from the automobile survey in Example 1. This was an anonymous survey with no personal data. In the column labeled "When buy," only the third and fourth rows have values because this column will only have a value when the reply to the previous query, "Buy car," is "yes." The column labeled "Preferred characteristics" allows for multiple responses. The category descriptions in the table are the same as in the questionnaire in order to make them easy to understand. While the table is representative of a real-world database table, in practice, the responses are usually stored in a coded form, such as A, B, C, D or 1, 2, 3, 4, to save memory space. Typically, the codes and descriptions are stored in a set of small auxiliary tables related to the main data file by secondary indexes.

Table 3.3 shows the data from the survey in Example 2, where customers have the option to identify themselves. All of the data consists of categories except for field three, "info utility," and the last field, "customer name," which is free format text. This last type of field can be detected by applications that process surveys and have text processing software. Again, in a real-world relationship database the category descriptions would be coded and stored in auxiliary tables.

Table 3.4 shows four records collected from the insurance company cancellation form in Example 3. The data captured will not be anonymous given that, in order to cancel an account, the customer has to be identified. Also, as the customer's principal interest is to cancel the account, the customer may be unwilling to complete the reasons for canceling, so there may be a significant amount of missing values in the overall records. Multiple reasons can be given for canceling; the reason code is conveniently stored in a vector format in the first column of the data table, and data in columns two through six depend on the reason code, which may not have been given in the form. Several of the fields from Example 3 are free format text, unlike Examples 1 and 2. This will make the processing and information extraction more complex, if the company wishes to make use of this information.

A common key is needed in order to fuse separate data sources together. Hence, data collected from anonymous surveys cannot be directly related to customer records by a customer ID. The next section discusses how to collect data that includes a unique identifier for the customer.

Issues When Designing Forms

How a data capture form is designed has an important effect on the quality of the data obtained. Chapter 5 examines in detail how to evaluate and guarantee data quality, which includes controlling the consistency of the data format and types, and ensuring that all the information variables included are relevant to a given business objective. That is, the form's designer should have a given data mining business objective in mind when choosing which variables to include and which data types to assign to each variable. Chapter 4 addresses how to assign the best data type for each data item. Two ways to improve data input quality are to

TABLE 3.2 Data collected from automobile survey

Buy Car	When Buy	Make	Model	How Long Had for	Use of Car	Preferred Characteristics	Price
No	-	Chevrolet	Volt	1	Work	ABS brakes, economical, ecological	$25,000–$50,000
No	-	Ford	Fusion Hybrid	2	Work	Economical, ecological	$25,000–$50,000
Yes	Year	Chrysler	200	5	Leisure	Security, ABS brakes	$15,000–$25,000
Yes	Year	Ford	Explorer	8	Leisure	Power, security	>$50,000

TABLE 3.3 Data collected from bank survey

Learn about	Bank info	Info utility	Info Readability	Reply speed	Best characteristics	Customer?	Customer Name
B	Yes	9	Easy	Normal	Interest, period	Yes	Bob Jackson
C	Yes	8	Easy	Normal	Interest	Yes	Karen Dinensen
C	Yes	7	Easy	Normal	Period	No	-
C	Yes	8	Difficult	Slow	Period, down-payment	No	-

TABLE 3.4 Data collected from cancellation form

Reasons 1 to 8	Specify conditions	Specify service	New address	New company	Explanation	Date
{1, 2, 3}	No claims limit	-	-	-	-	10/20/2014
{1, 2, 3}	Problems during incident resolution	Car insurance	-	21st Century Insurance	-	03/05/2013
{3, 7}	-	-	-	Merchants Insurance Group	-	07/15/2012
{1, 7}	-	-	-	-	-	02/01/2012

oblige the user to choose preselected categories and to use free text fields only when absolutely necessary.

LOYALTY CARD/CUSTOMER CARD

The loyalty card serves two objectives: Firstly, it is a way of offering better service to customers by allowing them to buy on credit with a low interest rate; keep track of their spending with monthly statements; and accumulate bonus points, which can be exchanged for a range of gift products. Secondly, loyalty cards also allow a business to know more about its customers through the accumulation of data about them, and makes possible specific commercial actions based on the detected customer profiles. In terms of data mining business objectives, the derived information can be used to potentiate sales of specific products, cross-sell products and services, and develop customer loyalty campaigns.

Loyalty Card Program

Business Objective

When designing a loyalty card program, consideration must be given to what the specific data mining business objectives are and what the products and services are. The loyalty card program should be designed to gather and mine the most reliable and relevant data to support it. Consider, for example, a supermarket VIP program that discounts specific items at specific times. This may be done to gather purchasing habits in preparation for launching a new product or campaign or to better understand a specific demographic segment of the customers.

If key relevant and reliable data can be obtained about customer behavior relative to discounting items, then it can be used to leverage or modify the existing loyalty program.

Two companies who supply loyalty cards are www.loyaltia.com and www.globalcard2000.com.

Registration Form for a Customer Card

How is data about customers obtained through a loyalty card? First the customer completes a detailed form in order to obtain the card. This form is designed with questions that give valuable information about the customer while keeping within the limits of confidentiality, respecting the privacy of the individual, and knowing the current laws related to data protection and processing. The following section gives practical examples of registration forms for a customer card. The questions that customers answer vary depending on the product, service, and sector.

Data mining business objectives are always a consideration when choosing what information to include in a loyalty card registration form. The forms in Examples 4 and 6 obtain demographic information that can be used for targeting specific products; Example 5 obtains information for segmenting customers and evaluating the effectiveness of sales channels; Example 7 obtains demographic and product-specific data that can be used for customer profiling, together with information about the competition, which can be used to improve market awareness.

Key questions should be chosen to obtain basic contact information and data that is highly relevant to the business objective. Reliability of the data obtained is an essential aspect: it is easier to obtain reliable data based on categories and limited multiple choice options than it is to get data from free text fields.

Example 4 Internet/Television-Based Home Products Company – Registration Form for Buyer's Club

Name/Surname: _____ / _____
Address: _____
City: _____
County: _____
State: _____
Zip code: _____
Telephone: _____

Number of people who live in your household (including yourself): _____
Age of each person in household (including yourself): _____
Gender of each person in household (including yourself): _____
Comments: _____
_____

Example 5 Website for Automobile Accessories – Registration Form for Customer Card

Name/Surname: _____ / _____
Address: _____
City: _____
County: _____
State: _____
Zip/postal code: _____
Country: _____
Telephone: _____
Email: _____
Date of Birth (MM/DD/YYYY): _____

You are:
  ○A. Interested in mechanics
  ○B. Interested in car racing
  ○C. Interested in karting
  ○D. Working in the automobile sector
How did you hear about us?
  ○A. Searching the Internet
  ○B. Through a friend/colleague
  ○C. Through publicity in magazines

Example 6 Perfume Chain Store – Registration Form for Customer Card

Name and Surname: _____
Address: _____
Town or City: _____
County: _____
State: _____
Zip/post code: _____
Telephone: _____
Email: _____
Date of birth: _____

Language:
  ○A. English
  ○B. Spanish
  ○C. French
  ○D. Other
Specify language if other: _____
Skin type:
  ○A. Greasy
  ○B. Mixed
  ○C. Normal
  ○D. Dry

Example 7 Airline – Registration Form for Frequent Flyer Card

Name/Surname: _____/_____

Date of birth: _____

Gender: _____

Marital status:
- ○A. Single
- ○B. Married
- ○C. Divorced
- ○D. Widowed

Number of children: _____

Dates of birth of children: _____

Mailing address:
- ○A. Home
- ○B. Workplace

Address: _____

City: _____

County: _____

State: _____

Zip code: _____

Country: _____

Cell phone: _____

Email: _____

Company name: _____

Language you prefer to receive correspondence in:
- ○A. English
- ○B. Spanish
- ○C. Other

If other, please specify: _____

Who normally makes your flight reservations?
- ○A. Me
- ○B. My secretary
- ○C. Other person or entity

Are you a member of other frequent flyer programs?
- ○Yes
- ○No

If you answered yes to the last question, please indicate which ones:
- ○Delta
- ○United
- ○British Airways
- ○Air France
- ○Other

Approximately how many international flights do you take in a year? _____

Seating preference:
- ○A. Window
- ○B. Aisle
- ○C. Indifferent

Examples 4 to 7 have several items of data in common: name, address, and telephone. There are also questions specific to the kind of business, such as this item from Example 5:

> You are:
> ◌A. Interested in mechanics
> ◌B. Interested in car racing
> ◌C. Interested in karting
> ◌D. Working in the automobile sector

Some questions require the selection of just one of the available options, for example:

> Marital Status:
> ◌A. Single
> ◌B. Married
> ◌C. Divorced
> ◌D. Widowed

Some questions allow for the selection of more than one option, such as the Example 5 item above, where the customer might choose "interested in car racing" and "working in the automobile sector." Some questions are obligatory, such as name, address, and specific data of special interest, whereas other questions are optional (age, number of children, etc.). Obligatory fields are normally indicated by an asterisk or other mark.

The form for the airline's frequent flyer card is the most complete and sophisticated. When designing a questionnaire, it is important to not omit key information. In Example 4, even though the business is Internet-based, there is no field for the customer's email address.

In terms of data types, the questionnaires are mainly free text (name, address) or categories (questions with various options, such as A, B, C, etc.). Only the number of children, age, and number of flights a year have numerical answers, and the date of birth is a date field type. From a data quality point of view, categorized data is easier to control, whereas free text fields may need additional post-processing, given that data may be entered inconsistently by different users.

Customer Card Registrations: Data Table Population

This section examines data tables populated with the data captured from the registration forms of examples 4 to 7. Table 3.5 includes data that identifies individuals and contains personal information, which is a different type of data from that in Tables 3.2 to 3.4. This is because the data of Table 3.5

TABLE 3.5 Data collected from the registration form for a buyer's club

Name	Surname	Address	City	County	State	Zip	Telephone	Number of persons	Ages	Gender	Comments
Essie	Roudabush	6220 S Orange Blossom Trl	Memphis	Shelby	TN	38112	901-327-5336	1	31	female	
Bernard	Fifield	22661 S Frontage Rd	Phoenix	Maricopa	AZ	85051	602-953-2753	3	40 42 12	male female female	
Valerie	Haakinson	New York	New York	New York	NY	10001	212-889-5775	2	25 27	female male	
Marianne	Dragaj	14225 Hancock Dr	Anchorage	Anchorage	AK	99515	907-345-0962	4	45 47 15 18	female male male female	

corresponds to the customer card registration form for the Internet/television-based home products company's buyer's club card. If a customer wants the card, all the obligatory information must be given. Some people may consider their telephone number and data about the members of their household as sensitive and would not wish to give those details. However, for this type of business, household information is very important, although the telephone field could be eliminated and substituted with the email address. The registration form can be designed to elicit the household information responses by offering an incentive or free gifts for the kids if the information is completed, for example. In this way more complete information is obtained for the data mining project.

Table 3.6 shows a sample of the data collected from the registration form of a website dedicated to car accessories. The majority of the data is identification information, with just one field related to the business ("you are interested in …") and one field to indicate the channel through which the customer learned about the business. This last field can be important if the company wishes to evaluate the effectiveness of publicity spending. Unlike the data in Table 3.5, this data has a "country" field. Consequently, it should be taken into account that the country, state, and zip code may have different formats and meanings in different countries. In the third row, CAT has been included in the "state" field for a location in Spain, and signifies the autonomous region of Catalonia. Also in the third row, "Barcelona" as "county" is a municipal region and the zip code is commonly known as the "codigo postal." In the Spanish addresses, the number of the house (or block) comes after the name of the street, followed by the floor number and the apartment number, if necessary. The fourth row, with an address in Australia, follows a structure similar to United States addresses. The telephone numbers in the third and fourth rows include the country code prefixes. Getting the format right by, for example, including format controls in the data fields, significantly affects data reliability. These details require careful consideration when designing the customer loyalty registration form. Chapter 5 goes into more detail about these considerations.

Table 3.7 shows a sample of the data collected from a perfume chain store's customer card application form. The majority of the fields contain data about the applicant and only one field (skin type) is specifically related to the product. The data types are textual, date, and categories. The name and surname are together in the same text field, which might make address formatting more difficult for mailings. Clearly, since the business sells perfume, the majority of its customers are probably female; hence, no gender field is included in the data. However, if the business also sells deodorant and other skincare products, the gender field would have to be considered.

Table 3.8 shows a sample of the data collected from the airline frequent flyer card applications. Of the example forms discussed, this is the most complete in

TABLE 3.6 Data collected from the registration form for an automobile accessories website

Name	Surname	Address	City	County	State	Zip	Country	Telephone	Email	Date of birth	You are	How did hear
Haley	Sharper	100 E Broad St	Evansville	Vanderburgh	IN	47713	US	812-421-4804	haley@sharper.com	12/23/1960	A	A
Allyson	Seid	1722 White Horse Mercerville R	Trenton	Mercer	NJ	8619	US	609-584-1794	allyson@seid.com	01/01/1995	A	A
Joan	Pujol	Av. Pedralbes, 33, 1º 1ª	Barcelona	Barcelona	CAT	08034	Spain	(+34) 93-105 01 22	Joan.pujol@yaho.es	06/15/1980	A	A
John P.	Smith	78 James Street	Salisbury	Adelaide	SA	5108	Australia	+(61) 8 8406 280922	Jpsmith55@egcit.au	12/12/1975	D	A

TABLE 3.7 Data collected from a perfume chain store's customer card application form

Name/surname	Address	City	County	State	Zip	Telephone	Email	Date of birth	Language	Skin type
Colin Evertt	645 Church St	Grandview	Jackson	MO	64030	816-765-0961	colin@evertt.com	12/30/1984	A	C
Jannie Crotts	101 US Highway 46	Denver	Denver	CO	80202	303-292-5477	jannie@crotts.com	05/15/1970	A	C
Jacklyn Catino	1092 Saint Georges Ave	Fairfield	Essex	NJ	7004	973-882-3960	jacklyn@catino.com	07/12/1963	A	C
Mariano Argenti	1201 18th St	Altamonte Springs	Seminole	FL	32701	407-332-9851	mariano@argenti.com	11/15/1995	B	D

TABLE 3.8 Data collected from an airline Frequent Flyer Card application

Name	Surname	Date of birth	Gender	Marital status	Number of kids	Mailing address	Date of birth, kids	Address	Cell phone	Email	Company name	Preferred language	Person flight res	Other freq fly	Which companies	Int flights	Seating pref
Gracie	Gidley	12/30/1975	F	S	0	B		2255 Kuhio Ave #1203, Lander, Fremont WY, 82520		gracie@gidley.com	United Waste Systems	A	B	N	-	0	A
Karla	Cieloszyk	05/18/1985	M	M	2	B		22343 Se Stark St, Pensacola, Escambia FL, 32503		karla@cieloszyk.com	Manpower Temporary Services	A	B	N	-	2	A
Tyree	Blumenthal	07/09/1968	M	M	2	B		104 N Aurora St, New York, New York NY, 10028		tyree@blumenthal.com	P C Systems	A	B	N	-	2	B
Bertie	Norris	02/15/1955	F	S		A		108 Washington St, Houston, Harris TX, 77040		bertie@norris.com	Ackerman Knitting Products Inc.	A	A	Y	Delta	5	B

that it asks for detailed personal information together with specific information (five data items) about the type of service offered. Defining which fields are obligatory is a sensitive issue. For example, it may be reasonable to request as obligatory the name, surname, date of birth, and gender of the applicant. However, asking for marital status and the number and ages of children may be considered excessive by some applicants. Therefore, these fields could be defined as optional for the applicant.

A mixture of text data, dates, categories, and numerical data is seen in Table 3.8. There are also some errata in the data: the home address includes the street, number, city, county, state, and zip code all together in the same text field, which might make address formatting difficult for mailings, and the "date of birth, kids" and cell phone fields are blank in all the records. The definition of the form must be checked to see if there was an error during data capture or processing.

Questionnaire Design

References

A discussion of detailed questionnaire design is out of the scope of this book. The following references are recommended for further reading:

Brace, Ian. 2008. *Questionnaire Design: How to Plan, Structure and Write Survey Material for Effective Market Research.* London, UK: Kogan Page Publishers. ISBN: 9780749450281.

Questionnaire Design. 2005. Adapted by Eiselen, R. J. and Uys, T. from Eiselen, R., Uys, T., and Potgieter, N. *Analysing Survey Data Using SPSS13: A Workbook.* Johannesburg, South Africa: University of Johannesburg. Accessed at: http://www.uj.ac.za/EN/Research/Statkon/Documents/Statkon%20Questionaire%20Design.pdf.

Transactional Analysis of Customer Card Usage

Together with the data capture process when the customer applies for a loyalty card, another key aspect is the customer's use of the card itself. As the customer uses the card, a log is generated of the products and services purchased, the amount of money spent, and the exact date and time of the card's use. This data is very useful for large department stores, for example, or gasoline stations, for whom customers are otherwise completely anonymous. Once the customer has been pinpointed with the customer card, transactional data can be accumulated and a transactional profile can be created. (For example, 80 percent of customer purchases are made between 2:00 pm and 8:00 pm; 70

percent are in New Jersey, 20 percent in Newark, 10 percent other; etc.) The transactional profile can then be related with the customer's demographic profile and personal data (the data captured by the card registration form). In terms of data mining business objectives, this information can be used in a department store or supermarket environment to adjust the store layout, product placement, and product mix based on the detected tendencies and preferences of the customers. Specific types of customers can be sent mailings with promotions of products related to what they have bought in the past.

Data Capture

Customer Data Protection

Customers may have the sense that a commercial enterprise could obtain too much information about them. (This has become a key issue regarding data collection from applications on the Internet.) Fortunately, the consumer is protected by current laws of data protection and privacy. These laws restrict the dissemination of data to third parties without the explicit consent of the person involved. The laws also define the type and extent of customer data that can be maintained, restrictions about the usage of the data, and a customer's explicit acceptance if a company wishes to send publicity about new promotions, and so on. However, in reality, there are cases of bad practices, such as when a customer is obliged to return a postpaid reply to reject an offer. If the reply is not made, the customer will be included in the mailings by default. This topic is discussed in more detail in Chapter 18.

Table 3.9 shows four records from a supermarket's transactional data log. The information is compacted by using customer and product IDs. The

TABLE 3.9 Transactional data from customer card usage

CID	Date	Time	Center	Product ID
C01500	12/10/2013	12:31	New Jersey	P34Z212
C03782	12/10/2013	12:31	New Jersey	P34Z212
C09382	12/10/2013	12:32	New Jersey	P95Q622
C01500	12/10/2013	12:33	New Jersey	P71A250

customer data is held in a separate customer table indexed by the customer ID (CID) and includes any special discounts to be applied. Similarly, the product data, including price, is stored in a separate product table. The amount a given customer spends and the products purchased can then be calculated for each visit to the store.

DEMOGRAPHIC DATA

Demographic data includes general statistics about the population and characterize different groups and subgroups. It can refer to a whole country, a region, a city, or individuals who are the targets for a given product or service. Basic demographic data about individuals consists of such information as age, gender, ethnicity, type of employment, education, marital status, and so on. A data mining business objective requiring demographic data would be, for example, a customer segmentation model that adds a socioeconomic category and an education level category to the customer record.

The national census is available at the United States Census Bureau, which is a public source of demographic data available online at www.census.gov and http://2010.census.gov. The data can be filtered by various criteria, such as topics, geographies, population groups, and industrial sectors, at http://factfinder.census.gov. Twelve United States regional census offices maintain specific statistics, such as the US Census Bureau – New York Region at www.census.gov/regions/new_york. In Europe, Eurostat serves a similar purpose and can be found at http://epp.eurostat.ec.europa.eu. Other statistics bureaus include:

- Japan: http://www.stat.go.jp/english/
- China: http://www.stats.gov.cn/english/
- Australia: http://www.abs.gov.au/
- Russian Federation: http://www.gks.ru/wps/wcm/connect/rosstat_main/rosstat/en/main/
- Brazil: http://www.ibge.gov.br/english/default.php
- India: http://mospi.nic.in/Mospi_New/site/home.aspx

A complete list can be found at the World Trade Organization website at www.wto.org/english/res_e/statis_e/natl_e.pdf. Note that some of these links may change over time.

In addition to public domain information sources, there are private companies dedicated to collecting and selling a diversity of demographic information. Companies that specialize in sector-specific data include the Population Reference Bureau (www.prb.org), USA Data (www.usadata.com), and US Data Corporation (www.usdatacorporation.com).

Demographic Data

Business Objectives

Demographic data has many uses. It can be used, for example, for market studies to launch a new product or service, or a business can relate the data to its own customer and business data. An example of a specific business objective would be to gain market presence in a new geographical region by evaluating a product for medium-income families with more than three children. Another example would be to identify residential areas with a high concentration of commuters who have to travel more than 30 miles to reach their workplaces.

The Census: Census Data, United States, 2010

This section discusses data included in the US census from 2010; the format is similar to the census data collected by the majority of countries. The US Census Bureau conducts a diversity of surveys that cover different areas. For instance, to study individuals who are either unemployed or working, the bureau conducts the Survey of Active Population (SAP). A survey called Family Budgets is conducted to study the household consumption of services and goods. The Survey of Fertility studies the characteristics of women in the context of fertility. The Survey of the Disabled, Deficiencies, and Health Conditions determines the number of people with a physical or mental limitation, and so on.

The Residence Questionnaire collects the most important characteristics of principal residences (that is, the habitual residence of a person), either rented or owned. The Household Questionnaire consists of the census variables collected for everyone and includes such information as marital status, education level, municipality of residence since the last census, and so on. The Individual Questionnaire is given to people over 16 years of age who are employed or are in school. It contains information about the type of employment or study and the place where the activity is carried out.

From census information can be derived conclusions such as:

- The population of the country and how it is distributed with respect to gender, age, place of birth, marital status, place of residence, and so on.
- The way households are structured, taking into account various forms of cohabitation.
- The number of people who are employed classified by activities, professional status, and so on, as well as the number of people who are unemployed and searching for employment and the number of people who are studying, what they are studying, and the types of qualifications they possess.
- The number of daily journeys (commutes) and the forms of transport used to reach the workplace or school.
- The characteristics of residential housing, offices, and other types of buildings.

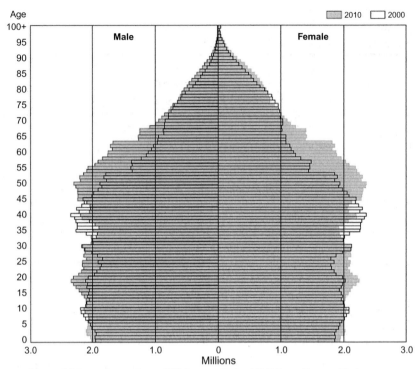

Sources: U.S. Census Bureau, *Census 2000 Summary File 1* and *2010 Census Summary File 1.*

FIGURE 3.1 Population pyramid based on age and gender (United States census, 2010)

- The problems or deficiencies of habitual residences and their neighborhoods, the types of installations the residences have, access to elevators, and so on.
- The possession of a second residence.

Figure 3.1 shows the demographic profile of the population of the United States for the year 2010 in terms of age and gender. This graph supplies a wealth of information, such as the location of concentrations or scarcities of population frequencies for given age ranges. For example, from 65 years and up there is a marked difference between the numbers of men and women (more women survive into old age). The bulge of baby boomers between 45 and 65 years of age is also visible. This bulge has moved proportionately upward over time, which is illustrated by contrasting the 2000 census data with that of 2010 (indicated by different shadings).

MACRO-ECONOMIC DATA

Companies and their businesses do not lead an isolated existence; on the contrary, they reside in a complex and interrelated environment within their own business sectors and further afield within their regional, national, and

TABLE 3.10 Example of macro-economic data
Macro-Economic Indicators, 2007–2011

Year	Consumer Price Index (US)[1]	Inflation (US)[1]	Industrial Production Index (US)[2]	Effective Interest Rate (US)[2]	GDP US[3]	GDP EU[4]	GDP UK[5]	GDP China[6]
2011	224.94	3.16	93.80	0.10	1.04	1.50	0.20	9.20
2010	218.06	1.64	90.07	0.18	1.04	2.00	0.42	10.4
2009	214.54	−0.36	85.55	0.16	0.97	−4.30	−0.22	8.7
2008	215.30	3.84	96.29	1.92	1.02	0.00	−0.67	9.6
2007	207.34	2.85	100.00	5.02	1.05	3.00	0.60	11.4

Sources:
[1] US Bureau of Labor Statistics;
[2] US Federal Reserve (www.federalreserve.gov);
[3] US Bureau of Economic Analysis (www.bea.gov);
[4] Eurostat (http://epp.eurostat.ec.europa.eu/);
[5] UK Office for National Statistics;
[6] National Bureau of Statistics, China Statistical Yearbooks (www.chinability.com/GDP.htm).

international geographical contexts. Therefore, some of the key factors that influence profit, costs, and customers are external factors.

The economic data about a given business sector includes the increase or decrease in total sales, sales for given products and services, and sales in a given sector with respect to previous periods (quarters, years). On a national level, the economic data includes the industrial production index; industrial prices; labor cost index; GDP (Gross Domestic Product); activity index; unemployment index; general consumer price index; harmonized consumer price index; base interest rate; inflation rate; national debt level; household debt index; consumer confidence index; price of oil; price of gold; price of raw materials (copper, coal, etc.); cost of basic energy supplies and services such as electricity, gas, and telephone; energy consumption indices; cement production (which is an indicator for the construction industry and is related to other economic areas); volume of car sales; national trade balance (imports versus exports); national stock exchange index; stock values of specific companies; currency exchange rates; and so on. For an import/export company, the currency exchange rates for the countries it trades with is a key factor. Specific values for some of these indices (with references) are shown in Table 3.10, and data source Internet references are listed at the end of the section.

External data can be found in the economic press, such as *Reuters Finance*, *Bloomberg*, and *Financial Times*. Similar data can be found for the European Economic Union, Asia, Japan, China, and other major economies.

External Data

Unifying with Internal Data

When a company wants to relate external data with its own transactional data, it needs a common index, such as a specific time period. Macro-economic data, such as interest rates and GDP, are typically published on a monthly, quarterly, or yearly basis, which means that the company must match the time stamps for these columns with its own data if it wants to have all the indicators together in one file.

Table 3.10 shows a sample of macro-economic data with one year per row. The table illustrates, for example, that China has a high relative GDP value over the given four-year period, and the US GDP has maintained a positive value, in contrast to the GDPs of the UK and the Euro zone. This information is important for businesses that depend on import/export with other countries.

Other data values that could be added to this table include national indices of imports/exports; trade balance; labor costs; active population; national debt level; consumer debt level; major stock exchange indices such as the NASDAQ, NYSE, Dow Jones (US), LSE (UK), DAX (Germany), and Hang Seng (Hong Kong); and so on. Thus, a company should not restrict itself to relevant variables in its own database but should also consider the business objectives. Internal data can be complemented with external data, which are public domain and easily accessible from the Internet and in various formats such as plain text, spreadsheet (e.g., Excel), or html.

Macro- and Micro-Economic Data

Business Objective

To illustrate how macro- and micro-economic data work together, consider, for example, a data mining project for the Port of Barcelona. The business objective was to incorporate and control uncertainty while guaranteeing precise and reliable information as the end product. The micro-economic data for the Port of Barcelona includes shipping volume and types of cargo along principal maritime routes. The macro-economic data includes GDP, interest rates, and consumer price indices for specific countries over the specified time period. The micro and micro-economic variables were unified in a unique table using a common timestamp, then all the variables were given as inputs to a clustering and correlation analysis.

From: Nettleton, D. F., Fandiño, V. L., Witty, M., and Vilajosana, E. 2000. "Using a Data Mining Workbench for Micro and Macro-Economic Modeling." Proceedings Data Mining 2000, pp. 25–34, Cambridge University, U.K.: WIT Press.

The following websites are relevant to external macro-economic data (these links may vary over time):

- National Statistics Institute: www.stats.gov. This website lists the principal United States, European, and international economic indicators. All industrialized countries have some equivalent of the National Statistics Institute available online. International organizations such as the OECD also provide overall outlooks on a worldwide level.

- US Department of Commerce: www.commerce.gov
- European Central Bank: www.ecb.int
- US Department of the Treasury: www.treasury.gov
- Institute for International Research: www.iirusa.com
- World Bank: www.worldbank.org and data.worldbank.org
- International Monetary Fund: www.imf.org
- IMF World Economic Outlook 2012: www.imf.org/external/pubs/ft/weo/2012/02/
- IMF Data and Statistics: www.imf.org/external/data.htm
- Economic forecasts, news, and indicators for Latin American economies: www.latin-focus.com
- Asian Development Bank – Data and Statistics: www.adb.org/data/statistics
- Asia-Pacific Economic Cooperation: statistics.apec.org.

City, state, and chamber of commerce websites also have pertinent information at a local level.

DATA ABOUT COMPETITORS

General data about specific business sectors are available through the public domain, as are summaries and yearly reports from the principal companies in those sectors. These reports include total sales data as well as turnover; number of offices or outlets; personnel; locations of offices, stores, and production centers; suppliers; number of employees; market strategy; number and types of products and services; principal customers; approximate number of customers; market share by product type; and so on. A business can measure the impact of a competitor's new product launch and adapt to the new situation; if the product launch is a success, then the business can launch similar products into the market. The business can also compile information about the best practices used by similar companies.

In order to compete in the marketplace, a good-quality database must be maintained, with information about the characteristics of competitors, their products and services, and their summarized business data. Many companies publish summaries of their business data and other data about their commercial activity on their company websites, which provide easy-to-access sources of information. However, companies do take care to not give away key information that, to the company's detriment, could be used by competitors.

Figure 3.2 shows rankings, in terms of sales (in millions of dollars), of the ten most important supermarket chains in the world. Kroger, for example, needs to know its relative ranking worldwide, for the prestige value and for the effect this information has on its stock price in the financial markets. However, a company operating only in, for example, the United States will be interested in just the competitors who have a presence in that country.

Principal supermarket chains worldwide
Sales in millions of dollars

1	Wal-Mart Stores	US	217.800	
2	Carrefour	France	67.721	
3	Ahold	Netherlands	64.902	
4	Kroger	US	50.098	
5	Metro AG	Germany	48.264	
6	Albertson's	US	37.931	
7	Tesco	UK	37.378	
8	Safeway	US	34.301	
9	Costco	US	34.137	
10	Rewe Gruppe	Germany	33.640	

FIGURE 3.2 Typical example of data about competitors

In addition to sales, other useful information that gives a company a richer profile of its competitors includes: total turnover, net benefit, profit margins, number of employees, number of stores and their total selling area in square feet, debt and loans, level of diversification, and so on. In this way, a profile can be built of a competitor's profitability, strategy, and approach to the market. This information can also be compiled by companies who are preparing takeover bids and, in order to strengthen their presence in the sector, are looking for competitors to buy.

Figure 3.2 does not give any information about the evolution of sales over time. For this, sales data must be obtained for the last X periods of interest. In this way, the evolution of the rankings can be ascertained, detailing which businesses have gone up in sales, which have gone down, and which have kept constant.

The following articles are relevant to competitive intelligence (these links may change over time):

Fahey, L. Feb. 2007. "Focus On: Competitor Analysis – Turning Data to Insight." CBS News. Available at: www.cbsnews.com/8301-505125_162-51053003/focus-on-competitor-analysis–turning-data-to-insight. (This article is on the use of data for competitor analysis.)

Kaushik, A. Feb. 2010. "8 Competitive Intelligence Data Sources & Best Practices." Available at: www.kaushik.net/avinash/competitive-intelligence-data-sources-best-practices. (This is a guide to competitive intelligence data sources.)

Manion, J. "Collecting and Utilizing Competitor Data." n.d. Stratigent, LLC. Available at: www.stratigent.com/community/websight-newsletters/collecting-and-utilizing-competitor-data. (This article is on collecting and using competitor data.)

Data Sources

Considerations

There are two questions a company should ask about each online data resource it is considering: "How easy is it to save search results?" and "Can I export the data?"

There are several tools available for finding data sources, including Google's advanced search options, individual states' corporate search engines and their international counterparts, individual states' incorporation filings and their international counterparts, and the Securities and Exchange Commission's EDGAR database and each country's equivalents.

FINANCIAL MARKETS DATA: STOCKS, SHARES, COMMODITIES, AND INVESTMENTS

If a company is listed in a stock exchange, if it is interested in following the share prices of companies in its sector, or if it is interested in investing, then the stock exchange is a key source of data for that company. Other types of businesses may not have any interest in or utility for following the evolution of share prices.

Commodities include raw materials and agricultural products and can be monitored, bought, and sold online. Commodities data includes the current (spot) or future prices of specific commodities such as gold, silver, oil, coffee, wheat, platinum, copper, and so on. Commodity prices are particularly relevant to businesses dependent on specific raw materials or primary goods, and historical and future commodity values could, for example, serve as input to a "what if" data model. There are conglomerate indexes for key commodity categories such as fuel, food, and metals.

Two websites that provide such listings are: CNNMoney at http://money.cnn.com/data/commodities/ and Index Mundi at http://www.indexmundi.com/commodities/.

Financial Data

Data Mining Objectives

Financial data is important for some data mining business objectives; for example, a company may be interested in obtaining situational awareness of its market, suppliers, customers, and competitors, or it may wish to create alerts related to stock prices and raw material movements. Perhaps a business analyst is interested in exporting data in spreadsheet format from Google Finance or Yahoo Finance to use as input for a data model. A small- or medium-sized business (SMB) may be interested in tracking the share price of one of its major customers it supplies products or services to. This data can be related with information about how well the customer's business is doing, possible takeovers, mergers, restructuring, and so on. Keeping track of current and future oil prices may be a key concern if a business

Continued

involves transportation. Creating predictive models for stocks and commodities is a specific genre that is out of the scope of this book.

For further reading, see:

Azoff, E. M. 1994. *Neural Network Time Series Forecasting of Financial Markets.* Hoboken, NJ: John Wiley and Sons Ltd.

Wikipedia: Stock Market Prediction. See: http://en.wikipedia.org/wiki/Stock_market_prediction.

Major composite indices are barometers of national economies and, often, of the world economic situation. However, certain sectors, such as finance or technology, can perform above or below the general indices, which are usually composed of a representative spectrum of the major business sectors.

Stock prices in general can be quite volatile and can easily be influenced by a declaration from a key institution or individual, such as the head of the US Federal Reserve or the head of the European Central Bank. These declarations often create an excessive optimism, which in turn creates a "bull run", or an excessive pessimism that spooks the markets. In recent years the interest rates on government bonds for different countries have become key factors. These rates fix how much countries have to pay investors (those who buy government bonds or debt) in order to raise capital to finance the country's debt, for example.

One way to analyze a company's stock value data is to plot its share price over time. This graph can then be overlaid with the general index for the stock exchange, for the sector, and for principal competitors. However, the evolution of the stock price is not enough data to make decisions about whether a company is really performing well as a business. In order to evaluate the underlying performance of a company, the price-to-earnings ratio, expected dividends, and other background information about the company must be examined. Such background (or fundamental) information can include the market capitalization, gross and net profit margins, level of indebtedness, and so on.

The task of evaluating a company's stock is made much easier by the many online applications now available. The most well-known applications are:

- Yahoo Finance (http://finance.yahoo.com/)
- Google Finance (http://www.google.com/finance)
- Market Watch (http://www.marketwatch.com/investing)
- Reuters (http://www.reuters.com/finance/stocks)

These applications allow the user to choose a specific stock, normally by searching for its name or typing in its ticker name (stock market abbreviation) directly. Then a graphic of that day's stock value evolution is displayed, together with a summary of the company, its principal competitors, analysts' evaluations (buy/hold/sell), and a ticker with the latest news items in the

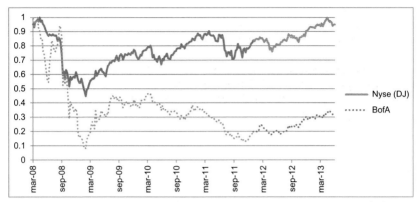

FIGURE 3.3   Stock price evolution (2008–2013) of Bank of America versus the NYSE Composite Index

financial press related to that company and the business sector in general. Data can be exported in spreadsheet format from applications such as Yahoo Finance and then imported into a company's own applications and analysis or modeling software.

External Data

Stock Market Data

There are several good sources of stock market information, including The Motley Fool (www.fool.com) and Warren Buffet's website (http://www.warrenbuffett.com/). (Warren Buffet is known as the "Oracle of Omaha" for his uncanny ability to pick winning stocks.) Two of the most well-known online television channels dedicated to finances are CNBC and Bloomberg. Analyzing Google search terms is a recent area of study for predicting stock market moves. For more details, see http://en.wikipedia .org/wiki/Stock_market_prediction.

Figure 3.3 shows a plot of the stock price over the last five years for Bank of America (ticker: BAC) on the NYSE (New York Stock Exchange) index. It is overlaid with the value of the NYSE Composite Index for the same period. Both values have been normalized (ranged between 0 and 1) to facilitate their comparison. The NYSE Composite Index is designed to measure the performance of all common stocks listed on the NYSE. BAC is a typical example of the trend in stock prices of the banking sector, which has taken a huge beating since 2009 due, to a large extent, to bad loans in the real estate sector, whose bubble burst in 2007–2008.

Chapter 4

Data Representation

INTRODUCTION

The analysis of commercial data is an activity that requires a series of steps, each of which builds a solid platform for the steps that follow and on which depends the quality and integrity of the whole data processing project. Thus, once a business objective has been selected and the necessary data identified, the next step is to decide how to represent the data variable by variable and as a whole. This chapter discusses the ways data can be represented in order to facilitate its interpretation and visualization. The chapter is divided into two main parts: basic representation and advanced representation.

BASIC DATA REPRESENTATION

This section addresses basic data types; visualization methods; and the topics of normalization, distributions, and outliers. The different visualization methods include pie charts, histograms, graph plots, and radar diagrams. Other topics covered include representation, comparison, and processing of different types of variables; principal types of variables (numerical, categorical ordinal, categorical nominal, and binary); normalization of the values of a variable; distribution of the values of a variable; and identification of atypical values and outliers.

Basic Data Types

It is convenient to consider data in terms of a file, which is normally defined in two axes: the vertical axis (length) is defined by the number of records available, and the horizontal axis (width) is defined by the number of variables used to describe those records. Normally, the raw data is stored in a flat file in plaintext format such as a spreadsheet file (e.g., Excel) or as a database table (e.g., Access, DB2 or MySQL), and usually the descriptive variables have different types (numbers, categories, etc.).

Assuming that the data was generated by some process or randomly extracted from a database, the first thing is to look at it and explore it. This is where the initial decision is made with respect to the data: in order to visualize data and give it meaning, each variable must previously have been assigned a type. In statistics, a type is often assigned that makes it easiest to process the data, rather than reflecting the nature of the data. If the data has already been generated, the types of variables might already be defined (for example, in a database table with its schema, or an Excel file with format masks). In this case, the task is to check that the assigned format is the most adequate for the current needs. If it is not, the data will need to be transformed.

As an example of a variable of (nominal) categories whose ordering cannot be used to compare the categories, consider the variable "zip code," which could have values such as 20037-8010, 60621-0433, 19020-0025, and so on. Another example is a list of states: although the states can be ordered alphabetically, the fact that one state comes before another in the list says nothing about the states themselves. For example, New Jersey does not have a greater population than New York, and Alabama is not bigger than Alaska.

On the other hand, "experience level" is an example of a variable that does have an implicit ordering (ordinal) among its values and would have values such as 1, 2, 3, 4, or low, medium, high. If variables of different types are to be compared, it is essential to dedicate time to assigning the initial types; otherwise, the meaning of the data may be lost. In this chapter, variable types are discussed in detail using examples that are relevant to commercial data. For a more academic and detailed introduction to variable types, see http://turner.faculty.swau.edu/mathematics/math241/materials/variables/.

Once a type has been assigned to each variable, and assuming the type assigned is the most adequate, then each variable can be explored individually. The way to visualize a variable depends on its type: numerical variables work well with a line plot, categories with a frequency histogram or a pie chart. The statistics generated for each variable again depend on its type: for numerical variables the maximum, minimum, average, standard deviation, and so on are suitable; for categoricals, the mode, frequency for each category, and so on work well.

Comparing Variables

Variables of Different Types

It is easier to analyze variables of the same type together and make direct comparisons between them. Visualization is a useful technique to compare variables of different types for frequencies and distributions. For example, for clients who have been customers for up to two years (numerical variable), the distribution of the variable "customer type" (categorical variable) is visualized using a pie chart. In this way, differences and tendencies between different ranges of customer lifetime can be identified.

Once the exploration phase is finished, which could involve normalizations, elimination of unknown or erroneous values, readjustment of distributions, and so on, the next step is modeling. To start modeling, the dataset can be partitioned into groups or segments (clusters) or directly created with a classifier or predictive model. The simplest algorithms that model the data require all the input variables to have the same type (for example, numerical). Often, a categorical variable (ordinal or nominal) is assigned values 1, 2, 3, and so on, and from then on it is considered numerical; however, this goes against what was discussed earlier about respecting the nature of the variables. So another approach is to convert all the variables to categories. The numerical variables are categorized by defining numerical ranges for a given variable and then assigning each record to the appropriate category.

For example, to categorize the variable "salary," some ranges or bands must first be defined. For this example, three ranges are described: 0 to 100, 101 to 999, and 1,000 or more. Next, three names are defined, which will give an intuitive meaning to the categories: 0 to 100 will be "low salary," 101 to 999 will be "medium salary," and 1,000 or more will be "high salary." The ranges and names can be defined by inspecting the distribution plot for the variable "salary," or an expert in salaries can be consulted to define the ranges and name them appropriately.

There are more sophisticated modeling techniques that are able to process input variables with data types. Some of these algorithms calculate true distances based on each type, whereas others simply convert (internally) all the data into a unique format.

In order to explore and model a dataset comprised of variables with different types, the difference, similarity, and grade of relationship between these variables must be measured. It is easy to interpret differences between a client who is 35 years old and another who is 75 years old. It is also easy to differentiate between a utility car and a sports car. But it is not so easy to understand a comparison between a blue utility car and another car for which the only information known is that it was built eight years ago. This difficulty does not arise because the data is incorrect, nor because the data types have been incorrectly assigned: it is due to the inherent difficulty of comparing variables of different types.

Variable Types

Numerical and Categorical

There are two basic types of variables that can be taken as starting points: numbers and categories. A numeric variable would be, for example, "age," with values 35, 24, 75, 4, and so on. A variable with categories is, for example, "marital status," with four possible values: "married," "single," "divorced," and "widowed."

Representation, Comparison, and Processing of Variables of Different Types

Assigning a type to a variable must be done before the data can be explored or modeled. Some of the most well-known representations, which take into account different data processing needs, are looked at next, starting with an example of typical customer data in a financial institution.

A bank's customer data consists of one record per customer containing the basic commercial data such as name, address, telephone number, account balance, products and services that the customer has, credit rating, date the customer record was created (customer lifetime), and so on. A derived variable (or factor) could be an indicator for loan concession, and another could be an indicator for the targeting of publicity information for a given marketing campaign. This data may contain a diversity of variable types: categorical (nominal and ordinal), numerical, binary, and variables with a probabilistic interpretation, for example, "probability that a client will pay back a loan" or "grade of interest of the client for a given financial product."

Principal Types of Variables

There are five principal types of variables: numerical, ordinal categorical, nominal categorical, binary, and date and time. The following descriptions refer to the examples in Chapter 3.

Numerical variables include, for example, age, account balance, and credit-to-debt ratio. This type of data contains whole numbers, such as 35, 24, 75, 4, and decimal point numbers, such as 35.4 and 24.897. The "year" variable in Chapter 3's Example 1 would clearly be represented as a numerical variable, whereas the utility scale variable in Example 2 could be represented as a number or as an ordinal categorical variable. In Figure 4.1, a three dimensional plot is shown of three numerical variables.

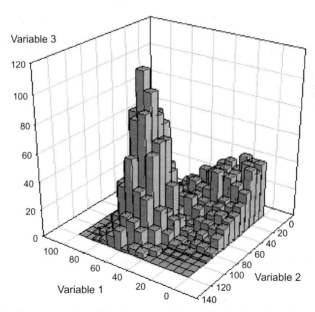

FIGURE 4.1 A representation of three key numerical variables in three dimensions

Ordinal categorical variables include profitability (high, medium, low) and time as client (long, medium, short). For this type of variable, there is a meaningful ordering among the categories. For example, debt level = 1 indicates a higher debt level than debt level = 2, and so on. In Example 1, for the variable related to question 2 (when thinking of buying a car), the first three categories are ordinal, whereas the last category is nominal. Also in Example 1, for the variable related to question 7 ("What price would you pay for a car?") all the categories are ordinal.

Nominal categorical variables include, for example, car manufacturer (Chevrolet, Ford, Mercedes, Opel) and zip code (20037-8010, 60621-0433, 19020-0025). This variable's type is categorical, but it is not possible to meaningfully order its values. As discussed earlier, alphabetic ordering is not considered meaningful in the sense that it is not based on a value that the category represents. Hence, it cannot be said that Alaska is bigger than Nebraska because it comes first in alphabetical order. In Example 1, the categories of the variable related to question 6 ("Which characteristics are most important for your car?") are all nominal. In Figure 4.2, a radar-style diagram is shown of a profile in terms of variables with different types.

Binary variables include, for example, has a mortgage (Yes, No), client cancellation (Yes, No), and gender (M, F). This type of variable can be considered as a special case of the nominal type, for which there are only two possible categories. There are often many variables of this type for data captured using questionnaire forms. For example, there may be a series of yes/no questions relevant to the client's specific services, products, attributes, and so on. In Example 1, the categories of the variable related to question 1 ("Are you

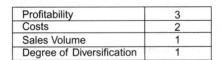

Profitability	3
Costs	2
Sales Volume	1
Degree of Diversification	1

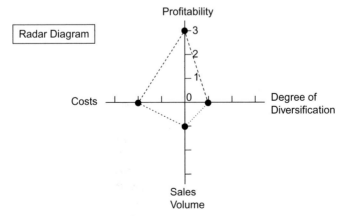

FIGURE 4.2   Radar-style diagram: representation of the values of four variables with different types describing a profile

thinking of buying a new car?") and question 5 ("What do you principally use your car for?") are both binary.

Date/time variables are usually collected together. A date can be considered a subtype of a numerical variable, and internally, it is processed as a number. What can vary is the format it is shown in: MM/DD/YYYY (United States), DD/MM/YYYY (UK, Europe), YYYY/MM/DD (ISO International Standard 8601), and so on. Also, the day and month can be displayed as names instead of numbers. For transactional data, the date and time stamp are often essential pieces of information. As they are internally stored as numbers, simple arithmetic can be performed on dates: subtract one from another to obtain the time difference, compare dates to know if one value is before or after another, and so on. Care must be taken when processing this type of variable, especially when importing and exporting from text or spreadsheets, during which it may unexpectedly be converted into a text string.

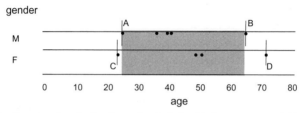

FIGURE 4.3   One way of evaluating the grade of relationship between two variables of different types is by visualization: the relationship of the numerical variable "age" is shown with respect to the categories of the variable "gender"

Time, on the other hand, can be a subcomponent of the date, or it can be a separate variable. It may be in 24-hour format (e.g., 23:56), or in am/pm format (e.g., 11:56 pm). International time zones (Greenwich Mean Time +/– 12hours) may also have to be taken into account. The time/date may be accompanied with the time zone as additional information. This information should be recorded for company databases whose clients' transactions are in any of the four time zones in the United States. If it is not directly available, it can be derived from the state's location (e.g., New York = EST, or Eastern Standard Time).

Figure 4.3 shows that the range of values for gender = M is between points A and B, whereas the range of values for gender = F is between points C and D. The overlap of the two ranges occurs between points A and B, indicated by the region colored in gray. In this way, the extent to which the values of the two variables overlap can be calculated and thus the strength of the relationship between them can be evaluated.

Figure 4.4 shows the characteristic distribution for the variable "days since last purchase," which measures the time in days since the customer's last purchase. There is a peak at 10 days, with the number of clients decreasing until reaching 50 days, at which point the number of clients remains more or less constant until reaching zero at 90 days.

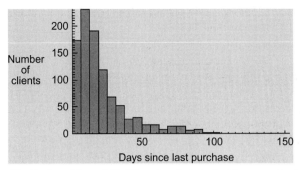

FIGURE 4.4   Distribution of the variable "days since last purchase"

Figure 4.5 shows a pie chart representation. For the variable "clients by state," the ratio of clients located in New York is approximately 10 times that of Pennsylvania. Figure 4.6 shows tendencies over time and compares the relative sales of different products.

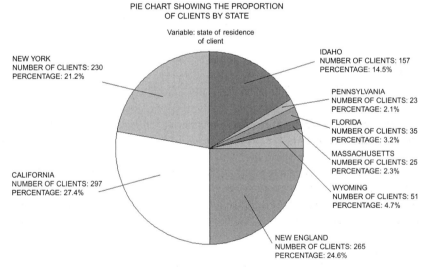

FIGURE 4.5   Distribution of the variable "clients by state"

Categorical Variables

Loyalty Card Registration Form

The loyalty card registration form in Chapter 3's Example 7 has categories of several variables that could be represented as pie charts: marital status (four categories), who makes the flight reservation (three categories), and other frequent flyer programs (five categories).

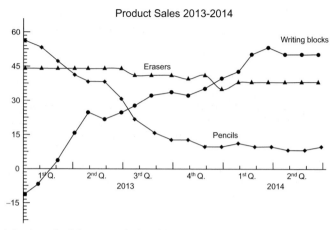

FIGURE 4.6 A graph of three numerical variables

Normalization of the Values of a Variable

In order to compare different datasets, or input them as variables to a predictive model, it is useful to have them in the same range. One of the simplest techniques to do this is called normalization, which configures the numerical data to fall into the same limits, for example, from 0 to 100, or from 0 to 1.

Data is normalized in order to avoid biasing toward extreme values. Consider, for example, a dataset with two variables, "income" and "age": the income range is from $0 to $50 million, and the age range is from 18 to 90 years. Hence, if these values are input to a data modeling technique, depending on how the technique is implemented, the model might give much more importance to the variable with the biggest numerical values. To avoid this, both variables are put onto the same scale by normalizing them. Another reason to normalize two or more variables is to plot and visualize them on the same scale in a graph plot.

To normalize the age value of the variable "age," subtract the minimum value for "age" from the age value and then divide by the maximum age minus the minimum age, that is, (age − min_age)/(max_age − min_age). Consider, for example, when age is equal to 35, the minimum value is 18, and the maximum value is 65. Then, the normalized value of age (35) will be (35 − 18)/(65 − 18) = (17)/(47) = 0.36. If age is equal to 18 (the minimum value), its normalized value is 0, and if age is equal to 65 (the maximum value), its normalized value is 1. There are other normalization techniques, such as subtracting the mean and then dividing by the variance.

There are some tools and models that automatically normalize the data as part of the preprocessing stage, whereas other methods (such as some neural network tools) require that the values already be normalized. Having all the variables on the same scale also makes it easier to compare one variable with another. If two histograms of two normalized variables are generated and placed one alongside the other, clearly their interpretation becomes easier.

Transformation of Variables

Normalization

Variables should not be automatically normalized, given that some of their characteristics may be lost. In rule-based models, for example, normalization will make the data more difficult to interpret. Therefore, the requirements for the modeling technique to be used must first be determined and the reasons for wanting to get the variables onto the same scale must be considered. Or, a non-normalized version may be used in part of the analysis phase and then normalization performed before inputting to a predictive model.

Distribution of the Values of a Variable

The distribution of a variable is related to the normalization process just discussed. It shows how the values of a variable are distributed, from the smallest to the largest. For example, consider the variable "number of visits of a given customer by quarter": the minimum value would be zero, and the maximum value could be 25. However, perhaps the majority of customers (60 percent) tend to visit the store between five and ten times a quarter. Thus the mean value will be seven or eight times a quarter. Graphing the values ("frequency of visit" versus "number of cases") results in a distribution with a weight toward the left (mean of 7.5) with respect to the complete range, which is between 0 and 25.

Statistical Principles

Standard Deviation

In statistics, standard deviation shows how much variation or dispersion there is from the average (mean) or expected value. A low standard deviation indicates that the data points tend to be very close to the mean; a high standard deviation indicates that the data points are spread out over a large range of values. For example, if a dataset consists of three customer records with ages of 20, 21, and 22, the mean value is 21 and the standard deviation (around the mean) is 1. If the ages were 20, 40, and 60, the mean value is 40 and the standard deviation is 20. Standard deviation, together with other statistical values, can be calculated directly on a column of numbers in a spreadsheet by using the appropriate function. (See the following website for examples: http://www.mathsisfun.com/data/standard-normal-distribution.html.)

Other distributions are possible, such as center-weighted toward the minimum, center-weighted toward the maximum, or a symmetrical distribution around the mean. For the initial analysis of the data, a symmetrical distribution is desirable, because it avoids the problem of bias or skew in the data. Other distributions are a Gaussian bell curve and a distribution with multiple peaks. Distribution of the values of a variable is covered in the next section.

Statistical Principles

Normal (Gaussian) Distribution

The normal, or Gaussian, distribution has a bell-shape that is, ideally, symmetrical about the mean value in the middle. A graph showing a normal distribution for a variable in a dataset has the variable values on the x-axis and the number of records with that value (frequency) on the y-axis. A symmetrical distribution around the mean implies that the majority of the records in the dataset are close to the mean. When showing the distribution of a numerical value, the values tend to be grouped into ranges (0–10, 11–20, etc.) and the distribution displayed as a histogram. (See the following website for examples: http://www.mathsisfun.com/data/standard-normal-distribution.html.)

Atypical Values – Outliers

One problem that can occur with the distribution of the values of a variable is the presence of extreme or non-representative cases. For example, consider the variable "age" with expected values of between 18 and 70 years. Suppose that a value of 250 is found among the data. This is clearly an error, and the value might be corrected by finding the data value in the original data source and re-entering it, or, if it is erroneous in the original data, the record may be eliminated altogether. For the variable "age," an error of this type is obvious. However, for other variables the error may not be so evident. For a large volume of records, there may be various extreme values and it might be necessary to identify and eliminate them. If they are not eliminated, these values would skew the overall statistics of the data set.

Figure 4.7 shows the distribution for average monthly customer spending on the x-axis with respect to number of customers on the y-axis. The distribution is

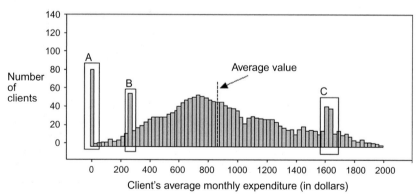

FIGURE 4.7 Typical distribution for numerical values for "average monthly customer expenditure" versus "number of customers," with atypical value groups A, B, and C

approximately Gaussian or normal with respect to a spending value of $875, which represents the mean expenditure value for these customers. From $750 onward the number of units sold reduces progressively. The same tendency is seen below $750. There are three groups of suspicious data values seen in the figure, which may impact the quality and the integrity of the data. Group A has an expenditure value of zero, which may be due to omission, a data processing error, or some other reason. For group B, the values do not behave in accordance with the general distribution. It would be necessary to investigate the cases to establish why there is a high frequency of customers with a relatively low expenditure level of between $250 and $275. A similar situation is evident for group C, but in this case it represents customers with a relatively high expenditure level of between $1,600 and $1,675. The records for groups B and C must be studied in more detail to check their characteristics and to establish whether they do not fit into the distribution due to an error in the data or due to some legitimate characteristics that differentiate them from the majority of customers and the general tendency with respect to the spending level. Chapter 5 discusses in more detail possible data content errors and how to deal with them.

Statistical Principles

Inferential Statistics

Statistical inference is a process for drawing conclusions from sample data that can then be generalized to the whole population. Inferential statistics is a tool specifically for this purpose and is used to test hypotheses and make estimations using sample data. For example, inferential statistics can be used to infer from sample data what customer sentiment is about a new product. Another use could be to evaluate the probability that an observed difference between groups of customers is a reliable one (it can be generalized) or one that might have happened by chance for a given dataset (a specific case). Descriptive statistics, on the other hand, describe characteristics of the data itself, such as the maximum, minimum, mean, standard deviation, and so on. The strength of relationship between independent (causal or input) variables and dependent (effect or output) variables can also be evaluated. Chapter 6 and Chapter 8 cover several of these topics in more detail. (For more information about inferential statistics, see: http://www.socialresearchmethods.net/kb/statinf.php.)

Figure 4.8 shows three main product types sold: pencils, with 27.3 percent of the total; notepads, with 25 percent; and ballpoint pens, with 22.7 percent. However, there is a remaining 25 percent of the total with doubtful values for "product type"; 14.5 percent of the products are assigned as "XX." This could be a data entry or processing error, or perhaps "XX" indicates that the product type is pending assignment, or it could have some other significance. Also, 4.7 percent of the product types are " ", that is, blank, or "null." A decision must be made on whether to include the values "XX" and " " in the data analysis and modeling or eliminate those records from the sample. If they are included,

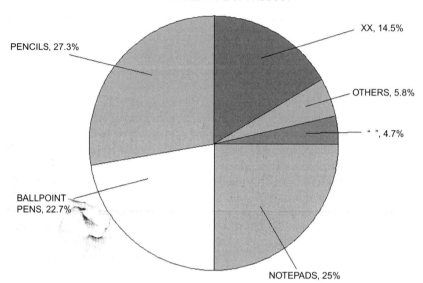

FIGURE 4.8 Distribution for the nominal categorical variable "product type"

an attempt should be made to assign the missing values by finding the real values from an alternate data source or deriving them from other variables.

Lastly, 5.8 percent of the product types are "others." This is not necessarily an error, given that many graphical systems create this category for a pie chart by grouping the values that have a very low percentage. On the other hand, it could be that the values are erroneous. Therefore, they must be checked. This section has focused primarily on the visual identification of outliers, which is a convenient approach. However, there are also computational models that can identify and filter outliers automatically.

Data Quality – Outliers

Outliers as a Business Objective

Sometimes outliers are precisely the data values of interest as a business objective. For example, in fraud detection, the majority of normal transactions follow standard patterns, whereas a fraudulent transaction has an atypical pattern with respect to the majority. Also, some small niche, high-profit customer groups that are differentiated from the major customer groups may be the target for a given product or service offering.

ADVANCED DATA REPRESENTATION

The following section discusses more advanced ways of representing data, which may be required for some special types of data and/or data that has a more complex structure. Four advanced types of representation are briefly presented: hierarchies, semantic networks, graphs, and fuzzy. Details on how to implement the data entry and data processing are given for each type.

Hierarchical Data

As its name suggests, hierarchical data has a series of levels that are organized hierarchically, normally top-down, and can be represented as a tree-like structure. For example, a company's commercial offering may be defined at the most generic level as products and services. Within products, there may be different types of products such as personal hygiene, domestic cleaning, bed linen, and so on. Different types of services may be hairdressers, beauty care, optician, and so on. Figure 4.9 represents this information as a tree-like structure.

In order to implement this type of representation, a tree-like structure is needed for which there are specific data types and libraries in various programming languages. Alternatively, the data could be represented as an XML document. Extensible Markup Language (XML) is a data definition format that follows a set of rules for structuring documents, with the advantage that they are understandable by humans and can also be directly processed by a computer program. (For more information about XML, refer to: http://en.wikipedia.org/wiki/XML.)

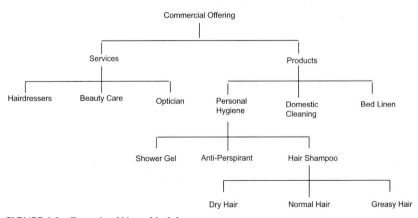

FIGURE 4.9   Example of hierarchical data

Hierarchical Data Representations

Treemaps

Treemaps are a specialized way of visualizing hierarchical, tree-structured data as a set of nested rectangles. The major branches of the tree structure are assigned rectangles, on which smaller rectangles are then superimposed to represent the sub-branches, and so on. The areas of the rectangles are usually proportional to the given data values and will have an appropriate color scheme to differentiate the underlying structure. (For more information about treemaps, refer to: http://en.wikipedia.org/wiki/Treemapping.)

Semantic Networks

Semantic networks are a type of data representation incorporating linguistic information that describes concepts or objects and the relationship or dependency between them. For example, financial products can be described by their duration, risk level, and other characteristics: a mortgage is a financial product that is long-term and has a dependency on other financial products such as home insurance, life insurance, and current accounts. Figure 4.10 illustrates a simple semantic network where the principal concept is "financial product," which can

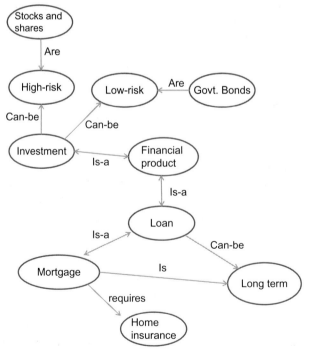

FIGURE 4.10   Example of ontological data

be a loan or an investment. An example of a long-term loan is a mortgage, and an example of a low-risk investment is a government bond.

With respect to implementation, this type of representation is somewhat different from the tree structure discussed in the previous section. A semantic network has a graph-like structure that can have connectivity horizontally as well as vertically between the represented objects. Again, there are specific data types and libraries in languages, such as Java, Python (Network X), and C++, for graph processing, as well as ontology libraries. Data structures such as matrices and linked lists are most frequently used to represent the nodes and links between them, and to efficiently perform queries on the objects and relationships.

Graph Data

Graph data represents objects as nodes and the relationships between the objects as edges in a graph. Communication between nodes can be represented by information related with the edges. For example, an online social network can be represented as a graph where the nodes are people and the edges are friendship links that have been established. The number of messages sent and received (by writes to a wall, email, or some other medium) between two nodes on a given link can be represented by a number associated with the edge. (Information about Facebook's social graph can be found at: http://en.wikipedia.org/wiki/Social_graph.)

A graph is comprised of nodes and edges, but it is easy to misrepresent an OSN (online social network). Some of the issues are: (i) choosing the type of activity between nodes to define a link, (ii) key data may be unavailable, (iii) related to the first point, establishing the minimum activity level (by frequency or latency) in order for a link to appear between two nodes, (iv) the information that is available about each node individually and the nature of the graph as a whole, and (v) what the user wishes to do with the graph once the OSN is represented.

In the upper graph in Figure 4.11 the existence of an edge implies that both users have mutually accepted a friendship request in the OSN application. The edges have no additional information associated with them. In contrast, in the lower graph a rule has been defined so that an edge implies at least five messages have been sent/received over the last three months. In this case, the information associated with the edges indicates the number of messages sent/received.

Hence, as seen in Figure 4.11, if an OSN graph is defined based just on the "friendship accepted" links, a false idea of the true relationships or lack of relationships may be given. Consider the case of the two users who have a "friendship link" but never communicate on the OSN. Key information may be missing or impossible to capture about how people really communicate. For example, two users who have no communication in the OSN (via writes to a wall or

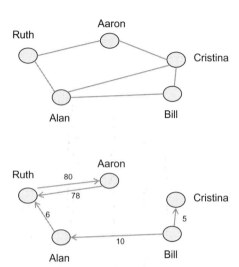

FIGURE 4.11   Graphical data representing an online social network with friendship links (*upper graph*) and communication activity (*lower graph*)

the OSN's internal email system) may work together in the same office and conduct constant verbal communication. With respect to implementation, the same comments apply as for the semantic networks in the previous section.

Fuzzy Data

In the real world, a given data item, such as a customer, may not fit exactly into just one category. The customer may have attributes that belong to two or more customer profiles a company defines to categorize its customers. In this situation, one can say that a customer partially belongs to profile A and partially to profile B, or that the customer belongs to profiles A and B, but is predominantly profile A. However, it may not be appropriate to just assign the customer to profile A and discard the customer's information characteristic of profile B, because that information may also be useful to know. One solution for this type of ambiguous classification is a "fuzzy" assignment, which allows for a "grade of belonging" or "grade of membership" to multiple profiles at the same time. Fuzzy grades are typically defined on a scale from 0 (no membership) to 1 (total membership) to a given profile or category. The sum of the grades of membership of all the categories to which a given item belongs must equal 1.

For example, a customer may belong to the category "slight risk" with grade 0.4 and the category "moderate risk" with grade 0.6. Figure 4.12 shows a graphical representation of the four risk categories "none," "slight," "moderate," and "high." The categories are represented by triangles and trapeziums, which overlap so that each customer could have memberships to two or more categories. On the x-axis the "linguistic" categories can be quantified on a numerical scale.

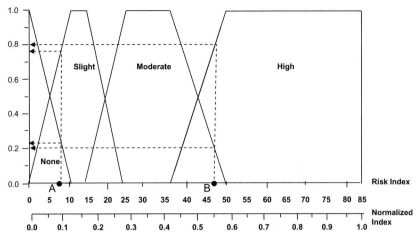

FIGURE 4.12   Example of fuzzy data

The membership grade can be read from the y-axis for a given point on the x-axis for each of the "fuzzy" categories. The risk index value on the x-axis is calculated by another process or data mining model.

The x-axis has two scales: the upper one represents the original calculated risk index, which goes from 0 to 85. Underneath it is the normalized version of the risk index, which goes from 0 to 1. Therefore, the value "40" on the upper index corresponds to 0.47 on the lower, normalized index. The four risk categories overlap: with reference to the upper risk index, "none" goes from 0 to 10, "slight" from 0 to 25, "moderate" from 14 to 50, and "high" from 37 to 85.

To understand how to read the grade of membership for points on the x-axis, consider points A and B in Figure 4.12. Client A is at 7.5 on the x-axis. The lines immediately above that point are the two fuzzy risk categories, "none" and "slight." By following the dashed lines vertically up to each category line, and then horizontally to the y-axis, the grade of membership for each fuzzy category can be read. Client A's grade of membership to "none" is 0.24 while the grade of membership to "slight" is 0.76. A vertical line drawn from client B crosses two lines in the fuzzy categories "moderate" and "high." By drawing a horizontal line across to the y-axis, the grade of membership can be read for each fuzzy category. Client B's grade of membership to "moderate" is 0.2, while its grade of membership to "high" is 0.8.

Fuzzy categories can, of course, be designed as desired by defining the size, form, and degree of overlap of the trapeziums that represent them. Then the grades of membership can be used in business rules to make decisions. For example, if a bank customer's membership grade for the fuzzy category "high" is greater than 0.4, then the bank will not give credit to that customer.

With respect to implementation, assume a data input file that is made up of numerical data. A grade of membership can be derived for each of the fuzzy categories by reading in the numerical data and using the fuzzy technique from Figure 4.12. Hence, the original data does not have to be in any special format. The processing is done by a set of "fuzzy rules" that mathematically represent the trapezoids of the fuzzy categories. Once the grade of membership of a given data item has been calculated for each of the fuzzy categories, the non-zero grades are stored together with the categories. The original data value and a unique reference to its record are also stored.

Chapter 5

Data Quality

INTRODUCTION

Data quality is a primary consideration for any commercial data analysis project, with the definition of quality including the availability or accessibility of the data. This chapter discusses typical problems that can occur with data, including errors in the data content (especially textual data), errors introduced in the data capture and transformation steps, the relevance and reliability of the data, and how to quantitatively evaluate data quality. Finally some typical errors due to data extraction and how to avoid them are discussed by examining a practical case study.

In order to consider quality, it is essential to have previously chosen a business objective, for example, "reduce the loss of existing customers by 3 percent." (Refer to Chapter 2 for the process of selecting business objectives.) This particular business objective is commonly known as "customer churn" and refers to the number of customers who stop trading with a business over a given period of time. Once there is a business objective, the next step is to evaluate the available data for that objective. Following the evaluation, the company may conclude that it does not possess sufficient data with respect to the objective. Given this situation, there are two alternatives to consider: (i) postpone the project and undertake the task of obtaining the necessary data (see Chapter 3), or (ii) abandon the chosen business objective and find another one for which the necessary data is available. If option (i) is chosen, then the cost of obtaining the data should be evaluated, and whether the cost is within the available budget should be confirmed.

Once it is established that the necessary data is available to go ahead with the project, the company is still not on firm ground, as it must then evaluate the quality of the data. For example, are there many data items for which the value is unknown or missing? What is the percentage of data values which are erroneous or unreliable? Are there too few variables that are really relevant to the business objective?

Consider, for example, the objective "reduce customer churn by 3 percent." What data is needed to create a predictive model that would anticipate customer loss and allow the business to take some preventive action? Some initial data could be the client ID, the total time as a customer, the date of the last purchase or commercial activity, and some indicator of the frequency of purchases in the last year. With respect to demographic data, if the customer is an individual (as opposed to a company or organization), the age, gender, marital status, and home zip/post code could be used. If the customer is a company, descriptive data about the company can be compiled, such as where it is located, its business sector, size (turnover, number of employees), and so on.

Let's say that to assemble this data, a single data file is created with one column per variable and one row per customer. When the file is opened with a spreadsheet program, it is immediately obvious that the "zip code" column is virtually empty. The same is true for the column labeled "marital status." Clearly the zip codes and marital status of customers are not habitually captured. In the column for "age," there are some records with values that are zero, negative, or greater than 100. So, although the "age" column is complete, it is not reliable.

During the process of analyzing unknown data, there are various alternatives, depending on the percentage of missing data and the characteristics of the variable being considered. If a variable has more than a given percentage of missing data values, for example, 50 percent, the company could decide to completely eliminate this variable. If the variable is numerical, a statistically simple solution would be to fill the missing values with the average value of the known values. A more sophisticated method is to generate a graph of the variable's distribution and identify gaps in the distribution, whose values would be candidates to fill in the missing data values. An even more ambitious method is to predict the missing data using a model whose inputs are the variables that have a high correlation with the variable with the missing values.

In order to identify and process erroneous data, a distribution of the values of the variable being studied can be generated using a graph plot or histogram to establish the general tendency of its values. Then cases can be identified that do not have the tendency or order of magnitude of the given variable. For example, if the amount of the monthly invoices for a customer normally varies between $60 and $150, an invoice for $2,700 would be suspicious. Other types of erroneous data are less easy to spot: one approach is to use segmentation models to distinguish clusters (groupings) of normal cases and abnormal cases. Segmentation models are discussed further in Chapters 6 and 8. Also refer to the discussion of data distributions in Chapter 4 for more details about identifying atypical values.

Outliers and Atypical Values

Business Objective

Sometimes, a business objective may be precisely that of identifying the outliers and atypical values. This must be taken into account in the initial data processing stages so as to not filter out the values of potential interest.

Another data processing task often performed early in a data mining project is extracting structured information hidden in fields that do not have a defined structure. For example, consider a text field that contains the complete address of a customer with the house number, street name, town, county, state, and zip code, all together. In this situation, a new data structure would be created with the fields "house number," "street," "town," "county," "state," and "zip code" defined separately. Then the data would be transferred from the original field to the new fields. Techniques such as lexical analysis, semantic analysis, and pattern detection can be used to achieve this. Some software tools that do this automatically (or semi-automatically) are commercially available for a reasonable price (for example, see Daedalus: http://www.daedalus.es/en/).

Text Mining – Data Quality

Data Sources

Several cases were discussed in Chapter 3 where a user had to enter personal details (e.g., name, address, telephone) in text fields in order to fill out loyalty card registration forms. The quality of the input data entered by the user can be guaranteed by format controls for these fields. However, in Chapter 3's Example 3, several of the fields allowed free-format text where the user could describe motives for changing companies. Although it is more difficult to control the input quality for these fields, they may contain highly useful or relevant nuggets of information for the business. Recall that, in many cases, a limited number of predefined response items were used in the survey/questionnaire examples, which facilitates the control of the input values and of the resulting data quality.

Text Mining

Chapter 11 specifically discusses the topic of text mining. For further reading on text mining, consult:
   Witten, I. H. 2005. "Text Mining." In: *Practical Handbook of Internet Computing.* M.P. Singh, ed., pp. 14.1–14.22. Boca Raton, FL: Chapman & Hall/CRC Press.

EXAMPLES OF TYPICAL DATA PROBLEMS

In practice, a diversity of problems associated with data that are caused by "concept errors" may occur, including: different formats in different data sources, hidden information in free-format fields, and the confused use of key indices, all of which make data access and understanding more difficult.

For example, consider the problems associated with having different formats in different data sources. In file 1 a company is named as "CARS, INC." and in file 2 a company is named as "CARSINC." It is possible that the two names refer to the same company and the different names are due to a subjective interpretation or a typing error by the person who entered the data.

Another problem associated with textual data is inconsistency. For example, if there are three lines of text assigned for the "address," the name of the city may normally appear in line 3, but occasionally in lines 1 or 2.

TABLE 5.1 Typical problems associated with data integrity

Name Field	Address Field 1	Address Field 2
McBRIDE, CARRIE	————————————	1 LAKE PARKWAY, CHICAGO IL 60621-0433
CHESAPEAKE, Inc.	205 108TH **AVN** NE, Suite 100	**AMBLER PA**
STEPHEN, J., BERNSTIEN	**316** STATE BOULEVARD	**WASH** 20037-8011

Table 5.1 illustrates some typical problems associated with the textual data of names and addresses of customers. There is one case of a truncation error ("WASH" should be "WASHINGTON"), one case of an abbreviation error ("AVN" should be "AVE."), one address has no zip code ("AMBLER PA"), one has a typing error ("Bernstien" should be "Bernstein" and "316" should be "361"), the mixing of company names with names of people in the same field (CHESAPEAKE, Inc.), and one customer with the "address 1" field left blank.

Semi-automatic software tools are available that use reference tables and dictionaries for names, addresses, and zip codes to correct this type of problem. However, given that they are often based on static tables, these tools cannot fix all the possible errors that may occur in real data and therefore require customizing for the specific data domain.

Content Errors in the Data

A content error is typically due to inconsistency between the description of a field, such as "person name," and the data that the field contains. For example, it is possible that company names and people names are found in the same field. Similarly, name fields may contain unexpected relations and information about locations. For example, an indication such as "take the first turning on the left" might be found in an address field.

Other frequent errors are, for example, finding texts that have been truncated and inconsistent use of spaces, hyphens, and field delimiters. In the case of field delimiters, an address field may contain a surname, or a street name may be truncated at the end of one line and continue on the next. This type of error makes it more difficult to know where data and text fields start and finish.

TABLE 5.2 Examples of inconsistent formats inside text fields

Person Name	Address	Work Telephone
(WARREN AND ASSOCIATES)	BAYVIEW AVENUE	914-349-1033 (OFFICE).
DWAYNE CARTER, JR.	PROMOTION 443, 60621-0433	481.696.3124
JAMES- REAL ESTATE	1400 AMPHITHEATRE PARKWAY, SAN JOSE, SANTA CLARA, CALIFORNIA – ZIP 95101-408	(011)(718)-123 -4567 (cellphone)
5333 FARNAM STREET	IN THE CITY CENTER	(408) 741-0901
"JLC ASSOCIATES"	ONE MACROSIFT WAY	215-761-4007

Table 5.2 shows how the fields of name, address, and telephone number change format from one record to the next.

A software product that is specialized in preprocessing data in order to guarantee its quality is the IBM Data Integration Platform; see www.ibm.com/software/data/integration. Another software product that can be used to extract, filter, and guarantee data quality is ETI Standard, which can be consulted at "www.eti.com."

RELEVANCE AND RELIABILITY

Two key concepts that influence the quality of a data model and the quality of the data itself are relevance and reliability. Relevance usually refers to the variable itself, whereas reliability refers to the current data assigned to a given variable. For example, the variable "age" might be relevant to "income level." On the other hand, perhaps 80 percent of the data for the variable "age" might be reliable: that is, the values are not null, they are not out of range (between 1 and 100), and they have been checked by two different people on data entry.

Table 5.3 shows a representative, randomly selected sample of 10 records for the variables of a given business objective. In the age column, the value for the third record is 0 and that of the fourth record is 99. Clearly, these two values are incorrect. Therefore, out of 10 records, the value of "age" is unreliable in two cases, giving a reliability grade of 0.8 for "age." This is an initial evaluation based on what is immediately evident. However, it may be that the age value of "55" for row 6 should be "45." To evaluate this would require some other type of cross-check or feedback from the customer. The next variable, "marital status," has three of the values missing, hence an initial reliability of $10/7 = 0.7$ can be assigned. Each dataset would have to be checked

TABLE 5.3 Data sample for evaluation of reliability of each variable

								Variables
Customer ID	Age	Marital Status	Gender	Time as Customer	State of Residence	Income Level	Office	Has Mortgage?
C2013-81	21	S	F	22	MA	2	2	N
C2012-12	42	M	M	145	NY	4	8	Y
C2011-17	0	-	F	10	NY	-	8	Y
C2013-03	99	D	M	12	CA	-	1	N
C2008-99	35	M	F	120	CA	4	1	Y
C2011-51	55	M	M	800	MI	5	3	Y
C2013-24	28	-	M	60	MI	3	3	Y
C2012-92	62	W	F	900	MA	3	2	N
C2012-65	38	-	F	122	MA	4	2	Y
C2013-58	50	M	M	106	NY	5	8	Y

individually in order to evaluate the missing values. For multiple datasets, an average value could be calculated for percentage of missing values and therefore the reliability. If the assigned values are correct, the same would apply as for the age values: they may require cross-checking. A third variable that also appears to have some problems is "income level," with two missing values. The other variables, "gender," "time as customer," "state of residence," "office," and "has mortgage" all seem correct, with no missing or erroneous values.

Table 5.4 shows the grades of reliability for the variables in Table 5.3. Each variable has a grade, which indicates its relevance (with respect to the likelihood of a client contracting a pension plan) and its reliability. The relevance is

TABLE 5.4 Relevance and reliability of available data

								Variables
	Age	Marital Status	Gender	Time as Customer	State of Residence	Income Level	Office	Has Mortgage?
Grade of relevance	0.81*	0.9	0.72	0.82	0.79	0.71	0.87	0.84
Grade of reliability	0.8	0.7	1	1	1	0.8	1	1

*1 = totally relevant/reliable and 0 = totally irrelevant/unreliable

considered with respect to the likelihood of a client contracting a pension plan. The least relevant variable is "income level" (0.71), and the least reliable is "marital status" (0.70). These values can be initially calculated from the correlation with the business objective (for example, contract pension plan: yes/no) in the case of relevance, and the percentage of missing or erroneous values found in the sample, in the case of reliability.

But how are relevance and reliability used in practice? Data modeling techniques that do not take relevance and reliability into account usually assume that irrelevant variables and unreliable data records have been eliminated and filtered out, respectively. In contrast, modeling techniques that do take these factors into account avoid the elimination of variables or complete records. These models allow for the fact that the influence of the variables and records on the overall result can be reduced or augmented, depending on the calculated grade of relevance and reliability.

- It is clear that if an input variable has a relevance of 0.1 with respect to an output variable (business objective), it would probably not be included in the data file to be analyzed. For example, perhaps only those variables with a relevance value of 0.7 or above will be considered for inclusion.
- The reliability value means that some records (for example, those that include atypical values or outliers) do not need to be eliminated; instead, their impact on the overall result can simply be reduced. In this way, the informative value of the other variables for a given record is not lost.

Another approach would be to eliminate *a priori* all the values that fall outside given limits for each variable and use a data file that has been filtered as much as possible, having accepted the cost of possible information loss. Clearly, different approaches exist, and the one used depends on the evaluation, in each situation, of the state of the available data.

QUANTITATIVE EVALUATION OF THE DATA QUALITY

After revising the available data, it can be concluded qualitatively that the data is okay, acceptable, unreliable, and so on. However, in order to get a more precise evaluation, the data quality must be calculated; that is, a quantitative evaluation must be obtained. In the following, one practical and simple approach is described. For each data item (variable/field of a data table), the following information is elaborated:

Data item/information:
Table of origin:
Input/output:
Input: Grade of relevance (h=high, m=medium, l=low)
 Grade of reliability (h=high, m=medium, l=low)
 Distribution (g=good, m=medium, b=bad)

Stability (h=high, 1 year or more; m=medium, 6 months; l=low, 1–3 months)

Expert support: The availability of an expert to give support in explaining the data and extracting and processing the data.

Once this information has been obtained, the grade of relevance and grade of reliability for each data variable can be inspected and, for example, the percentage of highly relevant variables that have a low reliability can be calculated. If this percentage is more than 40 percent, the conclusion could be reached that the quality of the available data is not good enough for the project to go ahead for the given business objective. Two options would be to (i) try to improve the reliability or distribution of the affected variables, and (ii) select alternative variables that have a similar grade of relevance but with greater reliability and/or better distribution.

With respect to the grade of stability, a low value does not make a project less viable from the point of view of the quality of the result, but it does increase the indirect costs. This is because a low grade of stability indicates that the environment being studied is changing quickly and it will therefore be necessary to rebuild the model or repeat the analysis with greater frequency. It is clear that the more often the analysis must be repeated or the data model rebuilt, the more expensive the overall project becomes. For example, one sector where there is a volatile environment is that of telecommunications. In the last decade there have been significant changes in the way the general public uses fixed and mobile telephones and devices, with the incorporation of online functionality, services, messaging, social networks, and so on. Thus, any model of telephone customer's behavior created ten years ago would have to be updated constantly over this period of time in order to incorporate the new tendencies of usage, hardware, and software as they became available.

DATA EXTRACTION AND DATA QUALITY – COMMON MISTAKES AND HOW TO AVOID THEM

This section discusses a common source of errors in the data: the data extraction phase. One may be lucky enough to be presented with a dataset for analysis that has already been extracted from the raw data, cleaned, formatted, and validated. On the other hand, some or all of these steps may still need to be done. This can be particularly tricky when dealing with online weblogs. Using an example of data extraction from an online bookstore query log, it will be shown that the required data fields have to be distinguished from other components of the weblog. Also, a way of identifying the users and the query search sessions that are of interest needs to be established.

Data Extraction

The following small case study gives an example of data extraction from an online bookstore's weblog. Table 5.5 shows the raw weblog data. The first field is the IP (Internet Protocol) address of the visitor; the second field is the date and

TABLE 5.5 Original data file for an online bookstore's weblog

IP Address	Date/ Time	Time Zone	Action	Action Detail	Action Code
187.421.421.12	20/Sep: 08:45:02	-05	SELECT	/xyz.jpg	-1
99.710.414.120	20/Sep: 08:45:54	-05	SELECT	/z21q49j12b95/99/1? isbn=1558607528&Run. x=12&Run.y=14	1
412.27.32.92	20/Sep: 08:45:55	-05	SELECT	/ e1k1t681nutr/pp/L? su=mql	1
99.710.414.120	20/Sep: 08:47:09	-05	SELECT	/ z21q49j12b95/pn/ 0120885689	1
99.710.414.121	20/Sep: 08:54:42	-05	SELECT	/ z21q49j12b95/pn/ 0321303377	1
99.710.414.120	20/Sep: 08:56:31	-05	SELECT	/ z21q49j12b95/pn/ 0750660767	1

time stamp; the third is the time zone (-5 means five hours before Greenwich Mean Time); the fourth is the web page action; the fifth contains the user session ID, actions details, and parameters; and the sixth field contains the action code. The records are ordered chronologically by the second field.

Table 5.5 shows six records with four different IP addresses. In the action detail field column, the second record contains the ISBN number 1558607528 and user session ID z21q49j12b95. The user session ID is made up of the first twelve alphanumeric characters after the slash "/" in the action detail field; however, the first six characters are the unique identifier and the last six characters vary on each distinct access. So, in the first row, the extracted user session ID is z21q49. Table 5.5 shows that, in general, the IP address agrees with the user ID (except in one case), but different users (with distinct user IDs) can have the same IP address. This is the case when the IP address corresponds to an ISP server or a server to which several different user PCs are connected. Also, some users have dynamic IPs (which change over time); hence a unique user may have different IP addresses in the IP field for different accesses. Based on this analysis, it can be concluded that, compared to the IP address, the user ID provides the most reliable unique identifier for distinguishing separate users and user query sessions.

In terms of data extraction, the date/time field and the action detail field must be processed in order to obtain a reformatted version of the date, time, user session ID, and ISBN number. Table 5.6 shows the information extracted into database fields in the desired format for user session ID z21q49. Table 5.7

TABLE 5.6 Extracted and processed data

IP Address	Date	Time	Time Zone	User ID	ISBN
99.710.414.120	20/09	08:45:54	-05	z21q49	1558607528
99.710.414.120	20/09	08:47:09	-05	z21q49	0120885689
99.710.414.121	20/09	08:54:42	-05	z21q49	0321303377
99.710.414.120	20/09	08:56:31	-05	z21q49	0750660767

TABLE 5.7 Data from a user session

User ID	Time	Category	Publisher	Title
z21q49	08:45:54	TK5105.8883 Elect. Eng.	Elsevier	Web Application Design Handbook: Best Practices
z21q49	08:47:09	QA76.76.D47 Maths.	Morgan Kaufmann	Effective Prototyping for Software Makers
z21q49	08:54:42	TK5105.888 Elect. Eng.	Addison-Wesley	The Non-Designer's Web Book
z21q49	08:56:31	TK5105.888 Elect. Eng.	Elsevier	Introduction to Web Matrix: ASP.NET Development for Beginners

shows the data that has been synthesized into a user session, that is, a sequence of book queries all formulated by the same user, which runs from 08:45:54 to 08:56:31 and consists of four book queries.

This all seems quite straightforward, but in order to obtain the data in Table 5.7, that is, the query sessions for a given user, a series of data extraction and interpretation problems had to be solved. And not all users have data of interest to extract. It was observed that users with high query frequencies (for example, hundreds) were not individual users but were either robots or APIs (Application Programming Interfaces). Hence, the data was sampled based on frequency of occurrence for books and users in order to eliminate high volume users.

Extensive study of the records showed that the sessions consisting of less than 23 queries were always coherent, individual sessions. Therefore, the data extracted included user sessions made up of users identified by a unique session ID whose frequency was less than 23 queries in a given 10-hour period (8:30 am to 6:30 pm). Table 5.7 shows that the sessions are usually coherent with respect to the types of books searched for. From this it was clear that the analysis should deal with the medium-frequency book and user queries. This gave an average of 5,800 distinct books and 4,300 distinct users in the 10-hour period. For the data file from 20/09, there were a total of 1,420,300 records, from which were extracted 109,368 valid records.

Data Validation Filters

Based on the analysis and extraction in the previous section, the data validation filters and rules are summarized as follows:

1. Action code (see Table 5.5) must be 1 (okay): gives a total of 1,320,879 records.
2. There must be a valid ISBN in the action field: gives a total of 924,615 records.
3. Only users whose total number of queries is less than 23 for a given time period: gives 109,368 records.

The second record in Table 5.5 includes a valid ISBN number in the action detail field, whereas the first record does not and will therefore be discarded.

Derived Data

The International Standard Book Number (ISBN) is a unique identifier for books and has been adopted as an international standard. The weblog in the case study contains the 10-digit version, which has four components: (i) a group/country/language identifier, (ii) the publisher code, (iii) an item number (title of the book), and (iv) a checksum character or check digit. For example, if the ISBN is 817525766-0, the group is 81, the publisher is 7525, the title is 766, and the check digit is 0. The length of the publisher code is variable, which, in the example, is equal to 4.

Other derived data for this case study was obtained by writing an API in JavaScript to access the Library of Congress's online catalogue using the ISBN number to obtain the title, topic classification (LCC), and publisher for each book. This additional information, which was not available in the original log file, was important to interpret the results and identify the books by topic and publisher.

Summary of Data Extraction Example

In summary, four key actions can be identified without which the quality of the extracted data would have been unacceptable and the subsequent analysis and modeling would have reached erroneous conclusions. The four key actions are:

1. Use of the user session ID instead of the IP address to identify the users
2. Filtering out high-volume user records: robots and APIs

3. Filtering out invalid records: those with no ISBN number and/or invalid action code
4. Enriching the data records with additional information: book category and publisher derived from ISBN number

HOW DATA ENTRY AND DATA CREATION MAY AFFECT DATA QUALITY

This chapter has considered how to evaluate data quality in terms of relevance and reliability, assuming that the dataset obtained has already been created. However, consideration may be given to how the dataset is created in the first place and the impact of that process on the data quality is also worth considering. Chapter 3 discussed surveys, questionnaires, and loyalty card registration forms, which can be implemented online in a website (thus offering much more format control and quality guarantees) or completed by hand on paper and then entered manually into a computer system. Presumably, a significant amount of data still has to be entered manually at an initial stage. Hence, the quality of the data operator's work and of the subsequent cross-checking and validation is essential. Data may also be automatically generated by an IT process, as in the weblog case study discussed in the last section of this chapter. An automatic process should guarantee data of greater quality with no errors. However, a computer process with a bug may generate large volumes of data with the same error, such as an incorrect data format or the time stamp overwritten with zeroes. Alternatively, it may create sporadic errors, which are more difficult to detect: for example, an incorrect configuration of the NTP (Network Time Protocol) by the administrator of a server cluster may affect the reliability of the log data, or an IP address conflict may result in missing records from the activity log. In order to mitigate these problems, a combination of automated checking software and manual inspection is the usual procedure. In general, the same criteria mentioned for evaluating the reliability and relevance of manually entered data can be applied to machine-generated data.

Finally, the more familiar a person is with the data being checked, the more easily that person can detect errors and anomalies. That is, a user who is looking at a data log or a customer record for the first time may not be able to evaluate whether the data values are correct or not.

Chapter 6

Selection of Variables and Factor Derivation

INTRODUCTION

This chapter deals with an aspect of commercial data analysis that may be difficult for newcomers: selecting and deriving key factors from a large number of variables. On the one hand, the novice analyst may think that this is a totally intuitive process performed by business experts. On the other hand, the novice may consider the process to be completely statistical. The reality is found somewhere between the two approaches. From a practical point of view, two different starting points can be considered: (i) "What data do I have and what can I do with it?" and (ii) "I know the final goal or result that I am interested in and I am prepared to obtain the necessary data to achieve it."

The first two sections of the chapter consider the approaches from these two starting points and present some of the basic statistical techniques for selecting variables and deriving factors. The third section discusses how to use data mining techniques for selecting the most relevant variables. The final section considers the alternative of obtaining a packaged or proprietary solution of preselected variables and factors for a specific business area. In practice, one or more of these approaches can be employed in order to guarantee that the best possible data and variable selection for the business objective is obtained.

Variable Selection

Why Select Variables?

Why select variables in the first place? Why not just use everything the business has to analyze and create data models? Chapters 2 and 5 discuss choosing variables based on their relevance to a given business objective and in terms of their quality (reliability). In practice, variables are selected and factors derived in order to obtain a reduced set of the most relevant and reliable variables from an initial larger set of variables, many of which may not be so reliable or relevant to the business objective. Also, working with a reduced set of quality inputs makes the data modeling much easier and results in more precise models. This chapter discusses selecting variables and considers the creation or generation of new factors, which are usually derived from the previously selected variables.

The topics of variable selection and factor creation recur throughout several chapters of this book, given their importance in the different phases of a data analysis project: from the initial definition of the business objectives, the data quality, the analysis, and selection *per se* through to the modeling phase. Recall that in Chapter 2 the initially identified variables were evaluated one by one in terms of their correlation with the business objective. Also, Chapter 5 introduced aspects of evaluation of the variables in terms of their relevance and reliability, which could also be used as selection criteria.

Appendix Case Studies

Variable Selection, Deriving New Factors, Input Data Processing

The appendix has three case studies that discuss in depth three different aspects of data mining. Case study 1 discusses customer loyalty, case 2 goes into cross-selling, and case 3 explores audience prediction. Each case study features real-world projects that use many of the techniques described in this chapter.

SELECTION FROM THE AVAILABLE DATA

This section considers approach (i): "What data do I have and what can I do with it?" The first step is to consider the basic elements common to almost all commercial data analysis projects. The business has: customers; products or services with retail, wholesale, and cost prices; product characteristics (for example, a packet of twenty-five 500-mg aspirins); and sales data. It also has available the costs associated with the infrastructure, logistics, initial investment, and so on. The company can include or exclude the costs, depending on whether it wants to calculate profitability figures or not. It also has information about its own commercial structure: sales channels, offices and locations, regions, salespeople, sales campaigns, and so on. The aspects of supplies, suppliers, delivery time, associated costs, and quality may or may not be included, depending on the focus and objectives.

Any commercial enterprise, from the smallest to the biggest, must know the key variables that affect its business. This set of variables is often called a control panel or dashboard and is normally comprised of ratios with a time or comparison factor. It allows a manager to visualize the current situation of the business, make provisions, and take appropriate actions. To start, the control panel uses the basic data summarized in the previous paragraph.

A typical control panel in the marketing area may contain one or more of the following:

- Sales: total sales; sales by product or product lines, geographical region, salesperson, customer type, market segment, sales volume, and sales territories; sales through intermediaries; and percentage change in sales.
- Costs: total costs; costs by products or product lines, geographical region, salesperson, customer type, market segment, order volume, sales territory; and intermediary and percentage changes in costs.

- Profits: total profits; by product or product line, geographical region, sales-person, customer type, market segment, order volume, sales territory, and intermediary.

These indicators for sales, costs, and profits are complete, but the business is confronted with a habitual problem: it is saturated with data and it cannot see the "forest for the trees." Also, this data has to be replicated for earlier time periods (quarterly, yearly, etc.) in order to make comparisons and see where the business is growing or shrinking, and then this growth or shrinkage must be related to the business actions taken. The actions are executed by the business managers (opening of a new commercial center, launch of a new product or service, and so on), and/or are due to external causes (expansion or recession of the market, strategy of the competitors, and so on).

Therefore, in order to distinguish the forest from the trees, the business needs a second level of indicators, or "meta indicators," which provide it with alerts about key variables. A second level indicator might be "the region with the greatest increase in profit with respect to the previous quarter." The name of this indicator would be "region." Another second level indicator would be "products with a negative growth greater than 25 percent of the average growth for all products." Two key aspects to define indicators of this type are: (i) the comparison with previous periods of time and/or with other products, regions, etc.; and (ii) the use of upper and lower limits to specify triggers if a variable exceeds or falls below a target value. Indicators (or alarms) can provide a warning when a value exceeds a given limit. For example, a rule to activate an alarm could be: if the average delivery time of product Z is greater than 30 days, then delivery time alarm = on. Another rule might be: if the percentage of returned type B products is greater than 15 percent, then returned goods alarm = on.

Figure 6.1 shows a screen from a contemporary EIS software dashboard, the Strategy Companion Analyzer, which is designed to graphically display a set of key business indicators. There is a category of software tools known as business intelligence systems or executive information systems that incorporates this type of presentation. These tools appear to imitate control panels of cars or airplanes (depending on the complexity of the business). Consider the analogy to a vehicle dashboard: its indicators for speed, RPM, water temperature, oil and fuel levels, and so on, with the key indicators for a business (cash flow, stocks, productivity, etc.). The default dashboard configuration will probably need to be customized for each particular business and its available data.

Statistical Techniques for Evaluating a Set of Input Variables

This section discusses techniques that evaluate input variables without having to compare them to an output variable (business objective). In this way the business can identify which pairs of variables are interrelated and which will give clues for possible data analysis and modeling objectives. Once this is done, the company can use the techniques presented in the second section of the chapter to validate candidate output variables and factors as business objectives. The

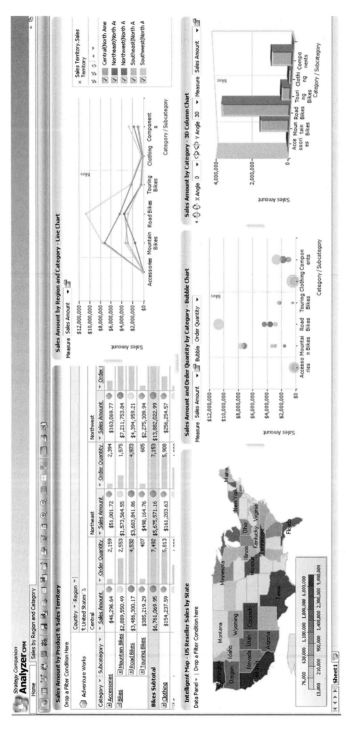

FIGURE 6.1 A control panel, or dashboard, display *Reproduced with permission from Strategy Companion Corporation (http://strategycompanion.com/company/)*

techniques described in this section, such as correlation and data fusion, can also be used to compare input variables with an output variable (business objective).

The following example looks at a retail bank's customers, but the methodology can be generalized to any business sector by, for example, adapting the product vector and substituting the bank account balance data for product or service billing accounts. Table 6.1 shows an initial set of variables taken from the data that is immediately available in the bank's database. All the variables

TABLE 6.1 Initial list of candidate input variables for a bank's data mining project

Variable	Type	Simple or Derived	Possible Values	Reliability
Age	Number	Simple	0 to 100	1.0
				0.9
Avg. monthly income	Number	Simple	Calculated from current account	
Avg. monthly expenses	Number	Simple	Calculated from current account	0.8
Avg. monthly bank account balance	Number	Simple	Calculated from current account	1.0
Cell phone usage	Number	Derived	Calculated from cell phone bills charged to current account	0.3
Profession	Category	Simple	Student, university student, employee, self-employed, manager, entrepreneur, retired, etc.	0.9
Marital status	Category	Simple	Single, married, divorced, widowed	0.9
Children	Category	Simple	yes/no	0.7
Gender	Category	Simple	male/female	1.0
Products/ services	Vector of categories	Simple	Products and services this client currently has contracted with the bank*	1.0

*This list of products varies depending on the type of business.

are above the reliability threshold, which the IT manager defined as 0.7, with the exception of the variable "cell phone usage." Hence the latter variable is a candidate for elimination based on quality (reliability) grounds. Presumably, the reliability for each variable has been evaluated using a procedure similar to that described in Chapter 5 in terms of percentage of data missing, percentage of errors, and so on.

Correlation

The Pearson correlation method is the most common method to use for numerical variables; it assigns a value between -1 and 1, where 0 is no correlation, 1 is total positive correlation, and -1 is total negative correlation. This is interpreted as follows: a correlation value of 0.7 between two variables would indicate that a significant and positive relationship exists between the two. A positive correlation signifies that if variable A goes up, then B will also go up, whereas if the value of the correlation is negative, then if A increases, B decreases.

For further reading on the Pearson Correlation Method, see:

Boslaugh, Sarah and Paul Andrew Watters. 2008. *Statistics in a Nutshell: A Desktop Quick Reference*, ch. 7. Sebastopol, CA: O'Reilly Media. ISBN-13: 978-0596510497.

Considering the two variables "age" and "salary," a strong positive correlation between the two would be expected: as people get older, they tend to earn more money. Therefore, the correlation between age and salary probably gives a value over 0.7. Figure 6.2 illustrates pairs of numerical variables plotted against each other, with the corresponding correlation value between the two variables shown on the x-axis. The right-most plot shows a perfect positive correlation of 1.0, whereas the middle plot shows two variables that have no correlation whatsoever between them. The left-most plot shows a perfect negative correlation of -1.0.

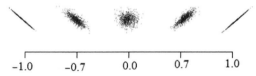

FIGURE 6.2   Correlations between two numerical variables

A correlation can be calculated between two numerical values (e.g., age and salary) or between two category values (e.g., type of product and profession). However, a company may also want to calculate correlations between variables of different types. One method to calculate the correlation of a numerical variable with a categorical one is to convert the numerical variable into categories. For example, age would be categorized into ranges (or buckets) such as: 18 to 30, 31 to 40, and so on.

As well as the correlation, the covariance of two variables is often calculated. In contrast with the correlation value, which must be between -1 and 1, the covariance may assume any numerical value. The covariance indicates the grade of synchronization of the variance (or volatility) of the two variables.

For further reading on covariance, see:

Boslaugh, Sarah and Paul Andrew Watters. 2008. *Statistics in a Nutshell: A Desktop Quick Reference*, ch. 16. Sebastopol, CA: O'Reilly Media. ISBN-13: 978-0596510497.

TABLE 6.2 Correlations between candidate variables

	Age	Income (US $)	Profession	Cell Phone Usage
Age	1	0.81	0.38	0.60
Income (US $)	0.81	1	0.85	0.25
Profession	0.38	0.85	1	0.28
Cell phone usage	0.60	0.25	0.28	1

Table 6.2 shows correlations between four business variables taken from Table 6.1. The two variables that have the highest correlations are profession with income (US $), with a correlation of 0.85, and age with income (US $), with a correlation of 0.81. The lowest correlations are cell phone usage with income (0.25) and cell phone usage with profession (0.28). Hence the initial conclusion is that cell phone usage doesn't have a high correlation with any other variable, so it could be considered for exclusion from the input variable set. Table 6.1 also shows that cell phone usage has a significantly lower reliability (0.3) than the other variables and this could have repercussions on its correlation value with the remaining variables. Also, profession only has a high correlation with income; however, it will be seen that this correlation pair (income, profession) is important to the type of business. Given that each variable has a correlation with every other variable, the values are repeated around the diagonal. Therefore, the values on one side of the diagonal can be omitted. Note that all the values are equal to 1 on the diagonal, because these are the correlations of the variables with themselves.

Factorial Analysis

Factor analysis is a statistical method applied to the values of an initial set of input variables that are known to have mutual correlations in order to find a smaller set of factors that describe the underlying interrelationships and mutual variability. They are not compared with an output variable, only between themselves. Principal component analysis (PCA) is a specific technique for factor analysis that generates linear combinations of variables to maximize the variance between the variables. It successively extracts new factors (linear combinations) that are mutually independent.

For further reading on factor analysis, see:

Boslaugh, Sarah and Paul Andrew Watters. 2008. *Statistics in a Nutshell: A Desktop Quick Reference*, ch. 12. Sebastopol, CA: O'Reilly Media. ISBN-13: 978-0596510497.

Two factors that were extracted using PCA from the six initial variables seen in Table 6.1 are:

$$\text{Factor 1 (demographics)} : 0.581 \text{ age} + 0.566 \text{ profession} + 0.522 \text{ marital} - 0.263 \text{ children}$$

$$\text{Factor 2 (financials)} : -0.926 \text{ income} - 0.372 \text{ expenses} - 0.065 \text{ age} - 0.021 \text{ profession}$$

So the value of Factor 1 (for a given row of data) is calculated as being 0.581 times age value plus 0.566 times profession value plus 0.522 times marital status value minus 0.263 times children value. The coefficient in front of each variable in the formula acts as a weight that defines its contribution to the overall result.

Factor Analysis

Objective of Factor Analysis for Data Modeling

The objective of factorial analysis is to define a data model with the minimum number of input variables, each of which provides the maximum informative value with respect to a given business objective, which is the output of the model. In this way the complexity of the model is reduced and the quality of the result is further ensured. One initial problem confronted early on is how to choose which to include of the large initial number of candidate input variables and which to discard.

The statistical technique of factorial analysis can be applied systematically to variables to create a reduced number of factors of high predictive value, each factor being a composite of several basic variables.

Data Fusion

One aspect associated with creating a data base or data mart (see Chapter 12) for a business is the process of aggregation, which normally generates sums and averages with respect to specific attributes such as total sales by region. However, this does not really increment the intrinsic value of the information. To get less data with more value per data item, the process of fusion can be used. In fusion, two numeric values are unified to form a single variable that best represents a tendency or characteristic. Non-numerical variables can also be fused, but this is a more complex process. As an example of fusing two numerical variables, consider $V_1 = $ income and $V_2 = $ expenses: from these two variables, V_3 is defined as: $V_3 = V_1/V_2$. V_3 can be defined given that a significant relationship between V_1 and V_2 has been established. Having n variables and not knowing which would be the most appropriate to fuse, statistical techniques can be employed to identify relationships. For example, the correlations between all the numerical variables can be calculated.

> **Relation with Appendix Case Studies**
>
> *Derivation of Ratios*
>
> Case studies 1 (Customer Loyalty) and 2 (Cross-Selling) in the appendix have examples of the derivations of ratios for real-world project data.

Summary of the Approach of Selecting from the Available Data

From the initial analysis the business has made of the data, and calculating the correlations between variables and performing principal component analysis (PCA), the business can make initial conclusions about potential business objectives. Given that the business has some reasonable correlations between demographic and economic variables of its clients, it could try a customer segmentation model: this could imply a potential business objective of improving on the company's current understanding of its customer base. Also, given that the company has the vector of products that customers currently have, it could try a predictive model for cross-selling to its actual customers, using the product type as the output variable.

REVERSE ENGINEERING: SELECTION BY CONSIDERING THE DESIRED RESULT

This section discusses approach (ii): "I know the final goal or result that I am interested in and I am prepared to obtain the necessary data to achieve it." In contrast to the previous section, where there was no preconceived idea of a business objective, in this section a candidate business objective has already been determined. Hence the business's task is to analyze the input data to evaluate the relationship between the input variables and the output variable as the proposed business objective. As a starting point, the same retail bank example is used, along with the input variable set in Table 6.1. In this scenario, the bank would also consider obtaining new data (variables/factors) if necessary, using methods such as those described in Chapter 3.

Statistical Techniques for Evaluating and Selecting Input Variables for a Specific Business Objective

With an initial set of input variables such as those in Table 6.1 (although in practice the initial set may be considerably more extensive), the bank's general goal is to obtain a minimum subset of those variables that best predict an output variable. The business must also consider that the minimum subset may include one or more derived factors. For example, if two raw input variables are age and salary, then a derived factor, ratio_age_salary, could be a ratio of age and salary, that is, age divided by salary.

Returning to the minimum set of input variables or factors, the objective is that each input variable has a high correlation with what is to be predicted or modeled. There are various techniques for evaluating and quantifying the grade of relation of an input variable with an output variable.

Statistical Concepts

Grade of Relation versus Relevance

In the current context, relevance refers to relationships between input variables and business objectives (output variables). Grade of relation can be between any two variables. The same correlation techniques discussed in the first section of the chapter can be used to evaluate either grade of relation or relevance.

A typical analysis result is a list of all the input variables ranked by their correlation to an output variable (business outcome). For example, if the business outcome is "buys product A" and the input variables are "time as customer," "disposable income," "purchased product B," "marital status," and "home owner," a correlation table of the input variables with respect to the output variable might look like that shown in Table 6.3. The table shows that the key factors related to a customer buying product A (business objective) are whether the customer bought product B and what the disposable income is (correlations of 0.77 and 0.75, respectively, with the business objective), followed by whether the customer is a home owner (correlation of 0.65 with the business objective). Alternatively, marital status and time as a customer, with respective correlations of 0.45 and 0.32 with the business outcome, may have little influence over the purchase of product A. In this case, a correlation threshold above which the variables are considered relevant can be defined. This threshold could be assigned by, for example, manually inspecting the distribution of the correlation value (column 2 in Table 6.3) and then identifying an inflection point at which the correlation drops significantly.

Relevant Input Data

Obtaining Additional Variables

Table 6.3 shows that two new variables, "home owner" and "time as customer," have been incorporated, which were not present in the initial list in Table 6.1. Both variables could easily be obtained by deriving them from existing data. If the home owner information is not available for a significant number of clients, the bank could consider designing and launching a survey questionnaire to obtain it. (See Chapter 3 for details about obtaining data from various sources.)

TABLE 6.3 Input variables ordered by degree of correlation with output variable

Input Variable	Correlation with Outcome (buys product A)
Purchased product B	0.77
Disposable income	0.75
Home owner	0.65
Marital status	0.45
Time as customer	0.32

Business outcome = buys product A

For the correlation of ordinal categories (categories that can be ordered in some meaningful way, allowing them to be compared), such as high, medium, and low, different options can be considered. The ordered categories could be converted into numbers such as high=3, medium=2, and low=1, and then proceed with the Pearson correlation as before. However, it might be that the interval between the categories is not equal or linear in its ordering; for example, "high" might be ten times greater than "medium," so the values for each category would first have to be established. A more statistical approach is to use a metric designed for ordinal values, such as the Spearman correlation.

For further reading on the Spearman Correlation Method and the chi-squared test, see:

Boslaugh, Sarah and Paul Andrew Watters. 2008. *Statistics in a Nutshell: A Desktop Quick Reference*, ch. 5. Sebastopol, CA: O'Reilly Media. ISBN-13: 978-0596510497.

For the correlation of nominal categories, that is, categories that have no order, such as blue, green, and yellow, alternative methods have to be used in contrast to numerical and ordinal variables. One of the most common methods is called the chi-squared test, which can be used to measure a goodness of fit or independence. The goodness of fit compares two distributions, and the independence measures the degree of independence between the values of two variables, represented as a contingency table. An example would be the responses of a survey of different age groups whose objective is to see if a person's age group affects the responses. A contingency table holds the frequencies for each category and variable. Table 6.4 shows an example for two variables, "product category" and "profitability category." Another approach is to generate the frequency histograms for each variable and category and compare the distributions.

TABLE 6.4 Contingency table for variables "product category" and "profitability category"

	Most Profitable Clients	Least Profitable Clients	Totals
Product A	65	32	97
Product B	20	15	35
Totals	85	47	132

Variable Selection

Choosing Variables from a Contingency Table

Table 6.4 shows that product is relevant to client profitability, given that product A has 80 percent more of the most profitable clients than product B. Hence product category would be included as an input variable to a profitability data model.

Transforming Numerical Variables into Ordinal Categorical Variables

Often it is convenient to transform a numerical variable into an ordinal categorical type. (See Chapter 4 for types of variables.) This may be for one or more of the following reasons:

1. The categorical representation of the variables has a higher correlation with the business objective than the original numerical version of the variable does.
2. An ordinal category is easier to associate to the segments of a customer segmentation model.
3. The ordinal type has greater intrinsic information value.
4. The ordinal type can compare directly with other ordinal categorical variables.

The following section provides an example of categorizing the numerical variable "age," which will be used later as input to the customer segmentation model. Four options are considered for categorizing customer ages:

1. The bank may already have a categorization of the age of its customers, and it can use this data without any changes.
2. The categorization could be manually derived from an analysis of the distribution of the variable "age" for all the clients.
3. The classification needed for segmentation could be defined through a series of meetings with the data analysis consultants, the marketing department, the customer service department, and the IT department.

4. The statistical technique of percentiles can be used to generate the categorization automatically by using the distribution of the variable "age."

By using the percentiles technique, the bank can define how many categories it
wants to generate, depending on the range of values of the variable "age" (in this
case). Each percentile will be a category in which there are given percentages of
all the records. In order to define the percentiles, the bank must specify the number of percentiles it wants, and for each percentile, the percentage of the records
it wants to include.

The values of the numerical variable must be described in ascending (or descending) order. For example, consider seven percentages that are defined as
percentiles for the variable "age": 5, 10, 25, 50, 75, 90, and 95 percent. The first
percentile is the first 5 percent of clients ordered by age. The second percentile
is the first 10 percent, and the seventh percentile is the first 95 percent. What is
achieved by doing this? Given that the distribution is being cut at percentile
points, the categories should reflect the nature of the data. In order to obtain
exclusive categories, the records must be post-processed so that each case is
in just one category. That is, the categories are: from 0 to 5 percent, from 5
to 10 percent, from 10 to 25 percent, and so on.

Figure 6.3 shows a graphical representation for the variable "age of customer." The positions of the percentiles on the x-axis depend on the distribution
of the variable, and for this reason the relative positions can vary from one variable to another. If there is a greater density of individuals in a specific section of
the distribution, then the percentiles will be more closely spaced. Hence, by the
data in Figure 6.3, 50 percent of the individuals lie between the 25% percentile
and the 75% percentile (high density), which is an age range on the x-axis of
between 35 and 47 years of age, or a range of 12 years. Only 10 percent come
after the 90th percentile (low density), which is between 55 and 72 years, or a
range of 17 years.

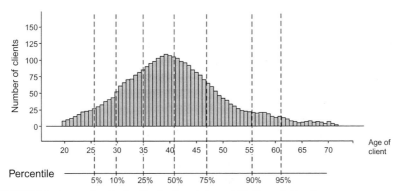

FIGURE 6.3   Percentiles for the distribution of the variable "age of client"

Clients ordered by age and percentiles

Client ID	Age	Percentile
C00101	20	5%
C00102	20	5%
C00103	21	5%
C00104	21	5%
C00105	22	5%
C00106	22	5%
C00107	23	5%
C00108	23	5%
C00109	24	5%
C00110	24	5%
C00111	25	5%
C00112	25	5%
C00113	26	10%
C00114	26	10%
....	....	....
C01356	53	90%
C01357	54	90%
C01358	55	90%
C01359	56	95%
C01360	57	95%

Using the percentiles from Figure 6.3, the categorization for the age of the bank's clients is: less than 26 years, from 26 to 29.5, from 29.5 to 35, from 35 to 42, from 42 to 47, from 47 to 56, from 56 to 62, and over 62. In this way, the bank has the numerical variable "age of client" defined in eight categories, which it can use as one of the input variables to the segmentation model.

For further reading on percentiles, see:

Boslaugh, Sarah and Paul Andrew Watters. 2008. *Statistics in a Nutshell: A Desktop Quick Reference*, ch. 16. Sebastopol, CA: O'Reilly Media. ISBN-13: 978-0596510497.

Customer Segmentation

This section looks at a specific example of choosing input variables with respect to a business objective. In this case, the business objective is not just a simple output variable; it is defined at a higher level. The business objective is to improve the segmentation and classification of the bank's current customers using segmentation techniques in order to more accurately market specific products and services.

The motivation for segmenting customers is that, if the bank classifies its diverse multitude of customers into the categories indicated by segmentation, it can improve its focus for offering products and services to its customers.

Assume that the initial hypothesis of the segmentation is guided by the classification that the bank already has and which it considers the best representation of its customers. The segmentation may be the product of a series of meetings between the data analysis consultants and, for example, the marketing director and the customer service manager. However, it is clear that the added value of the new segmentation is in providing the bank with a new vision of its customers. For example, a new segment may be discovered that was previously overlooked by the marketing department. Another added value is to create an automatic IT process that can classify the entirety of the bank's customer database using the derived data model, placing each individual customer into one of the segments.

Segmentation Model

Inputs and Output

A segmentation model is similar to a clustering model (see Chapter 9 and section 3 of this chapter) because it doesn't have an output variable, as such. All the inputs to a clustering algorithm are given to create clusters or groups based on the input variables. However, the cluster label could be considered as the output variable *per se* and the resulting customer profiles related with the various clusters.

Variable Selection – Reverse Engineering

Figure 6.4 illustrates a first attempt at clustering or segmenting clients using the input variables from Table 6.1. The four segments generated by the clustering algorithm are strongly influenced by the gender and cell phone income and

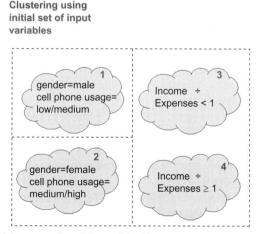

FIGURE 6.4   Initial segmentation of the retail bank's customers

expense inputs, due to the underlying statistical interrelations between the variables. However, the bank's business experts say that this result is nonsensical and does not match any current segmentation the bank has of its clients. In consequence, the analysts correlate all possible pairs of variables to identify those that have a high correlation with other variables in the dataset. It is found that gender and cell phone usage have very low correlations with the other variables. Hence the analysts try eliminating the cell phone usage and gender variables as input to the clustering technique. This time the segmentation produces groupings of clients that the business experts from the marketing and sales departments like much more. However, there is still a way to go before the bank has the best input variable set. New factors can be derived from two or more existing variables that have a higher correlation with the other variables. Also, the business experts suggest which additional variables would be useful to have as inputs in order to give the segmentation more business utility. An exercise can now be conducted to identify the most relevant variables in order to analyze and model the segments.

The bank can now move backward from the desired result to consider the variables necessary to give that result (hence the title of this section, "Reverse Engineering"). A series of brainstorming sessions could now take place between the data analysis consultants and the best "gray matter" of the marketing department. The data processing department should also participate in order to confirm which of the data and variables that have been selected are available in the company's data bases, along with their reliability.

Second list of candidate input variables for segmentation

Variable	Type	Simple or Derived	Possible Values
Age	Number	Simple	0 to 100
Avg. monthly income	Number	Simple	Calculated from current account
Avg. monthly expenses	Number	Simple	Calculated from current account
Avg. monthly bank account balance	Number	Simple	Calculated from current account
Home owner	Category	Simple	yes/no
Time as customer	Number	Simple	0 to 600 (months)
Profession	Category	Simple	Student, university student, employee, self-employed, manager, entrepreneur, retired, etc.
Marital status	Category	Simple	Single, married, divorced, widowed
Children	Category	Simple	yes/no
Products/ services	Vector of categories	Simple	Products and services this client currently has contracted with the bank*

*This list of products varies depending on the type of business.

Factor Derivation

Inventing New Variables

Determining variables to be used for data mining involves more than just defining basic variables such as customer age or existing ratios such as customer profitability; in all likelihood, new variables (factor derivation) will have to be invented with greater relevance to the analysis/modeling/business objective.

The marketing and business experts for the bank have selected several additional factors to add as inputs to the customer segmentation, including economic level (income and solvency) of the client and a special VIP indicator. If the income data is not available, a profile of the customer's economic level could be constructed based on a variety of factors: area of residence, zip code, number of automobiles, types of automobile, value of first residence, possession of a second residence, and so on. Other asset indicators could also be considered: pension plan value, investment plans, stocks and shares, insurance policies, and so on. The customer's solvency is calculated as the sum of assets minus debts (mortgage, credit card, other loans, etc.). To establish a customer's solvency, the client's cycle of income and expenses can be analyzed by assuming the salary or paycheck is received on a monthly basis and by asking the following questions: "Does the client have a positive balance in the current account at the end of the month?" and "Does the client's level of expenses make the current account go negative on a regular basis?" (Alternatively, the bank could formulate a survey to obtain additional related variables [see Chapter 3]). And finally, "How is a VIP client defined?" This could be a client with liquid deposits of more than $100,000 in a bank account, or a client could be a VIP because of profession, position of responsibility, or relationship with someone at the bank or in a given company.

No information about customer loyalty has been included. Toward this end, the bank could try including a factor such as "time as customer" or indicators that evaluate the value of the current products and services the customer has.

The end result of the input data preparation is shown in Table 6.5 and will serve as the inputs to the segmentation (clustering) algorithm.

For further reading on banking variables for customer segmentation, see:

Liua, Hsiang-His, and Chorng-Shyong Ongb. Jan. 2008. "Variable Selection in Clustering for Marketing Segmentation Using Genetic Algorithms." In: *Expert Systems with Applications*. Amsterdam: Elsevier, 34 (1), pp. 502–510.

A dataset can be created from the variables in Table 6.5. This can be done for all the bank's clients or for a representative sample of them. The next step is to validate this data for possible errors and incongruences, such as VIP clients who are also insolvent, or a retired person with an age category of 22 to 24 years.

TABLE 6.5 Final list of descriptive variables identified for the bank's customer segmentation project

Variable	Type	Simple or Derived	Possible Values	Derived From
Age	Number	Simple	0 to 100	
Age category	Category	Derived	Less than 22; 22 to 24; 24 to 32; 32 to 39; 39 to 54; 54 to 60; 60 to 65; more than 65	
Economic level (1)	Number	Derived	Income level 1: 0 to $600/month income level 2: $601 to $1,200/ month $1,200 to $1,300; etc.	Monthly income (salary, rents, etc.)
Economic level (2)	Category	Derived	Low, medium-low, medium, medium-high, high	Profession, education, area of residence, zip/postal code, number of automobiles owned, value of domestic property, second home owner, balance of pension plan, investment plans, insurance, etc.
Debt/insolvency	Category	Derived	Low, medium-low, medium, medium-high, high	Mortgage loan, credit card, other debts, characteristics of monthly expenses/income cycle, more than 30 days with current acct in debt, etc.
VIP	Category	Derived	yes/no	>$100,000 in cash, responsibility, profession, relationship
Retired	Category	Derived	yes/no	Age >65 years (males) or 60 years (females) and/or receiving pension
Profession	Category	Simple	Student, university student, employee, self-employed, manager, entrepreneur, retired, etc.	

TABLE 6.5   Final list of descriptive variables identified for the bank's customer segmentation project—Cont'd

Variable	Type	Simple or Derived	Possible Values	Derived From
Professional	Category	Derived	yes/no	Profession one of: executive, director, lawyer, architect, engineer, medic, or similar. Derived from the variable "profession."
Marital status	Category	Simple	Single, married, divorced, widowed	
Offspring	Category	Simple	yes/no	
Offspring minors	Category	Simple/derived	yes/no	Captured directly or derived from the age of offspring, if this data is available

When the company is confident that the data is good (that is, representative, without errors, missing values, or incongruence) then it can start generating segmentation models of its clients.

Final Segmentation Model

Figure 6.5 shows the final segmentation model, where the customers have been divided into seven distinct segments. Clearly, the age of the customer is a determining criterion in several segments: young in segments 1, 2, and 4 and retired in segment 7. The marital status is also significant: single in segment 4 and married in segments 2 and 3. Having offspring or not (binary indicator) is a criterion in segments 2 and 3, and segment 3 also requires knowing whether the offspring are minors. (Obtaining this information may have required launching a survey to obtain feedback from the customers.) For segment 7, the bank asked whether the customer is retired (binary indicator, yes or no), and segment 5 asked the customer's profession. Segment 5 requires defining the profession, such as executive, director, lawyer, architect, engineer, medic, and so on. The factor "income level" appears in two segments: segment 1, low income, and segment 5, affluent.

In Figure 6.5, an implicit client life cycle is indicated by arrows, where young clients get married, have children, earn more money, and so on. However, it is clear that this is not the only possible segmentation. The retired people segment is interesting because it is becoming an increasingly higher proportion

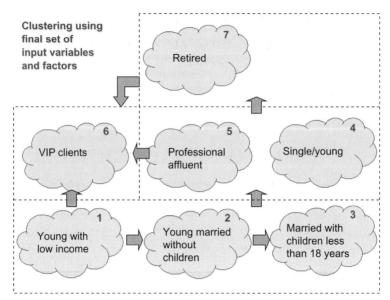

Clustering using final set of input variables and factors

7 Retired

6 VIP clients

5 Professional affluent

4 Single/young

1 Young with low income

2 Young married without children

3 Married with children less than 18 years

FIGURE 6.5 Final segmentation of the retail bank's customers

of the populace, especially in industrialized nations, and these people tend to have significant wealth: mortgage paid, pension plan liquidated, fewer expenses given that children have become independent, inheritance from their own parents, and so on. The segments for younger people are interesting because, although they may not be profitable at present, their lifetime value is potentially greater than that of older people.

If the bank has been correct in the initial hypothesis of the segmentation, as well as in the selection of input variables, then as a result, its clients will be categorized into coherent segments the business experts approve of. If not, then the company will have to revise the variables and maybe create or obtain new descriptive variables, change the definition of the segmentation, or extract new data samples.

Data Quality

Quality versus Cost

Data may not be perfect in every aspect; however, data quality is also a question of how much time and effort the business or project manager is prepared to invest in the data processing. Hence, data quality has an objective (measureable) component and an economic component: how much effort is a company prepared to spend on improving its data? Chapters 2 and 5 describe how to choose and evaluate business objectives and available (or non-available) data *a priori* in order to avoid reaching the data analysis stage and realizing the data is not good enough to proceed with the rest of the project.

Summary of the Reverse Engineering Approach

This section concludes by highlighting that the reverse engineering approach should be the final approach adopted in a data mining project. It is clear that a tangible and well-chosen business objective must be the end game of any commercial data mining project. However, the approach of selecting from the available data may serve as an optional first step in order to identify candidate business objectives.

DATA MINING APPROACHES TO SELECTING VARIABLES

The first two sections in this chapter described how to select variables based on a statistical analysis of the available data using statistical techniques such as correlation and factorial analysis. This section addresses how to use three data mining techniques for the same purpose. The three techniques are rule induction, neural networks, and clustering. They are described in more detail in Chapter 9, so the present chapter focuses on selecting the variables rather than on the techniques themselves. The following section briefly describes how each technique can be used to identify the subset of input variables that are the best predictors for an output variable (business objective).

Rule Induction

Rule induction is a technique that creates "if–else–then"-type rules from a set of input variables and an output variable. A typical rule induction technique, such as Quinlan's C5, can be used to select variables because, as part of its processing, it applies information theory calculations in order to choose the input variables (and their values) that are most relevant to the values of the output variables. Therefore, the least related input variables and values get pruned and disappear from the tree. Once the tree is generated, the variables chosen by the rule induction technique can be noted in the branches and used as a subset for further processing and analysis. Remember that the values of the output variable (the outcome of the rule) are in the terminal (leaf) nodes of the tree. The rule induction technique also gives additional information about the values and the variables: the ones higher up in the tree are more general and apply to a wider set of cases, whereas the ones lower down are more specific and apply to fewer cases.

C5 is an improved version of Quinlan's C4.5 algorithm. For further reading on the C5 Rule Induction algorithm, see:

Quinlan, J. R. 1993. *C4.5: Programs for Machine Learning*. Burlington, MA: Morgan Kaufmann (rev.). ISBN-13: 978-1558602380.

"Data Mining Tools See5 and C5.0." March 2013. Available at: http://www .rulequest.com/see5-info.html.

Figure 6.6 illustrates a tree induction applied to a set of input variables with respect to an output variable. The input variables are client_age_over_35yrs,

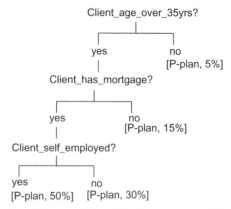

FIGURE 6.6 Induced tree of input variables related to an output variable

client_has_mortgage, and client_self_employed, and the output variable is P-plan (pension plan). The percentage after P-plan indicates the percentage of clients at the given leaf node who actually have a pension plan. As observed earlier, the variable highest in the tree is the most general, which in this case is client_age_over_35yrs; that is, the client's age is a key aspect that determines whether they contract a pension plan or not. The variable lowest in the tree is client_self_employed; that is, the type of employment is a more specific criterion related to contracting a pension plan. The other two input variables were given to the tree induction technique, but they were pruned from the tree because they didn't reach the minimum information support level. The information support level can be considered as a sort of relevance measure or correlation with the business objective (output label); hence the algorithm uses this threshold to decide whether or not to include a variable in the tree data model.

In this sense, the tree induction technique has been used as a filter to identify the variables most and least related to the output variable (contract pension plan). This technique is described in more detail in Chapter 9, in the context of data modeling.

Neural Networks

A neural network is a technique that creates a data model based on the interconnectivity of artificial neurons that become activated or inhibited during the training phase. (This technique is described in more detail in Chapter 9.) In the present context, a neural network will be used to rank the relevance of the input variables with respect to an output variable (the business objective). When a neural network is trained, some input neurons (input variables) get assigned a higher weight (activation), whereas other input neurons get assigned a lower weight and are therefore relatively inhibited from contributing to the overall result (output). The weights are a set of numbers that can be displayed, and from this the input variables can be ranked in terms of their activation with respect to the output. Graphing these numbers usually results in an inflection point, where the activation drops considerably. This inflection point can be used as a threshold below which the variables are not relevant to the output (business objective).

Clustering

The technique of clustering can also be used to select variables. (Clustering will be considered in detail in Chapter 9). Many data mining tools, such as Weka, the IBM Intelligent Miner for Data, and the IBM SPSS Modeler, let the user cluster input variables and then overlay an output variable on the resulting 2-D cluster plot. (The output variable should be categorical, with just a few categories. See Chapter 19 for details about and references for Weka, the IBM Intelligent Miner for Data, and the IBM SPSS Modeler.) The way the categories of the output variable fit on the clusters of the input variable can then be seen. Consider, for example, that the clustering generates three clusters (labeled one, two, and three) and the output variable has two categories (yes and no). When the output variable is overlaid on the clusters, all the values of the output variable from cluster one equal "yes" and all the values of the output variable from cluster two equal "no." Finally, of the values of the output variable assigned to cluster three, half are yes and half are no. From these results, one could conclude that the clustering of the input variables has quite a good match with the values of the output variable. If each cluster contained a mixture of yes and no in equal proportion, then one could conclude that the clustering of the input variables is not related to the values of the output variable.

So, how are the right combinations of input variables determined so that the clusters correspond to the values of the output variable? First, one or more candidate sets of input variables must be selected. Then an attempt can be made to cluster each candidate set and observe the degree of matching; then, depending on the results, different combinations of input variables can be tried until a good fit is reached. This technique can also be used in combination with the other variable selection techniques as a form of cross-checking, which will provide more confidence that the input variable set is relevant to a given output result under alternative conditions.

PACKAGED SOLUTIONS: PRESELECTING SPECIFIC VARIABLES FOR A GIVEN BUSINESS SECTOR

There is an alternative approach to variable selection for a given business objective, which is to buy a standard solution. Some suppliers of software analysis tools such as the SAS Enterprise Miner, the IBM Intelligent Miner for Relationship Marketing, and the IBM SPSS Modeler, offer sectorial solutions for banking, insurance, and telecommunications companies, among others. (See Chapter 19 for details of these products and their references.) These solutions are characterized by an easy-to-use interface, whose objective is to make the whole laborious process of preprocessing, data cleaning, sampling, and so on transparent to the user, inasmuch as this is possible. But their true added value is that they offer a preselection of variables for a given sector, such as banking, or for specific business objectives that require specialist, up-to-date know-how (such as for fraud detection), which saves a lot of time and ingenuity in the identification of the most significant variables.

In the following section a specific example of a packaged solution is explored. The idea is that there are some variables or derived factors that are common for a given sector, and knowing *a priori* which ones they are avoids having to reinvent the wheel. However, standard solutions require caution, because they can be upset by business idiosyncrasies and stochastic environments. It is easier to define standard libraries and default parameterizations with query and reporting, EIS (executive information systems), and OLAP (online analytical processing) approaches, than in the terrain of data mining. Chapter 10 looks in more detail at query and reporting, EIS, and OLAP in the context of deployment systems for data mining results.

Variable Preselection

Open Source Applications

Some open source applications offer algorithms for variable preselection. For an interesting survey about user choices, see:

Piatetsky, G. June 3, 2013. "KDnuggets Annual Software Poll: RapidMiner and R Vie for First Place." KDnuggets. Available at: http://www.kdnuggets.com/2013/06/kdnuggets-annual-software-poll-rapidminer-r-vie-for-first-place.html.

Despite their possible pitfalls, packaged solutions must be recognized for their ability to give a project a good head start; customizing where necessary is essentially a good idea. The variables used in packaged solutions are the result of many hours of effort and learning with real business data. As well as providing a set of business variables that are sector-specific, solutions may be subdivided by different aspects of CRM (customer relationship management) within the given sector, such as identification of potential clients, cross-selling, and customer attrition. One can assume that cross-selling for bank clients has variables in common with telecom clients, whereas other variables and ratios are only meaningful for a specific sector. For example, "time as customer" is common to all sectors, whereas "standard deviation of the duration of local calls in the last quarter" is only meaningful for customers in the telecom sector.

Depending on the economic interests and specific business problems in a given sector, systems have been developed that have acquired the status of industry standard. One example is FAMS (Fraud and Abuse Management System), which is used for fraud detection in the insurance industry. It includes its own methodology as well as a set of key variables and indicators for data analysis and the generation of predictive models. The following section examines the FAMS system in more detail.

The FAMS (Fraud and Abuse Management) System

FAMS is an IBM solution for the finance industry—specifically the banking, property/health insurance, and tax revenue sectors. It uses the neural network algorithm within the IBM SPSS Modeler data mining software, whose inputs are a set of selected variables and derived factors, to predict fraudulent transactions in an online environment. The system performs a scoring that identifies transactions as successful, on hold, or declined. The business objective in this case is to identify a greater percentage of fraudulent transactions faster and with a greater precision than current methods do.

For further reading on the FAMS system, refer to the official IBM Redbook on predictive analytics for fraud detection:

Ebbers, Mike, Dheeraj R Chintala, Priya Ranjan, and Lakshminarayanan Sreenivasan. Mar. 11, 2013. "Real-Time Fraud Detection Analytics on System z." *IBM Redbook*, 1st ed. IBM. SG24-8066-00.

FAMS also uses a historical data base for pattern reference in order to predict the fraudulent transactions based on the historical information. If the system produces a score, it can be assumed that a score above a given threshold will result directly in a decline, whereas a score below a given threshold will result directly in an accept. A score between the two thresholds will therefore result in an on-hold status. However, if the system is to produce a yes/no output, then the score will require some additional processing rules.

One of the difficulties of developing a system such as this is the need for it to run in an online environment; the online transaction processing has to be fast, whereas the analytical processing required to detect fraud tends to be slow.

The preselected variables used for fraud scoring are divided into three groups: the transaction data, the customer profile, and the customer card details.

The transaction data includes: the amount of the current transaction, the total number of transactions made with an amount greater than $500, the total number of transactions within the last three hours, the total transaction amount within the last three hours, and the time interval since the last transaction. Also, the last month's transaction data is compared with the current transaction to establish whether the current transaction represents an exception, and the last 10 transactions are compared with the current transaction in order to establish whether the current transaction represents an exception.

The customer profile includes the following variables: gender, education level, marital status, occupation, economic status, annual salary, and house owner. This data represents specific demographic variables of different types (recall Chapters 3 and 4): binary, categorical (nominal and ordinal), and numerical.

Finally, the customer card details include: the credit card ID, the credit limit of the card, the ratio of the current account balance to the credit limit, the total amount of the last billing to the card, the country code the issuing bank belongs to, and whether the card holder has previously conducted a transaction with the bank.

SUMMARY

This chapter has discussed several approaches for selecting variables and deriving factors related to a given business objective from a larger set of initial variables. The approaches considered include the data-driven approach, followed by the business objective-driven approach, where some of the basic statistical techniques for identifying key variables such as correlation and factorial analysis were addressed. The use of data mining techniques for variable selection was discussed, and finally, consideration was given to the option of obtaining a packaged solution that offers preselected variables and factors for a given business objective.

Chapter 7

Data Sampling and Partitioning

INTRODUCTION

Sampling is a method for selecting a subset of data from the complete dataset in order to analyze and create models, and where the subset is sufficiently representative of the whole data set. This is important when the total data volume is very high: for example, if a bank has five million clients, the models and the analysis will be able to relate to all five million clients with a well-chosen sample of 5 percent of them (250 thousand records).

A debate is happening in data mining circles about whether sampling is really necessary now that so much disc space and processing power are cheaply available. On the one hand, there are those who defend statistical sampling given that, if the sample gives just as good results as the whole dataset, it is common sense, from an economy of effort viewpoint, to use the sample. On the other hand, the Big Data movement proposes that, if the whole dataset can be processed in a reasonable amount of time and effort, then it should be done. Another justification for processing the whole dataset is to avoid missing outliers and small niches in the data. At the end of the day, the choice of processing the whole dataset may depend on how big the dataset is with respect to the available processing power and storage and what the business objective of processing the data is. The first aspect implies that the choice is a function of cost: presumably, the project could purchase as much processing power and storage as necessary if the project can justify the cost. Independent of whether or not data is sampled for reduction or manageability reasons, distinct train and test datasets will still have to be extracted for data mining, and subsets of the data based on different business criteria must be extracted. Data mining is usually performed with one or more datasets consisting of records used to train the model (called the training data) and a second type of dataset used to test the model created with the training data (called the test data). These concepts are explained in more detail later in the chapter.

The chapter looks at various types of sampling, such as random sampling and sampling based on business criteria (age of customer, time as client, etc.), discusses how to extract train and test datasets for specific business objectives, and considers the issue of Big Data, given that it is currently a hot topic.

SAMPLING FOR DATA REDUCTION

The first key consideration for extracting a sample is that it must be representative of the entire population. The easiest way to achieve this is by a random selection of x percent of the 100 percent. Several samples can initially be extracted—say, five—and then validated. One way of validating a sample is to look at the distribution of the values of the principal variables and determine whether they are the same in the complete population of data and in the sample. For example, if the total population of the dataset is 30 percent male and 70 percent female, then in the sampled dataset should also be 30 percent male and 70 percent female.

Sampling

Extracting Multiple Datasets for Data Analysis and Modeling

Sample datasets are extracted until a sufficient number are good with respect to the respective variables distributions. Normally, two datasets are needed for data modeling: one to train the model and another to test it. The number of sample datasets to extract depends on the cross-validation (comparison of results from distinct datasets to validate precision) to be performed, but could be three, five, or ten (10-fold cross-validation). (Cross-validation and train and test datasets are discussed in more detail in the context of data modeling in Chapter 9.)

The following example discusses extracting a dataset sample from a larger dataset, such that the distribution of the values for each variable will be the same in the sample dataset as in the larger dataset. Suppose a sample of 50,000 records is needed from a complete dataset of a million records. Almost all the statistical software and commercial data mining tools have sample extraction tools and usually offer several ways of extracting records. (Chapter 19 describes these software tools in more detail and provides their references.) For this example, the simplest way to extract the sample is to select the first 50,000 records from the file. Clearly, the risk is that these records are not representative of the whole one million. For example, the complete dataset may have 40 percent females and 60 percent males, but all the clients in the first 50,000 records are women because the complete dataset was ordered in that way. Perhaps the records had been ordered by one or more variables (such as gender), thus potentially biasing any samples extracted. To avoid this kind of mistake, an alternate method can be used, such as random extraction. For this method, records are selected and extracted using a random algorithm until a total of 50,000 are obtained.

Selecting Records from a Dataset

Random Selection

When a random function is used to select records from a dataset, the result may be software-dependent. Some random functions are more pseudo-random than others, so the software manufacturer's information about how the random function works should be read before using the software. For example, according to Microsoft, the rand( ) function of the Excel spreadsheet returns a real random number greater or equal to 0 and less than 1, uniformly distributed. Each time the spreadsheet is executed, a new, real random number is returned. To generate a real random number between limits a and b, use the formula: random( ) $\times$ (b − a) + a. Note that "real" in this context means the real data type (e.g., 3.1412 . . .) as opposed to an integer or binary type, for example. Java has a random generator that returns a floating-point, pseudo-random number in the range 0 to 1. The seed value or initialization value is a key aspect, and initializing with a value, such as a system clock's current time in milliseconds, is recommended. Finally, Oracle has two random functions, one for generating integers and another for real numbers. If the function is seeded twice with the same seed, and then accessed in the same way, it will produce the same results in both cases.

Another way of extracting sample data from a population dataset is selecting each *n*th record, in a cyclic manner, until 50,000 records are obtained. Once selected, a record would be marked so that it cannot be selected again. This method is susceptible to errors or bias caused by the ordering and nature of the records in the dataset.

For further reading on statistical approaches to sampling, see:

Lane, D. M. n.d. "Introduction to Sampling Distributions." Available at: http://onlinestatbook.com/2/sampling_distributions/intro_samp_dist.html.

Peck, Roxy, Chris Olsen, Jay L. Devore. 2008. *Introduction to Statistics and Data Analysis*, 3rd ed., ch. 2. Stamford, CT: Cengage Learning. ISBN-13: 978-0495557838.

Figure 7.1 illustrates the variable distributions for a complete dataset, and for two samples, one correct and another which is incorrect. The top row shows the distributions for three key variables of interest: average sales, sales by product type, and customer age. In the case of average sales, some specific traits for the complete dataset (top row) can be seen, such as the dip in August and the rise in the first semester and the last quarter. These traits are also present in the correct sample (middle row), but are distinctly different in the incorrect sample (lower row). Considering sales by product, observe that the proportions are similar for the complete dataset and the correct sample, but are very different for the incorrect sample, where the products ham and bacon have disproportionately large slices. Finally, the complete dataset and the correct sample have similar frequency distributions for customer age, with the greatest frequencies

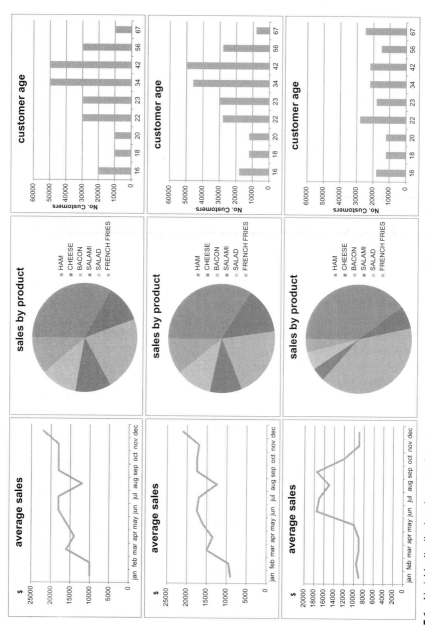

FIGURE 7.1 Variable distributions in a complete dataset (*upper row*), correct sample (*middle row*), and incorrect sample (*lower row*)

for customers between 22 and 56 years of age. However, the incorrect sample shows a much flatter overall distribution and a significant change in the absolute frequency values. In practice, an error tolerance margin could be set for, say, 10 percent for the observed difference between the statistics of the complete dataset and the statistics of the sampled dataset. In order to quantify this, the averages and standard deviations for the numerical values could be calculated, together with the correlations. The modal values and the difference in the frequencies for each category could be calculated for the categorical values.

COMPLETE DATASET	AGE	SALES	SAMPLE DATASET	AGE	SALES	DIFFERENCE	AGE	SALES
Average	44.2857143	1128.57143	Average	25.7142857	1357.14286	Average	18.5714286	−228.571429
Stan. Dev.	19.6698948	475.093976	Stan. Dev.	5.34522484	713.809365	Stan. Dev.	14.32467	−238.715389

Correlation	PRODUCT		Correlation	PRODUCT		Correlation	PRODUCT	
0.99237682	0.3	a	0.88299639	0.5	a	0.10938042	−0.2	a
	0.7	b		0.5	b		0.2	b

FIGURE 7.2 Comparison of the statistics of a sampled dataset with respect to the complete dataset

Now consider the values in Figure 7.2: On the left side of the table are statistics for a complete dataset for the variable's age, sales, and product. The average value for age is 44.28 years and the standard deviation is 19.66, while the average value for sales is 11.28.57 and the standard deviation is 475.09. For the categorical variable "product," 30 percent of its values are equal to a and 70 percent are equal to b. The correlation between the variable's age and sales is 0.9923.

The middle table of Figure 7.2 has the same statistics but for a sample dataset. The right-hand table shows the differences between the complete dataset statistics and the sample dataset statistics. The big difference is in the distribution of the categorical values of the product variable: in the complete dataset, the ratios are 30 percent and 70 percent for product types a and b, respectively; in the sample dataset the ratio is 50:50. Ideally, all the differences should be zero; that is, the statistics for the complete dataset should be the same as those of the sample dataset. In practice, there will inevitably be a small deviation, but the idea is to minimize it. Having said all this, there is an exception to the rule of keeping the class distribution of a variable the same in the sampled dataset with respect to the complete dataset. This is when the variable in question is the output variable for a supervised learning technique, and there is a class imbalance for that variable. This exception is explained later in the chapter.

For further reading about sampling and distributions, see:

Lane, D. M. n.d. "Introduction to Sampling Distributions." Available at: http://onlinestatbook.com/2/sampling_distributions/intro_samp_dist.html.

On the left in Table 7.1 is a random selection of customers, and on the right every fourth customer has been selected.

TABLE 7.1 Two methods of sampling from a customer database

	Type of Sampling		
(1) Random		(2) Each nth Record	
Client ID	Selected	Client ID	Selected
1		1	×
2	×	2	
3		3	
4	×	4	
5	×	5	×
6		6	
7		7	
8	×	8	
9		9	×
10		10	
11		11	
12	×	12	
13		13	×
14	×	14	
15		15	
...		...	

When extracting multiple sample datasets (where a sample dataset means a subset of records) from the complete data file, care must be taken to not extract the same records in separate sample datasets. That is, the records in each sample dataset must be exclusive and unique.

In order to check the validity and quality of the dataset samples, graphs can be generated of the distribution for the key variables (ideally they should have a uniform Gaussian, or bell-shaped, distribution), and a random inspection of the values made to ensure that they fall within the desired ranges. Extreme values—those that are very small or very large compared to the average value for a variable—must be watched for, given that they may distort the statistics of the sample.

If extreme or outlier values are found, one option is to delete them from the dataset, always taking into account the values of the other respective

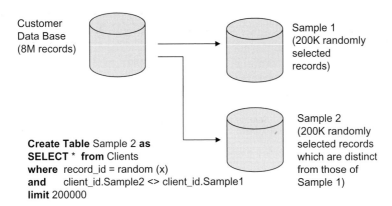

Customer
Data Base
(8M records)

Sample 1
(200K randomly
selected
records)

Create Table Sample 2 **as**
SELECT * **from** Clients
where   record_id = random (x)
and   client_id.Sample2 <> client_id.Sample1
limit 200000

Sample 2
(200K randomly
selected records
which are distinct
from those of
Sample 1)

√ Check with your version of SQL for the exact syntax of the "select."

FIGURE 7.3   A random sampling of two samples from the complete table of available data

variables in the record. If, on the other hand, the business objective is related to outliers (for example, fraud detection), then there may be specific interest in selecting a sample in which all the records are outliers or a mix of outliers and non-outliers.

Figure 7.3 illustrates the extraction of two samples of 200 thousand records from a total dataset of 8 million records. The selection of records is random. As mentioned earlier, many data processing tools have options for selecting data in this way. As an alternative, a counter could manually be created using a random value as an index. Although this process seems simple, there are several possible pitfalls. The first thing to confirm is that each final sample is exclusive, that is, that the records in sample 1 are not present in sample 2. To achieve this, when selecting the records for sample 2, one can specify the client identifier as "NOT IN" sample 1.

Sampling

Random Selection

A random value is used to select the records in Figures 7.3 and 7.4. To do this, a random value can be created as an additional variable, then the records can be ordered by the random variable and the first 200 thousand records chosen from the total of eight million. Alternatively, there may be a random generator function (such as in the SQL example) that selects customer IDs randomly, on the fly.

PARTITIONING THE DATA BASED ON BUSINESS CRITERIA

In certain cases a sample needs to be created with a distribution that is different from the complete dataset. Suppose, for example, that from a complete customer dataset, 85 percent are customers who buy product A and 15 percent are customers who buy product B. In order to obtain a distribution consisting of 50 percent of each product customer, the records for product B customers can be replicated until the proportion is equal to 50 percent.

Sampling

Class Balancing – An Exception

Class balancing clearly goes against what was discussed earlier in this chapter about keeping class proportions the same in the sampled dataset with respect to the complete dataset. An exception is made when the variable under consideration is the output variable for a supervised modeling technique, and a class imbalance exists for that variable that would impair the modeling result.

This procedure is useful when predicting both customer types using a supervised learning technique for those who buy product A as well as those who buy product B. If this redistribution isn't performed, the model will be much better at predicting customers with product A than those with product B. For example, suppose that 90 percent of all products are of type A and only 10 percent are of type B. If a model is trained with this variable as the output, a supervised learning technique may tend to go for obtaining the maximum precision in the easiest manner, which could be by classifying all the records as type A. This would give 100 percent precision for type A records but 0 percent precision for type B records, which would be useless. (These issues are discussed in detail in the context of data modeling in Chapter 9.)

Unbalanced Data

Supervised Learning Techniques

Supervised learning techniques are so named because they "learn" a model from the data by being given input variables and then being given the corresponding output variable for each data record. Two examples of supervised learning techniques are neural networks and rule induction. (These techniques are discussed in detail in the context of data modeling in Chapter 9.)

However, if the records of product B customers are replicated, the new distributions will have to be revised to determine that secondary effects have not been introduced in the data. For example, by rebalancing the categories of the variable "product," the previously balanced categories of another variable, "region," may become unbalanced.

Another type of extraction is nonrandom, that is, selection using business criteria. For example, one can extract from the complete dataset only the clients who live in Boston, who have been clients for more than one year, who have bought the product or service by catalogue, are between 20 and 40 years of age, and who have bought something in the last six months. Presumably, the sample datasets are extracted directly from the company database. In this case the complete dataset is usually much greater than the sample dataset. After this initial extraction, criteria can be applied to limit the data volume to be analyzed. Extraction methods could also be combined: first by making an extraction using business criteria to obtain a sample dataset A and then performing a random extraction on that dataset to obtain sample dataset B.

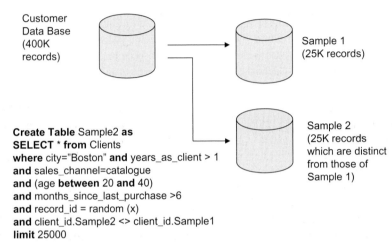

FIGURE 7.4   Extraction of two data samples from the client database, using fixed criteria together with a random selection

Figure 7.4 shows that sample 1 has been extracted using the following criteria: clients who live in Boston, have been clients for more than one year, have bought the product by catalogue, are between 20 and 40 years of age, and have made at least one purchase in the last six months. The records complying with these criteria are randomly selected until a total of 25,000 is reached (if that many exist). Sample 2 is extracted using the same criteria as sample 1, but with one exception: instead of clients with activity in the last six months, clients with no activity in the last six months (months_since_last_purchase > 6) are extracted. Figure 7.4 illustrates the full SQL selected for the business criteria.

Consider the business goal behind the months_since_last_purchase selection criteria. Sample 1, according to the criteria of activity in the last six months, contains the profitable clients, whereas sample 2, by the same criteria, contains the unprofitable clients. Thus, knowing which are which (by assigning them binary flags), various strategies can be carried out. For example, the profitable clients can be thanked for their loyalty and given some kind of gift, such as 100 bonus points as a discount on their next purchase. The non-profitable clients could, for example, be fired, but this is difficult in practice. So an effort could be made to improve their profitability, thus converting them into profitable customers. If the characteristics of the profitable customers are analyzed, non-profitable clients who have the same characteristics as the profitable ones can be identified—that is, non-profitable clients who should be profitable. For these clients, actions, incentives, and mailings can be carried out to wake up their consumer activity. Also, among the non-profitable clients, those who have characteristics contrary to the profitable ones could be identified. These clients are the truly unprofitable ones. Their data records can be flagged to exclude them from mailings so as not to waste publicity budget on them.

The types of sampling in Figures 7.3 and 7.4 create files that can be used for analysis or creating models. When creating a data model, samples must be extracted for specific purposes. Typically, three separate samples are needed: one sample of records used to train the model (the training data); a second sample used to test the model that is created with the training data (the test data); and a third set of real data, which is called the production set. The third dataset is different from the first two because the data is not historical data; it is data without a final result.

Extracting Train and Test Datasets

Cross-Validation

Cross-validation is a technique related to sampling, in which multiple files are extracted for training and testing in order to obtain a model that generalizes and has a good average precision for separate datasets of records. Chapter 9 discusses cross-validation in more detail.

For example, if a company were to study its customer loyalty, the production set would consist of all the customer data minus the indicator that tells whether the customer left to go to the competition or not. The samples for training and testing do include this indicator: that is, the outcome is known because the samples are taken from historical records. Figure 7.5 illustrates the extraction of the train, test, and production datasets.

When creating predictive models (also called supervised models), the training file is used to mold the model based on the profiles of the records or cases, which is known as learning by examples. The model is "told," this is an example of those who went to the competition, this is an example of those who didn't, and so on. In this way, the model learns the profiles of the "yes" cases and the "no" cases, in the same way as high school students learn from examples and counter-examples. Once this learning process is complete, when a new record is presented to the model without the data indicating whether the client is loyal or not, the model will automatically identify the new record with a high percentage of precision.

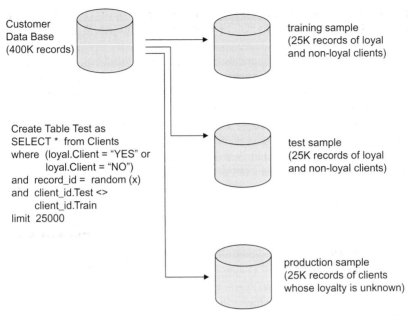

FIGURE 7.5   Extraction of samples for training, testing, and online use (production) of a data model. The output variable is "loyal," which is of binary type, and has possible values of "yes" and "no."

ISSUES RELATED TO SAMPLING

This section addresses issues and auxiliary topics related to sampling, such as traditional sampling methods for questionnaires and surveys, possible problems when performing sampling, and when it is advisable (or not) to perform sampling. Long before computer data became available for analysis, sampling, surveys, and censuses were being conducted. According to the article "The Census through History" (http://www.census.ie/-in-History/The-Census-through-History.150.1.aspx), the Babylonians conducted a census of population, livestock, and other property in 3800 BC. The idea of a census is to cover 100 percent of the population, whereas a survey or poll covers a sample population. A survey or poll typically assesses preferences of audiences, consumers, voters, and so on. (See "The History of Surveys" at http://www.squidoo.com/history-surveys for an interesting summary of these aspects.) Hence, when evaluating tendencies, the census is the only data capture method that considers the whole population.

With respect to problems that can occur with sampling, the chapter has addressed ways to guarantee a good quality sample in terms of representing the complete dataset. However, if business criteria are used to select a subset of the data, a quantity of records that is too small could be obtained.

For example, in an extreme case, a target analysis could be set so precisely that, from a million records, just twenty would be chosen that comply with the query definition.

When to perform sampling and when not to must also be decided. There is no clear-cut answer to this question, given that it depends on various factors. Clearly, it is common sense that, if a dataset of just 1,000 records exists, it would be unnecessary to sample it for volume reduction motives. Generally, the threshold of the number of records depends on the processing limit of the hardware and software. A business could try loading 50,000 records into its data mining tool, try executing whatever process it wishes to use, and see if the program freezes or doesn't terminate in a reasonable amount of time. If the program freezes, the business can try again with 40,000 records instead of 50,000, and so on. Again, what constitutes a reasonable amount of time is subjective. Some analysts think nothing of letting a process run overnight, whereas others require a result within an hour. There are users who have access to remote corporate disc clusters and multi-processors for their processing needs, whereas other users have just their desktop PCs.

Sampling versus Big Data

As mentioned in the introduction, there is currently a debate between the Big Data movement and the sampling approach advocates. Here the debate is not whether to partition data based on business criteria or divide the data into train and test subsets; rather, it centers on whether data reduction is a thing of the past, given that the processing power is now available to deal with a whole dataset. But as just mentioned, not everyone has access to high-performance hardware or software, and so Big Data will stay in the realm of those who do.

On the other hand, there is an argument that favors extracting a representative sample even if the whole dataset could theoretically be processed. This argument is related to the topic of data quality discussed in Chapter 5. That is, with a dataset of three terabytes, the cost of preprocessing will multiply for each action performed, and it is more difficult to double-check a large dataset than a smaller one for inconsistencies, erroneous data, and so on.

But Big Data is still an attractive option for those who wish to process large weblogs from Twitter or Facebook, or the transaction logs of all bank customers over the last year in order to find fraudulent transactions. The difference between the need for processing Big Data from a transactional and database storage point of view and the need for analyzing this data must be emphasized. According to Wikipedia (http://en.wikipedia.org/wiki/Big_data), Amazon.com and Wal-Mart process millions of customer transactions every hour, and the former have one of the largest database systems in existence. Software companies such as Oracle, IBM, SAP, and HP have developed and are continually improving solutions for processing large data volumes. Hadoop is a software system designed for processing Big Data and is based on the MapReduce algorithm, whose original purpose was for indexing the Web. The idea behind Hadoop is that, instead of processing one monolithic block of data with one processor, it fragments the data and processes each fragment in parallel. (See Wikibon at http://wikibon.org/wiki/v/Big_Data:_Hadoop_Business_Analytics_and_Beyond for more details.)

For further reading on the debate of Big Data versus sampling, see:

Swoyer, S., n.d. Big Data Analytics and the End of Sampling as We Know It. ComputerWeekly .com. Available at: http://www.computerweekly.com/feature/Big-data-analytics-and-the-end-of-sampling-as-we-know-it.

Chapter 8

Data Analysis

INTRODUCTION

Analysis can be considered as a prior step to creating data models, or it can be the final phase in itself, the objective of a project. This chapter discusses a diversity of ways to analyze data, methods that depend primarily on the type of data to be analyzed and the complexity of the analysis to be performed. The chapter starts with the simplest form of analysis, which is by visualizing the data in some way and inspecting the resulting presentation. A case study is followed in which visualization is combined with clustering and segmentation in order to contrast differences between datasets. The reader is then briefly introduced to the analysis of associations, transactional analysis, time series analysis, and data normalization. Finally, some of the typical mistakes when doing data analysis and interpreting results are discussed.

Data Analysis

Variable Selection and Creating New Factors

Chapter 6 covers a diversity of data analysis techniques (correlation, factor analysis, etc.) in the context of variable selection and creating new factors. Hence, these techniques can also be considered as part of the analysis phase.

The simplest type of analysis consists of looking at the characteristics, distributions, and values of the variables in a dataset. This can be done initially by a simple visual inspection of the tabular data displayed in a spreadsheet; then the distributions can be visualized using graphs. A histogram of the distribution can be generated for each numerical variable, with the most typical distribution being the bell, or Gaussian, curve. A pie chart graph can be generated for each categorical variable. In this way, the category values that occur most frequently can be identified and, in the case of the numerical values, what the maximum, minimum, and average are. This information provides clues about the nature of the data. If the data represents customers, tendencies can be identified in terms of age, gender, time as a customer, products a customer has purchased, frequency of purchases, and so on.

VISUALIZATION

Although it may seem obvious, one of the most important techniques in data analysis is visualization. This consists of generating different types of graphs and scrutinizing them to find tendencies, relations, exceptions, and errors, all of which can provide clues for creating derived variables, improving the quality of the data model, and adjusting distributions. Chapter 4 showed that, when discussing how to represent the data, a numerical variable can be represented by plotting it as a graph or as a histogram, whereas a categorical variable is usually represented as a pie chart or a frequency histogram.

This section does not pretend to describe an inventory of all the different ways of visualizing data. Rather, a diverse selection of visualization types is presented throughout the book. The reader can see more options in a typical spreadsheet application: select from the upper menu Insert → Chart and see the available options, including columns, bars, lines, pie, scatter, area, radar, surface, bubble, and stock, each one with its variants.

Analysis by visualization is a little like being a detective, especially when looking for differences or similarities between groups of data defined by business criteria. For example, consider two datasets of customer records: the first one consists of individuals who have been clients for five years or more (that is, they are the most loyal clients) and the second file consists of clients who canceled their accounts within the first year as a client.

The objective is to evaluate the differences between profiles of clients who canceled their accounts and those of loyal clients. To start, the distributions of the most relevant variables (numerical and categorical) can be generated for the first file, which contains the loyal clients. They can be conveniently displayed in just one window on a computer screen. Then the same is done for the second file, which contains the clients who canceled. The two windows can be placed side by side on the screen and the distributions scrutinized, variable by variable. There are many interesting trends that can be discovered with this procedure. For example, the age distribution for loyal clients can be identified as starting at 35 years and displaying a typical bell distribution. In contrast, the distribution of the same variable for those who canceled their accounts has a much sharper form, with a concentration of cases for clients between 18 and 35 years old and another around 60 years.

Figure 8.1 illustrates overlaying, which is a technique often used in data exploration, and which allows for relationships between pairs of variables to be identified. The figure shows a histogram of the binary variable "age category" on the x-axis versus number of clients on the y-axis. The two possible values of the output or result variable "client status" are overlaid (indicated by different colors) for each one of its possible values. The figure shows that, for the clients represented by the left column, with ages between 18 and 35 years, the cancellation rate is 40 percent. The right column shows that, for clients between 35 and 60 years old, the cancellation rate goes down to 18 percent.

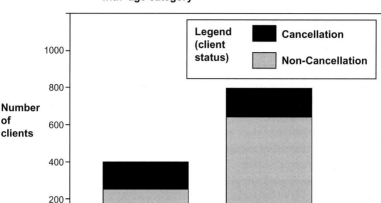

FIGURE 8.1   Distribution of the variables "age category" and "client status"

The results must be validated by business experts, in this case represented by the marketing and campaigns department. Case studies 1 (Customer Loyalty) and 2 (Cross-Selling) in the appendix give examples of using the overlay technique in real-world projects.

ASSOCIATIONS

The term "associations" refers to the relationships that may exist (or not) between the different values of the variables. For example, 65 percent of users who click on reviews of films in which Clint Eastwood is the director also click on reviews of films directed by Steven Spielberg. Associations are similar to rules, and they are identified by counting the frequencies between cases.

Associations can be identified manually, but tools are available that can automate the process. It is a technique that is particularly useful for "market basket analysis," which is typical for data of sales in supermarkets and retail stores in general, and identifies products that tend to be purchased together. As a consequence of the analysis, the identified products can be grouped physically close in the store (or on the website), thus making it easier for the customer to locate and purchase them.

The graphic in Figure 8.2 is a spider's web diagram based simply on occurrence frequencies, in which the strength of the relation is indicated by the thickness of the line. Clients who have a customer card tend to be higher spenders, and they make their purchases on the weekend or on Mondays and Fridays

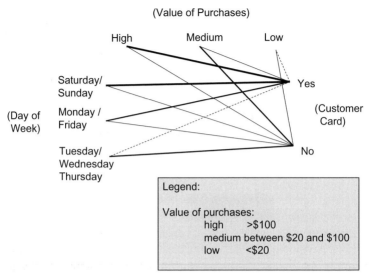

FIGURE 8.2   Spider's web diagram indicating the grade of relation between the values of different variables

(strong relation indicated by a thick line). Clients without a customer card tend to have a medium expenditure and purchase more often throughout the week. A secondary observation shows that people with a customer card don't tend to make purchases with a low expenditure (weak relation indicated by a dotted line) and avoid visits in the middle of the week. A general consideration with this type of diagram is that, if there are many variables and values, the number of lines may become excessive, making it more difficult to interpret the interrelations. In order to avoid this problem, groups of two or three variables at a time should be selected, each with just a few possible values. Case studies 1 (Customer Loyalty) and 2 (Cross-Selling) in the appendix give examples of the spider's web diagram used in real-world projects.

CLUSTERING AND SEGMENTATION

The basic concept of clustering is very simple: similar cases are grouped together and cases that are different are separated. The similarity or difference between two cases can be measured as a number or distance and there are many techniques that, as they perform the segmentation, also give the distances between cases and clusters.

A good segmentation creates clusters that are as compact as possible (distances between clusters within a group are minimized) and maximizes the distances between distinct groups (there is good separation between groups of distinct cases). In Figure 8.3, an example is shown of clustering the customers in terms of two key variables: profitability and time as customer.

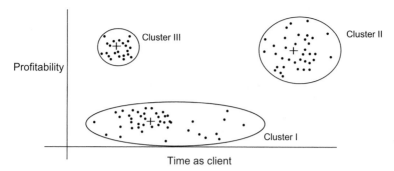

FIGURE 8.3   The objective of clustering is to maximize the distances between clusters while minimizing the distances within them

In contrast to a predictive model, a model based on segmentation or clustering does not have output variables. It only has input variables, and the grouping criteria try to group cases that are similar by using these variables. One golden rule is not to use an observation variable (for example, "contract new service Y/N") as an input to the clustering. This is because, if it is given as an input, it will influence the result of the clustering. Later, this variable could be used as the classifier output label for a predictive model. Many clustering methods let a variable of this type be defined as non-participative, allowing the variable's values to be visualized on the resulting graph plot of the clusters. In this way, it can be determined whether or not the clusters differentiate between values.

Consider a database of bank customers as an example. A useful segmentation would be in terms of profitability. For example, three groups could be identified: customers who are the most profitable for the bank, those with profitability around the average, and those who are the least profitable. Then a series of characteristics could be identified for each group; for example, in the most profitable clients group, the average age is 45 years, and in the least profitable clients group, the average age is 30 years. However, care must be taken when including new considerations to categorize the clients. The profitability, for example: if the profitability of clients is defined in terms of their commercial activity up to the present date, the aspect of lifetime value is lost, that is, a client's commercial potential over a lifetime. In the case of financial products, a young client has more potential in these terms than an older client does, although it may seem from the client's actual historical activity that the young client is not very profitable.

Another useful segmentation is in terms of the products or services that are purchased. This segmentation allows a business to identify clients who are most likely to buy certain products and provides information for cross-selling new products to existing customers.

Segmentation can also serve as a phase prior to creating predictive models. It is easier to create a predictive model for each major segment of a dataset than to create just one model for all the data. For example, in the case of a customer segmentation of high, medium, and low profitability, a predictive model could be constructed based on the high profitability segment.

SEGMENTATION AND VISUALIZATION

Segmentation and visualization create a powerful combination of techniques that facilitate the identification of differences between profiles and distributions of numerical and categorical variables, also making it possible to quantify those differences and create decision rules. As a next step, these decision rules can be written as SQL sentences and used to query the customer database.

Consider a situation where a series of client groupings have been obtained through the use of a segmentation technique, where some groupings have a high incidence of contracting a home delivery service and other groupings have practically no incidence of contracting. It would be interesting to know what differences exist between the profiles (or other factors) of clients who contract and those who don't.

The objective of applying a segmentation technique to the data is to establish homogeneous groups in the data. An example is two groups of clients, in which one group contains all loyal clients, and the other group contains clients who all leave within a year. Other tendencies between clusters and variables can also be looked for, which help to define new significant factors.

Figure 8.4 shows that the grouping technique (in this case, a "Kohonen SOM") has achieved a reasonable grouping in the sense that it has been able to distinguish groups of clients in terms of the variable of interest: "contract new service yes or no." A Kohonen SOM (self-organizing map) is a type of neural network that performs clustering. (Chapter 9 explains Kohonen SOMs in more detail, and case study 2 in the appendix gives an example of using the

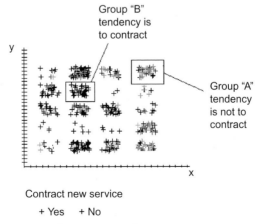

FIGURE 8.4   Customer groupings

Kohonen SOM in a real-world project.) Clients represented by the gray-colored crosses are those who don't contract the service. Observe that some groups are made up only of clients who do contract, whereas other groups have a majority of clients who do not contract, and still other groups have a mixture of clients who contract and those who do not. Clearly, in the case with mixed types, the segmentation has not been able to distinguish clients in terms of the "contract new service" variable. However, each group must be studied individually in order to see the characteristics and distributions of other input variables. Recall that the variable "contract new service" has been defined as non-participative in the clustering so that it doesn't influence the clustering process. However, it is available to visualize and study the relation of its values (yes/no) with the clusters generated in terms of the other variables.

TABLE 8.1 Clients from group B from the groupings in Figure 8.4

Time as Client (Months)	Age	Kids	Married	District of Residence	Number of Visits Last 3 Months
24	31	Yes	Yes	East	>20
19	37	Yes	Yes	East	>20
28	34	No	No	East	>20
36	41	Yes	Yes	West	11 to 20
41	51	Yes	Yes	South	5 to 10
33	45	Yes	Yes	East	11 to 20
21	40	No	No	West	5 to 10
25	38	Yes	Yes	South	>20
27	39	Yes	Yes	South	>20
31	48	Yes	Yes	North	<5
32	45	Yes	Yes	West	>20
28	37	No	No	East	>20
25	42	No	Yes	South	11 to 20

Visualization and Clustering

Inspecting Records inside a Cluster

Table 8.1 consists of 13 clients in Figure 8.4's group B. Notice that the client age varies between 31 and 51 years. Also, the time as a client varies between 19 and 41 months, 9 out of 13 have kids, 10 out of 13 are married, 5 out of 13 live in the EAST district, and 7 out of 13 have made more than 20 visits to one of the branch offices in the last three months.

The following discussion follows an example of how to display and analyze three figures that show the distributions of key variables in three different datasets. Figure 8.5 illustrates the distributions of key variables for the complete dataset of clients, Figure 8.6 shows the distributions of key variables for the dataset of clients who buy (contract a new service), and Figure 8.7 shows the distributions of key variables for the dataset of clients who didn't buy.

Visualization

Comparing Distributions of Variables

In Figures 8.5 to 8.7, the variables are ordered by the grade of relevance in the dataset with respect to a business objective variable, which, in this case, is "contracting of new service (yes/no)," and is the first variable on the left in Figure 8.5.

In this example, the grade of relevance is calculated using the chi-square measure, a statistical measure often used for categorical-type variables. Each variable is assigned a chi-square value with respect to the variable "contracting of new service." Then the variables are shown in descending order (from left to right) of their chi-square values.

Figure 8.5 shows the variables for all clients: the variable with the highest chi-square ranking with respect to "contracting of new service" (and therefore the most relevant variable to the business objective) is "time as client," followed by "age," "children," "number of visits last 3 months," and "married," in that order. The least significant variable with respect to the business objective is "area of residence."

The chi-square measure can be used to measure the relevance of categorical variables with respect to a business objective variable (which is also categorical). However, some of the variables in the figures are not categorical (e.g., time as client and age, which are numerical). In order to consider them in the same format, the numerical variables must be categorized by calculating their quantiles. As an alternative, the ranges could be manually defined for these variables. For example, "time as client" could be categorized as follows: category 1, one to six months; category 2, six to twelve months; category 3, twelve to eighteen months, and so on. Figure 8.5 shows two types of graphical representation for the variables: a histogram for the numerical variables and a pie chart for the category variables.

The objective is now to compare Figures 8.5, 8.6, and 8.7. A convenient way of doing this is to place them side by side on the computer screen. Any difference in the distributions or category frequencies may provide clues with respect to the customers who buy and those who don't buy, compared with the total number of customers. In this way, the profiles of the best clients can be defined, as well as those of low-value clients. Note that among the segmentation clusters in Figure 8.4, there is more than one group of clients who all bought. Therefore,

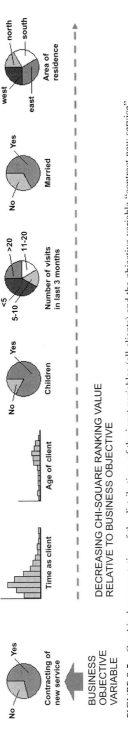

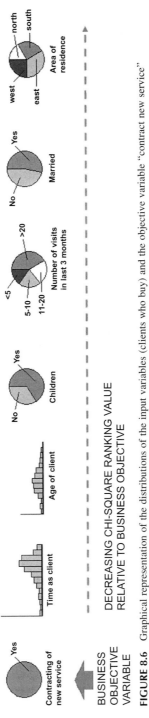

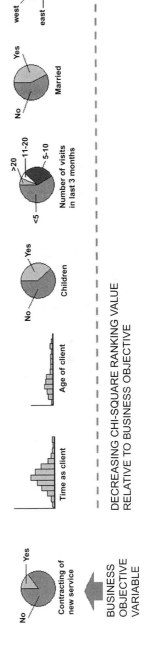

FIGURE 8.5   Graphical representation of the distributions of the input variables (all clients) and the objective variable "contract new service"

DECREASING CHI-SQUARE RANKING VALUE
RELATIVE TO BUSINESS OBJECTIVE

FIGURE 8.6   Graphical representation of the distributions of the input variables (clients who buy) and the objective variable "contract new service"

DECREASING CHI-SQUARE RANKING VALUE
RELATIVE TO BUSINESS OBJECTIVE

FIGURE 8.7   Graphical representation of the distributions of the input variables (clients who don't buy) and the objective variable "contract new service"

DECREASING CHI-SQUARE RANKING VALUE
RELATIVE TO BUSINESS OBJECTIVE

BUSINESS
OBJECTIVE
VARIABLE

BUSINESS
OBJECTIVE
VARIABLE

BUSINESS
OBJECTIVE
VARIABLE

there may be more than one customer profile who is a prototype buyer. That is, there will be one prototype for each cluster with a majority who buy.

Next, the distribution of the variable "time as client" is studied. For all clients in Figure 8.5, the tendency is toward a relatively short duration, with the main density and the maximum point being to the left and closer to the vertical axis. Now look at the same variable in Figure 8.6, but for clients who buy. See the difference? Now the tendency of "time as client" is toward the right, with an average value that is much higher. Now look at the distribution of the same variable in Figure 8.7, but for clients who don't buy. Again the distribution is different. In this graph there is a symmetrical distribution with a maximum more or less centered. This gives client profiles for those who buy and for those who don't buy and the difference between them and the total number of clients.

The idea is to repeat this brief visual analysis for the other variables in the figures. Notice that there are clear tendencies that differentiate clients who contract from those who don't. Observe that there is a variable whose value does not change: "district of residence." This means that the variable is not significant with respect to whether clients contract or not. The distribution is the same for all clients, those who buy, and those who don't buy. Therefore, this variable can be considered for elimination from the dataset.

In summary, the techniques of visualization and analysis explained in this section are important aspects of data analysis in general. This is emphasized because what human beings do well is visualize, and if this capacity can be potentiated using this technique, then the analysis can be made easier, especially when the data is complex.

In this section a previously created segmentation has been used as the starting point. However, the project could have commenced from just three basic files: total clients, clients who have been offered the service and contracted it, and clients who were offered the service and didn't contract it. Thus the need to segment is eliminated. However, the segmentation does provide the possibility of defining multiple profiles of clients who buy and creates the basis for future data modeling. But if this is the first analysis of the data and general trends are being looked for, it is possible that not much segmentation is needed.

This technique is very powerful for applications such as fraud detection for insurance companies, or for the evaluation of debt default for credit companies, as well as for identifying clients who do or don't contract a given service. For insurance fraud detection, time series aspects are often included as input factors in addition to basic client and insurance policy data, such as the periods of time elapsed between the occurrence of an accident, the presentation of the claim, and the different administrative dates of processing the insurance payment, together with the characteristics of the contracted cover and the relationship between the policy holder, the insured, and the beneficiary. For debt default, the idea is to identify cases of unpaid debt in which the client would be able to pay the debt (derived from the client's profile of estimated wealth), thus avoiding wasting effort on insolvent clients and taking into account the quantity of debt to be recovered. In these two applications, insurance fraud and debt default, clients are divided into two possible groups: fraudulent or not fraudulent and recoverable or non-recoverable, respectively. Once three datasets have been prepared for each application (all clients, clients who are, and clients who are not), the technique of graphic visualization discussed in this section can be applied.

This section addresses tools that make the analysis process easier. Again it must be emphasized that the more visual (as opposed to lists of numbers) the representation, the better. If a segmentation is performed first, a technique called *k*-means (traditional statistics) can be used or, alternatively, Kohonen (non-supervised learning) or some other method. IBM's SPSS Modeler is very agile for generating clusters, selecting a given cluster of interest, and extracting those cases, as shown in Figure 8.4. With respect to generating distributions in order to visualize and make comparisons between them, IBM's Intelligent Miner for Data is very adequate. Alternatively, the reader could acquire more economic tools such as Weka, and with a little skill, do something similar. (All of the tools mentioned here are discussed in detail in Chapter 19.) The trick is to add a tag or an indicator to each case indicating the cluster to which it belongs, and then generate the distributions of the variables one by one, putting the graphs side by side in a single screen as the last step.

ANALYSIS OF TRANSACTIONAL SEQUENCES

The analysis of transactional sequences can be seen as a sort of market basket analysis, where the products customers purchase together, and in what order, are analyzed. Imagine transactional sequences as long strings of product identifiers where the relative position of a product in the sequence represents the order and grouping in which it was acquired by an individual customer. For example, consider the sequence "diapers diapers beer diapers diapers diapers beer beer diapers diapers diapers diapers beer beer beer." Predicting what the following product in the sequence will be may be of interest, assuming that there is some underlying tendency that allows for the prediction of what will follow.

A little more complicated are multiple (two or more) sequences that are mutually interrelated. For example, consider two sequences, the previous one, "diapers diapers beer diapers diapers diapers beer beer diapers diapers diapers diapers beer beer beer," and a new one, "towels soap towels towels soap soap towels towels towels soap soap soap." In addition to each sequence having a given progression, observe that there is a relationship between the two: in the second sequence, "towels" appears in the same relative position as "diapers" does in the first sequence, and there is always one fewer "towels" than there are "diapers." Also, the occurrences of "soap" in the second sequence and "beer" in the first coincide and the number of occurrences is exactly the same.

How can this information be used? To see its utility in practice, consider some commercial transactional data of a supermarket, where each sequence represents a customer's purchases and the products the customer bought. From this, a prediction may be made for what will be bought and in which order, as well as what the affinities are between the products purchased. Also, with a minimum demographic profile of clients (obtained from customer card data), the tendencies and behaviors between different types of clients can be identified.

The analysis of sequences is also useful in other business contexts, such as banking transactions. Note that time has not been included as a dimension in the examples of transactional sequences. The time factor in data analysis is introduced in the next section.

ANALYSIS OF TIME SERIES

Things start to get more complex, or more interesting, when the time dimension is introduced. The idea is very simple: well-known time images are the line tendency graphs of the stock exchange indices, which rise and fall from one day to another. In a similar way to the analysis of sequences discussed in the last section, series of data can be analyzed over time to evaluate whether the next tendency will be upward, downward, or without significant change. Two or more time series can also be compared to evaluate whether there is mutual influence. For example, consider the variables "gross profit" and "product diversification index." The data could show that, over the last three months, there has been an increase in the product diversification index that has coincided with (but has not necessarily been the cause of) a rise in gross profit.

Published in www.tradingeconomics.com and derived from the US Bureau of Economical Analysis, February 2012.

FIGURE 8.8   Cycles over time: United States economic cycles 1960–2012

Figure 8.8 illustrates a time series that covers a 50-year period. It shows the year-on-year percentage change of the GDP (Gross Domestic Product) of the United States, with the recession periods indicated by the vertical gray areas. There have been two recessions in the 2000–2010 decade. The recessions occur with a certain frequency, and it is often said that the economy in general is cyclical: there are periods of growth (bull market) followed by periods of recession (bear market). Even though a business may be small, it should know which point it is at in the economic cycle in order to make opportunistic decisions.

Figure 8.9 shows three graphs with the same variables (time and stock price) but in distinct periods over time (for example, three different days of the same week). It is observed that what they have in common are characteristics A and B. Characteristic A, made up of one smaller peak and one bigger peak, occurs at the beginning of the time period shown in graph (i) and at the end of the time period shown in graph (ii). In graph (ii) the characteristic B appears at the beginning of the time period, whereas in graph (iii) it shows up more or less in the middle.

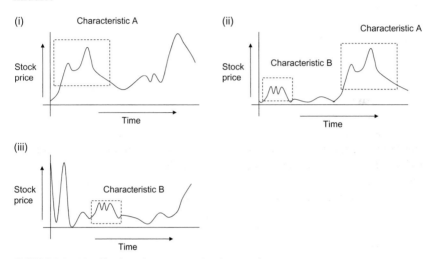

FIGURE 8.9   Identification of common tendencies over time

If tendencies of this type can be identified in time series—for example, that characteristic A is always preceded in time by characteristic B—in certain cases, what will happen to a stock price can be anticipated and appropriate actions taken (e.g., if it will probably go up, buy; if it will probably go down, sell). Relating these fluctuations and tendencies with other variables is also useful, enabling common variances or covariances to be identified. In chapter 17, time series analysis will be looked at in more detail.

Bank Current Account: Time Series Data Profiles

Various typical profiles exist for bank account data. Consider an individual with a current account into which the customer's salary is paid at the end of each month. The account balance will typically start at a maximum at the beginning of a new month and progressively reduce to a minimum at the end of the month, until the salary is again paid. In terms of outgoings, this same person will probably have one major, unique, regular expense for a mortgage repayment or rent for living accommodations. There may be other specific monthly expenses for a car loan repayment and other loan repayments. There will also be periodic payments related to gas, electricity, water, and phone bills, as well as insurance policies (car, home, life). Finally, there will be the day-to-day payments, typically via a debit card, to pay for food, public transport, gasoline, and any other small purchases. If the person uses a credit card to make some or all of the day-to-day purchases, then these payments will not appear in the bank account, but they will be represented by a lump sum debit at a specific monthly date.

Now consider an individual who is self-employed. This customer type may be further subdivided into (i) those who receive a fixed monthly payment (like a salary payment), (ii) those who receive a number of relatively large payments (similar to a salary) but at variable times, and (iii) those who receive a large number of relatively small payments continually. The second type of self-employed person may be an architect, a lawyer, a medical practitioner, a freelance engineer, and so on. Or the customer may have a small- or medium-sized business that provides professional services and products. A third type of self-employed person owns a retail business (such as a local store) that constantly sells a range of low-priced products.

Time Series

Current Account Profiles

Table 8.2 shows a summary of the various profiles just discussed. Although it is possible that some profiles may possess two or more of the types of characteristics shown in the table, in general, the majority of accounts would conform to one of these four types.

TABLE 8.2 Account profiles in terms of type of employment/work activity

Type	Income	Expenses
Salaried worker	Relatively large, unique, fixed periodic	Diverse: fixed low volume/ large and variable high volume/small
Self-employed #1 (similar to salaried worker)	Relatively large, unique, fixed periodic	Same as above
Self-employed #2 (professional, small- to medium-sized business)	Relatively large, low volume, variable time period	Same as above
Self-employed #3 (retail business)	Relatively small, high volume, variable time period	Same as above

Figure 8.10 illustrates three graphs of the same bank account over a 8-month period. The top graph shows the account balance, the bottom right graph shows income or credits, and the bottom left graph shows expenses or debits. The data has been normalized with respect to the maximum and minimum values of balance, income, and expense; hence the y-axis scale goes from 0 to 1. What distinguishes the different types of profiles detailed in Table 8.2 is the income profile, whereas the expense profile tends to be similar in all cases. In the top graph, the balance has specific points where it goes up or down, and these points have a certain periodicity. In the bottom right graph, some of the income is periodic and other income is not. In the bottom left graph, there is a specific periodic expense for the same amount, and other, smaller, ad hoc expenses.

The account shown in the figure displays a mixture of the attributes described in Table 8.2. Some characteristics are those of a salaried or self-employed regular-income person, and other characteristics point to ad hoc income throughout the month. A relatively large balance and large expenses are seen at the beginning of the 8-month period compared to the rest of the time. Possibly, the individual or business has more than one active bank account and, if this is the case, what is seen is a partial picture of the person's income and expenses. If this data is to be analyzed successfully, auxiliary information would be needed.

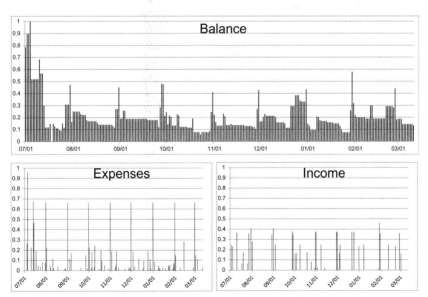

FIGURE 8.10   Three graphs of a bank account over time: current account balance (*top*), expenses (*bottom left*), and income (*bottom right*)

TYPICAL MISTAKES WHEN PERFORMING DATA ANALYSIS AND INTERPRETING RESULTS

"There are three kinds of lies: lies, damned lies, and statistics" was reportedly said by the nineteenth-century Prime Minister Benjamin Disraeli. "A statistician is a person who, with his head in the oven and his feet in the freezer, will say that, on average, he feels fine" is anonymous.

Presumably, an analyst is not intentionally wrongly interpreting the data being analyzed; the next section reviews some of the typical mistakes than can occur. By knowing these mistakes, they may be avoided more readily in analytical work.

Three general types of analysis errors are due to (i) bias in the data, (ii) errors in data processing, and (iii) wrong interpretation. The first type of error can be caused by incorrect sampling, or skewed data. Recall that samples should have the same distributions as the complete dataset. However, there are cases in which the distribution must be changed, especially with respect to the result (output variable). Consider, for example, that fraud cases are going to be studied: 99 percent of the cases in the initial data sample are non-fraudulent and 1 percent are fraudulent. If a balanced analysis of fraudulent and non-fraudulent cases is to be conducted (and later, a data model trained), a sample is needed in which the percentage of fraudulent cases is similar to that of the non-fraudulent ones. This can be done by (a) augmenting the number of fraudulent cases by replicating them, or (b) reducing the number of non-fraudulent cases by further sampling, until a dataset is obtained that contains 50 percent non-fraud and 50 percent fraud cases. That is, the sample size can be reduced by removing the most common cases or increased by duplicating the most infrequent cases. However, when this is done, the distributions of the other input variables must be rechecked so as not to introduce secondary biases. As discussed in Chapter 7, distributions of the sample must be rechecked with respect to the complete dataset. A similar situation occurs when wanting to study an output variable with five output categories, but in the dataset, 95 percent of the cases belong to just one of the categories.

Another error that can lead to incorrect interpretation is extrapolating or interpolating results, such as on a graph plot, with too few real values. A very incomplete picture is seen when there are results for only three months in the year, or for four commercial centers out of a total of 50. With luck, the missing results for the other nine months or 46 commercial centers will have values close to the known ones. But don't count on it!

For further reading on avoiding typical mistakes, see:

Cohen, Jason. Mar. 2010. "Avoiding Common Data-Interpretation Errors." A Smart Bear. Available at: http://blog.asmartbear.com/data-interpretation -mistakes.html.

King, Gary. 1986. "How Not to Lie with Statistics: Avoiding Common Mistakes in Quantitative Political Science." Workshop presentation. New York University, New York.

Moore, Robert J. Feb. 2013. "The 5 Most Common Data Analysis Mistakes." Inside Ecommerce. Available at: http://blog.rjmetrics.com/the-5 -most-common-data-analysis-mistakes/.

Authors have published lists of the "top 10 data mining mistakes" or the "five most common data analysis mistakes," and so on. The following is a selection from some of these lists, tailored for the commercial focus in this book.

- First, the lack of the right data for the task can be the problem. Choosing the right data for a given objective is covered throughout Chapters 2 to 7.
- Second, the analyst may rely on just one technique for data analysis, which may be a favorite technique or the one the analyst knows best. It is worthwhile to invest the time and effort to learn how to use a selection of distinct methods.
- Third, a classic faux pas is to include an output variable (that is, the future result) as an input variable and consequently get a fantastic predictive precision. Output variable means something that cannot be known at the present (it is a future value), or it is a variable that somehow has codified the business objective in a unique way. For example, if fraud is being analyzed, the output variable is a fraud flag (yes or no); however, there may be some other variable or code used by the insurance company that indicates risk level, type of cancellation, or something similar. These variables are sometimes not apparent at first sight.

For more information, consult the following references:

John F. Elder, IV. "Top 10 Data Mining Mistakes and How to Avoid Them." Salford Systems Data Mining Conference. New York, NY, March 29, 2005. Available at: http://docs.salford-systems.com/elder.pdf.

——. 2009. "Top 10 Data Mining Mistakes: Avoid Common Pitfalls on the Path to Data Mining Success." Adapted from: Robert Nisbet, John Elder, and Gary Miner. 2009. Handbook of Statistical Analysis & Data Mining Applications, ch. 20. Burlington, MA: Academic Press. Available at: http://www.sas .com/news/sascom/2010q3/column_tech.html

Another genre of misinterpretation can arise due to a false or myopic vision of data that is given in order to make a news headline or to sell a product, service, or idea.

For example, consider the statement, "The share price of bank x went up 65 percent last year." That sounds spectacular; however, additional data is then obtained revealing that the share price was $20 in January, dropped to $12 in April, and by December was up to $19.80. Hence, the headline is based on the interpretation that the share price had gone up by 65 percent in December relative to $12, the minimum reached in April of the same year.

For a second example, consider the statement, "Net profit in 2013 ($12 million) went up by 20 percent relative to 2012 ($10 million)." This is presented as a positive news snippet. However, when more profit data is obtained from the last four years, things look very different: 2009 ($40 million net profit), 2010

($30 million), 2011 ($20 million), and 2012 ($10 million). From this data, it now seems that the company has had serious problems over the last four years with a strong down trend, and the increase of $2 million in the period 2012–2013 pales compared to the loss of $30 million in the period 2009–2012.

Sometimes the inverse occurs; that is, a negative evaluation of a situation based on some statistics is actually false and the true situation is much more positive. This can give rise to undervaluing, which is sometimes done intentionally when, for example, a company wants to minimize its profit/net worth for tax reasons.

Sometimes, an innocent-looking factual statement can be illogically misinterpreted. For example, "In 2012, thirty percent of the total traffic deaths were alcohol-related." This could be conjectured to mean that "Thirty percent of car accidents are caused by drunk drivers," which could lead to, "Therefore, drunk drivers are not a significant cause of car accidents"!

Finally, here are three actual headlines from online news sources in 2013:

Electronic Cigarettes "Help Nine out of Ten Smokers Quit Tobacco Completely"
1 in 10 U.S. Deaths Blamed on Salt (excessive salt consumption)
New Survey (made by an IT company) Unveils Worldwide Innovation Gap: Only Five out of Ten People Are Satisfied with Innovations Currently Available

In each of these cases, the article would have to be checked to see who did the study, what methods were used, and what the findings were compared to. For example, the third headline may be biased by the interests of the company doing the survey.

Chapter 9

Data Modeling

INTRODUCTION

Creating a data model is the last step of a data analysis project, having already defined a good business objective; extracted and prepared the data; guaranteed its quality; and analyzed, segmented, and created new indicators and factors with greater information value.

This chapter discusses what is meant by a data model and introduces key associated concepts such as supervised and unsupervised learning, cross-validation, and how to evaluate the precision of the modeling results. A variety of techniques for modeling data are considered, from AI (Artificial Intelligence) approaches, such as neural networks and rule induction, to statistical techniques such as regression. The chapter goes on to discuss which techniques to use for specific modeling scenarios, how to apply models to real-world production data, and how to evaluate and use the results. Finally, guidelines are given for how to perform and reiterate the modeling phase, especially when the initial results are not the desired or optimum ones.

MODELING CONCEPTS AND ISSUES

What is a data model? A data model is essentially simple: it has some input variables, one or more output variables, and it contains an intermediate process that acts on the inputs to produce the output. Figure 9.1 shows the general schematic idea of a data model. A model typically predicts something in the future or clusters many individual records into meaningful groups, such as clients who are most likely to buy a new product, the prognosis of a patient, the most profitable clients, and so on.

Supervised and Unsupervised Learning

Modeling techniques are said to "learn" from data in an artificial intelligence sense of the word. The following describes two main ways these techniques learn.

The first method is called supervised learning because the model learns to predict or classify data items by being presented with examples and counter-examples. For instance, if an objective is to train a model to classify

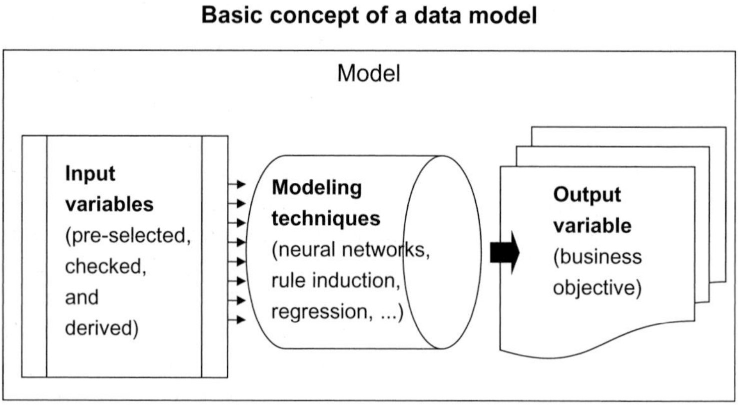

Basic concept of a data model

FIGURE 9.1   The basic idea of a data model

fruit, the model would be presented with examples of fruit (apples, pears, oranges) and other examples that are not fruit (potato, cauliflower, rice). Each example needs data characteristics (variables) that allow the model to differentiate between the fruit examples and the non-fruit examples. The model would be trained on some data, giving it the true classification for each example (fruit = yes) and counter-example (fruit = no). Then the model would be tested on a new dataset of examples and counter-examples, but without supplying the classifier label. The number of correct classifications on the examples and the counter-examples would allow for calculating the model's precision. Two examples of supervised learning techniques are supervised neural networks and rule/tree induction.

The second method is called non-supervised learning because the learning process is not supervised. That is, the classifier label isn't given to the model when it is training. The modeling technique has to figure out what the classification is from the input data alone. Unsupervised clustering techniques in general fall into this category, such as the k-means (statistics) and the Kohonen self-organizing map (neural network). By studying the data records assigned to each of the clusters, the analyst can then evaluate the criteria that the clustering technique has used to group them. For example, one cluster may contain all the profitable clients and another cluster may contain only the least profitable clients.

Cross-Validation

Chapter 7 discusses that the dataset is typically divided into two parts; for example, a dataset is proportioned into a sample of 60 percent for training and 40 percent for testing. However, if just one train and one test are run, it is not guaranteed that on other occasions the same precision will be achieved. Hence, several training processes and tests on different samples are typically carried out. In this way, some idea can be had of how the data model generalizes on new data-sets as well as ensuring that the model hasn't learned from a fluke sample.

"Over-fitting" can be another problem, meaning that a model has over-learned a given input data sample resulting in poor precision on the test data. It can also mean that the model's input variables are specialized for a given dataset and don't reflect the more general characteristics of future datasets. One corrective approach is to train a model and then test it on ten different datasets. The overall precision would then be the average of the ten tests.

A more formal solution to generalization testing is to perform what is called k-fold cross-validation. In k-fold cross-validation, the original dataset is randomly partitioned into k equal-size subsets. From those subsets, one is designated as the validation set for testing the model and the remaining $k-1$ subsets are used as training data. The cross-validation process is then repeated k times, such that each of the k subsets is used once as the validation set. The precision for each of the k tests is then averaged to obtain a global precision. A typical value for cross-validation is $k=10$. Some software implementations (such as Weka) include an automatic option for k-fold cross-validation when training a model.

Stratified k-fold cross-validation is a variant in which each subset of data is selected so that the distribution of the business objective variable is as similar as possible in all the subsets. For example, if there is a classifier variable (business objective "buy"=yes or no), then the stratified process would try to obtain the same proportions of cases of yes and no in each of the k subsets of data.

Evaluating the Results of Data Models – Measuring Precision

Recall that Chapter 2 discusses how to estimate the expected improvement of precision with respect to the current precision for a given business objective, the idea being to choose a business objective that offers a significant improvement with respect to the actual precision. As a baseline, consider that throwing a coin in order to predict something will give, on average, a precision of 50 percent. The minimum required precision for an analysis may, however, be defined by legal requirements, such as in the case of quality control processes.

Sometimes a small improvement in precision can translate into a large economic reward in sectors with small, finely adjusted profit margins, hence the importance of input from the business experts in evaluating what target precision is obtainable for a given business problem. For example, one could not be too disappointed with a 75 percent precision for cross-selling targeting of a given product or service if the industry average is 65 percent and the current precision using manual selection of potential clients is 60 percent. However, the precision given from predictive and clustering models must be correctly evaluated and interpreted; this topic is addressed in the following part of this section.

Evaluating the Results of a Data Model

Numerical Continuous Output versus Categorical Output

If output is a numerical continuous value, it may be correlated with a known true value. Hence, the correlation will measure the precision, with 1 being perfect precision. If the model produces a category label as output, the precision tends to be visualized using what is called a confusion matrix, also known as a contingency matrix, which is discussed in Chapter 6.

Some tools show other types of quality indicators, such as entropy, for the trained model. Entropy is based on thermodynamics (heating and cooling of gases) and refers to the state of equilibrium (maximum entropy) or total disorder (minimum entropy) for the internal state of a system. (For more details about entropy, consult Wikipedia: http://en.wikipedia.org/wiki/Entropy.)

The rows in Table 9.1 represent the true classes, and the columns represent the classes assigned or predicted by the data model. Assume a total dataset of 80 records used for training, of which 20 are labeled as High, 10 as Medium, and 50 as Low. Observe that, of the 20 records that are true High categories, the model predicts that seven are Medium. Likewise, of the 10 records that are true Medium categories, the model predicts one as Low and three as High. As seen in the matrix, the model found it difficult to distinguish between the High and Medium classes, while the precision for the Low category was relatively high (45/50). All the correct predictions are found along the diagonal of the table. This way of representing the results is much better than obtaining an overall precision for all classes, especially when there is a situation of class imbalance. For example, if there were 90 cases of High, five cases of Medium, and five cases of Low, the model might predict all the records as being High and obtain an overall precision of 90 percent. However, the precision for the other two classes would be 0 percent.

TABLE 9.1 Confusion matrix of true classes versus predicted classes

		Predicted Class		
		High	*Medium*	*Low*
True Class	High	13	7	0
	Medium	3	6	1
	Low	0	5	45

After studying the confusion matrix tables for all the classes, the next step is to prepare a confusion table for each class. This table shows four different versions of the results for a given class: true positives, false negatives, false positives, and true negatives. Table 9.2 shows the number of true positives is 13, that is, the

TABLE 9.2 Confusion table for the High class

True Positives: 13	False Negatives: 7
False Positives: 3	True Negatives: 57

number of true High that have been correctly classified as High. Likewise, the number of false negatives is seven; that is, the High that were incorrectly classified as other classes. Next, the number of false positives is three; that is, other classes incorrectly labeled as High. Finally, the number of true negatives is 57; that is, all the remaining classes correctly classified as not being equal to High.

Finally, the precision and the recall for the High class can be calculated from the values in Table 9.2 and are defined as follows:

$$\text{Precision} = (\text{true positives})/(\text{true positives} + \text{false positives})$$

$$\text{Recall} = (\text{true positives})/(\text{true positives} + \text{false negatives})$$

So, for the data in Table 9.2 the results are:

$$\text{Precision} = (13)/(13 + 3) = 81.25\%$$

$$\text{Recall} = (13)/(13 + 7) = 65\%$$

Note that Tables 9.1 and 9.2 would have to be formulated for the remaining classes, Medium and Low, and their precision and recall calculated. Then the final precision and recall would be the average value for the three classes.

NEURAL NETWORKS

This section examines two types of neural networks: the first is of the supervised learning type, used for giving a predictive value as output. The second is of the unsupervised learning type, used for clustering the data into groups containing records that are similar according to some key criteria.

Predictive Neural Networks

Neural networks fall into the category of techniques called black boxes, so-called because we cannot see inside the model to know how it works or which process has been used to obtain the result. Only the input and the output variables can be seen. Neural networks tend to be very precise, are able to model very complex data, and work better with numerical data as input and output. They also have the capacity to process and filter data that contains noise or erroneous or irrelevant data values. They have been used extensively in the financial sector for stock prediction: predicting the future values of shares, compositions of funds, and micro- and macro-economic indicators in general. They have also been used in numerical control systems. Neural networks are so named because they model the way the biological brain works, simulating an interconnected network of neurons that communicate with each other.

The training phase of a neural network may need a lot of computational resources, especially in elapsed time, depending on the complexity of the inputs and the number of records in the training set. Some tools, such as NeuroShell and the IBM SPSS Modeler, have automatic modes that find the best configuration and training parameters without user intervention. Expert users can try modifying the parameters, such as learning rate and number of hidden neurons, although it is out of the scope of this book to go into details about these configurations. The user should consult the documentation of the specific software used or a detailed, hands-on book such as:

Ian Witten, Eibe Frank, and Mark Hall. 2011. *Data Mining: Practical Machine Learning Tools and Techniques*. Burlington, MA: Morgan Kaufmann. ISBN 13: 978-0123748560.

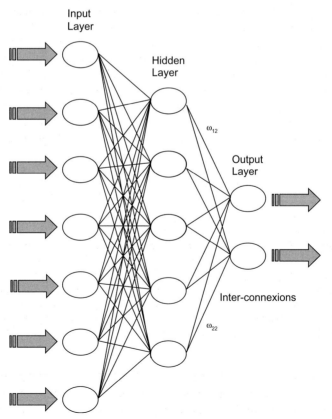

FIGURE 9.2 Example of the structure of a neural network

As mentioned earlier, modern commercial data mining software usually automates the configuration and parameter assignment of the neural network so the user can focus on preparing the input data and analyzing the output. For readers who are interested in knowing more about how neural networks process data internally, the following gives a brief description.

Figure 9.2 shows a simplified example of the structure of a predictive (supervised) neural network. It has three layers of neurons: on the left is the input layer, in the middle is the "hidden" layer, and on the right is the output layer. Observe that, in general, the input layer has the same number of neurons as the input variables (seven in the example). There is also a hidden layer consisting of five neurons. The number of neurons in the hidden layer is a function of the number of inputs and outputs. In general, the more inputs and outputs, the more hidden neurons are required to model the data. In some cases, more than one hidden layer may be required; however, in general, the objective is to minimize the number of hidden neurons used. The output layer consists of two neurons, or two output variables.

With reference to the interconnections between the neurons of different layers, the interconnections between the input layer and the hidden layer are denser than those between the hidden layer and the output layer. Also, a weight is assigned to each connection, which is used to influence the flow of data through the connection. The weight has a value between 0 and 1: a higher value will allow data to flow more freely, whereas a lower weight will restrict data flow along the connection. In neural networks this is related to the activation of a connection. During the training of the neural network, some areas of neurons become more activated, whereas other areas remain inactive as a consequence of the application of the input data. Clearly, the way in which the model is activated is molded by the data given to it.

Predictive Neural Networks

Basic Working Aspects

The neural network is typically defined by three aspects: (i) the interconnection pattern between different layers of neurons, that is, its structure; (ii) the learning process for updating the weights of the interconnections; and (iii) the activation function that converts a neuron's weighted input to its output activation. Other parameters are defined at runtime and are normally automatically assigned by the software tool: the learning rate that decides the speed at which the model assimilates the data, the momentum related to the learning rate, and the error tolerance that decides when the model has reached the desired precision.

The most general type of neural network is called a feed forward back propagation network. It is so called because it first feeds the data in the input layer in a forward direction through the hidden layer to the output layer. The back propagation part occurs when the predicted output values are compared with the correct output values, and the error rate is fed backward through the network in order to update the weights assigned to each connection. The idea is to minimize the output error by progressively adjusting the weights, through a large number of iterations, until the model converges to a state of minimum error, or the error doesn't change over a given number of iterations.

There are other types of neural network architectures for specific tasks. For example, a recurrent architecture is often used for processing time series data, in which the connections form a loop back between the hidden and input layers. The loop acts like a window on the data stream, enabling it to identify trends if the data represents a time series. (Case study 2 demonstrates using a predictive neural network in a real-world project.)

Kohonen Neural Network for Clustering

The second type of neural network is called a Kohonen SOM. Professor Teuvo Kohonen is the distinguished Finnish scientist who originally designed the algorithm, and SOM stands for self-organizing map. The Kohonen SOM has a neural network structure different from the predictive model, consisting only of an input node layer and an internal (map or matrix) layer where the clustering is formed.

This algorithm contains a matrix of nodes, which compete to win weight and to attract the given input data. As a consequence, after successive iterations, some groups of nodes (clusters) will become more highly activated, while other nodes will become relatively deactivated. The nodes are interconnected in a typical neural architecture, and the information propagates from an input layer to a layer (or matrix) of classification nodes. The Kohonen architecture has demonstrated its applicability to a diversity of data domains, especially those with large volumes and many attributes. It behaves well in the presence of noise and unknown values. (Case study 2 in the appendix demonstrates the use of a Kohonen SOM in a real-world project.)

Specific implementations have specific metrics in order to evaluate the clustering quality. The user can vary the matrix size and then compare the overall quality indicators to find the best configuration. For example, a 3 × 3 matrix would produce a maximum of nine clusters. The individual clusters can be analyzed for the composition of the records they contain, in terms of numerical variable distributions and category label frequencies. Rule induction can also be applied to the clusters using the cluster ID as the classifier label. Hence the induction process creates rules that explain the internal structure of the clusters.

CLASSIFICATION: RULE/TREE INDUCTION

Rule induction creates a model built from rules of the if–then–else type. In general, it can work with both numerical values and categorical values. As before, the models have a set of input variables and one or more output variables, but are different from the neural networks in that we can actually see inside the model and how it produces the result or output. For example, a very simple model would have five input variables: solvency, type of employment, marital status, mortgage, and savings account; and one output, contract pension plan. The two processing rules (inside the data model) could be:

"**IF** SOLVENCY IS HIGH
AND MARITAL STATUS IS MARRIED
AND HAS MORTGAGE = YES
THEN CONTRACT PENSION PLAN
→ YES (2500,68%)"
OR
"**IF** SOLVENCY IS MEDIUM
AND TYPE OF EMPLOYMENT IS SELF-EMPLOYED
AND HAS SAVINGS ACCOUNT = YES
THEN CONTRACT PENSION PLAN
→ YES (3400,76%)"

In rule induction data models, the models and rules are usually constructed from decision trees. A decision tree, as the name indicates, has decision branches (for example, "solvency equal to high" and "marital status equal to married"), which are read from the top down. The decision is placed at the end (output variable), for example, CONTRACT PENSION PLAN → YES. The decisions at the end are called leaves, following the same botanical terminology.

Figure 9.3 illustrates rules represented in a tree form. Many data mining tools allow for visualizing the model in both forms: as a tree and as rules. Rules are more convenient if, for example, the model will later be implemented in SQL and run on a native customer database. The alternative branches of each node have been omitted in the decision tree in the figure for the sake of clarity. That is, for the node "marital status," there is also a branch "marital status = not married" (which could signify single, divorced, or widowed). Also, the node "has savings account" has two possible alternatives: yes and no. This type of tree is called a binary tree, because each node has two possible options. In this example, the paths of interest are the ones that reach terminal nodes with CON-TRACT PENSION PLAN → YES.

In Figure 9.3, the two numbers after the YES on the terminal nodes indicate, first, the number of clients on this branch, and second, the percentage of clients who comply with all the conditions along the branch. There are 2,500 clients in the terminal node on the left, and 68 percent of them comply with all the conditions. In general, let's say that any terminal node with 65 percent or more compliance can be considered useful. In terms of the number of clients, the more who comply, the better, although the absolute number depends, of course, on the total number of clients in the dataset. In general, the interest lies in identifying precise rules for a large number of clients.

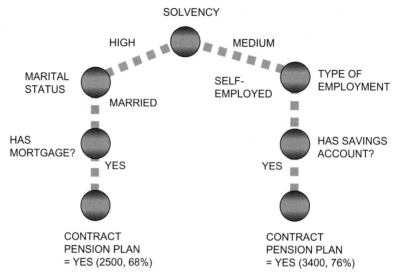

FIGURE 9.3   Schematic representation of a decision tree

Another interpretation of the tree in Figure 9.3 is the generality or specificity of the attributes: the most global attributes appear higher up in the tree and the most specific ones appear in the lowest part. Thus, in the figure, the most general attribute is "solvency" and the most specific are "has mortgage" and "has savings account."

The rest of this section on rule and tree induction goes into more technical detail about how specific algorithms work. (Readers who are not interested in or don't need to know how rule induction works in detail can skip this section and go directly to the next section about statistical models.)

In the following section, three algorithms (ID3, C4.5, and C5.0) by author Ross Quinlan are briefly described; they represent an evolution over time of how Quinlan introduced successive improvements to the rule induction technique in order to obtain an algorithm that now represents one of the best and most widely used of its kind for general data mining.

The ID3 Decision Tree Induction Algorithm

The ID3 algorithm, published by Quinlan in 1986, constructs classification decision trees using a top-down induction method and is the predecessor to another induction algorithm called C4.5, which is discussed in the following section.

ID3's objective is to construct a reasonably good decision tree (although not necessarily the best possible one) without too much computation. The type of dataset it works with has many attributes and objects. There is no guarantee of finding the optimum solution (best tree). ID3 is an iterative algorithm: it randomly chooses a data subset from the training set (called the window) and constructs a decision tree from it. This tree must correctly classify all the objects in the window. Then it tries to classify all the other objects in the complete training set using this tree. If the tree succeeds for these objects, then it is correct for the complete dataset, and the process terminates. Otherwise, a selection of the objects that were incorrectly classified is incorporated into the window, and the process is repeated. In this manner, the correct tree may be found after just a few iterations, even for big, complex datasets. The design of ID3 has an anecdotal component, given that Quinlan used a window on the subset instead of using the whole test data set, due to memory restrictions of the computers used at that time.

The C4.5 Decision Tree Induction Algorithm

The C4.5 decision tree induction algorithm was published by Quinlan in 1993, and an improved version was presented in 1996. It uses subsets (windows) of cases extracted from the complete training set to generate rules, and then evaluates their goodness using criteria that measure the precision in classifying the cases. (Examples of using the C4.5 rule induction modeling technique in real-world projects are given in case studies 1 and 2 in the appendix.)

> **C4.5 Decision Tree Induction Algorithm**
>
> *Heuristics*
>
> The main heuristics that are used in the C4.5 algorithm are the information value that a rule (or a tree branch) provides (calculated by a function called "info") and the global improvement that a rule/branch causes (calculated by a function called "gain"). The algorithm also has a function for evaluating the information loss caused by missing values in the data.

The algorithm is executed in successive iterations. In each iteration, the window size is incremented in a given percentage (in proportion to the complete set). The objective is to obtain rules that correctly classify a successively greater number of cases in the complete dataset. The proposal is that it is easier to identify rules in a smaller subset than in the complete dataset. Each iteration uses as its basis that which the previous iteration has achieved.

As in the case of the neural network technique described in the previous section, the majority of software implementations and commercial tools allow rule induction to be run in auto mode without having to worry about setting the parameters. However, it is useful to know two parameters the user, with some practice, may be able to usefully configure. The first one is the confidence factor, which is used for pruning the branches of the tree to obtain a simpler tree structure, for which a smaller value will result in a greater degree of pruning. The second parameter is the minimum number of instances required in order to form a leaf. A higher number of instances required will result in a smaller number of leaves.

C4.5 incorporates the following improvements with respect to ID3:

- C4.5 biases the selection to make the class distribution more uniform in the initial window instead of randomly choosing training cases to include in the window.
- ID3 uses a fixed limit for the number of erroneous classifications per iteration. On the other hand, C4.5 includes a minimum of 50 percent of the error cases in the next window, which results in a faster convergence toward the final tree.
- C4.5 terminates the construction of the tree if the precision is not improving, without having to classify all the classes.

C4.5 is based on the idea of "divide and conquer" and performs an evaluation of the candidate tests and questions that are formulated to partition the cases. Also, a benefit criterion is used to quantify and maximize the information increase in the global system. For each candidate division, the benefit is calculated and the one with the highest calculated benefit is chosen at each step.

The C5.0 Decision Tree Induction Algorithm

Quinlan released his new rule/tree induction algorithm, C5.0, in 2000. It includes the following improvements with respect to C4.5:

- The sets of rules generated occupy less memory and train faster.
- The training time for decision trees is reduced while the same accuracy as C4.5 is maintained.
- A boosting technique is used for generating and combining multiple classifiers in order to improve predictive accuracy.
- C5.0 allows a separate cost (penalty) to the misclassification of different classes, whereas in C4.5, all errors are treated using the same criteria. Hence, C5.0 constructs a classifier that minimizes the expected misclassification cost rather than a homogeneous error rate. This makes sense because, in real-world applications, an error with one class may have a greater impact or importance than an error with another class.
- The following new data types are included: dates, case labels, and ordered discrete values. In addition to missing values, values can be labeled as not applicable. Also, new attributes can be defined as functions of other attributes.

For further reading about the rule/tree induction algorithms described in this section, see:

Quinlan, J. R. 1986. "Induction of Decision Trees." *Machine Learning Journal* 1, pp. 81–106.

——. 1993. *"C4.5: Programs for Machine Learning."* San Mateo, CA: Morgan Kaufmann.

"Data Mining Tools See5 and C5.0." March 2013. RuleQuest Research. Available at: http://www.rulequest.com/see5-info.html.

TRADITIONAL STATISTICAL MODELS

This section divides statistical models into those used to predict something and those used to perform clustering or grouping. For prediction, regression modeling is considered, given that it is the most widely used technique. For clustering, k-means is discussed, again given that it is a widely used clustering technique. There is a certain analogy between the supervised and unsupervised learning techniques seen in the previous section; however, these terms (supervised and unsupervised learning) tend to be reserved for machine learning techniques and not for the statistical techniques.

Regression Techniques

Regression is the technique most often used to create data models in traditional statistics. It is a statistical modeling technique that examines the relation between a dependent variable and one or more independent variables. There are three main types: linear regression, for data whose distribution tends to adjust to a straight line; non-linear regression, for data whose tendency adjusts to a curve; and logistic regression, for data models whose output is a binary type.

Linear regression is a general technique that adjusts a line for a given dataset. For example, one could try to predict the total volume of purchases in a given quarter for a client (the dependent variable) using some independent variables such as age, income, (or some other socioeconomic indicator, such as district of residence), and time as customer. Both the dependent and the independent variables have to be numerical. Categorical variables such as gender or district of residence must be recoded as binary variables (two categories) or as numerical.

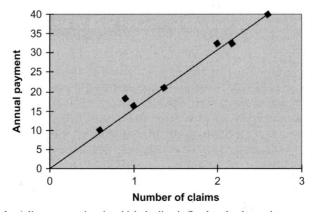

FIGURE 9.4   A linear regression, in which the line is fitted to the data points

In order to measure the grade of fit of the regression model with respect to the data, the residuals can be examined, identifying the values that least agree with the line (atypical values). Linear regression analyzes the relation between two variables, X and Y, and tries to find the best straight line that passes through the data, as seen in Figure 9.4. The gradient of the line and the point where it crosses the x- and y-axes can be interpreted in terms of the variables. The objective of linear regression is to find the line that best predicts Y given X by adjusting the values along the gradient and the crossing point of the line with the axes.

Non-linear regression is a general technique that adjusts a curve (instead of the line of linear regression) for a given dataset. It can adjust to any formula that defines Y as a function of X and one or more parameters. It finds the values for the parameters that generate the curve with the closest fit to the data (minimizing the sum of the squares of the vertical distances between the data points and the curve). When a suitable non-linear model is known, it is easier to determine the parameters; however, if a suitable non-linear model is not known, different ones must be tried until one is found that best fits the data. Figure 9.5 shows an example graph of non-linear regression.

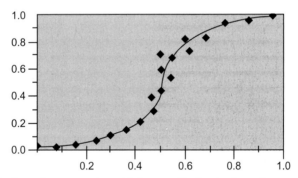

FIGURE 9.5   A non-linear regression, with the curve fitted to the data points

Logistic regression is a regression-based modeling technique in which the dependent variable has a binary type (1 or 0, yes or no, etc.). For example, a logistic regression model could be used to indicate what the tendency of the stock price of a company will be over the next three months (output variable: increase, decrease), based on current knowledge, previous performance, type of business, and geographical areas where the company operates (input variables).

As another example, one could predict the prognosis for the recovery of a patient (output variable: will recover, will not recover) based on the patient's characteristics and the type and severity of the illness or injury (input variables). In general, a variable selection technique is used to identify the subset of variables that are most highly related to the output variable. The selection of variables is normally accompanied by techniques that assess the precision of the model and the identification of atypical values. Logistic regression produces a formula that predicts the probability that a given event may occur as a function of the independent variables (the inputs).

Summary of the use of regression techniques

If the dependent variable has more than two categories (that is, it's not binary), a discriminant analysis can be used to identify the variables that best classify the data. If the dependent variable is continuous (numerical), a linear regression could be used to predict the values of the dependent variable from a set of independent variables.

If the formula to be fitted is known beforehand, and its parameters are non-linear, then a non-linear technique would be the most appropriate to use. If the dependent variable is binary, as is the case for a diagnosis whose result is positive or negative, then a logistic regression model would be used. If the variable is biased, as in "time since last purchase," appropriate techniques would include "Life Tables," "Kaplan–Meier," or a "Cox"-type regression.

K-means

K-means is a simple but effective algorithm that calculates a distance between records given as input, where a predefined number of records is selected to be used as seeds for the cluster construction process. Each record is assigned a cluster by an iterative algorithm, which is the closest cluster as defined by the distance between the object to be clustered and the mean value of all the clusters. The clustering stops after a predefined number of iterations, at which point the current clusters are settled as the result of the clustering.

K-means is included as-is in many data mining tools, such as Weka, although one restriction is that the number of clusters has to be given by the user at the start of processing. The user can make an informed guess of how many clusters, defined as the k value, should be derived from the given input variables. The user can also try different values of k and then look at the cluster statistics to see which gives the best quality clusters. Usually, the clustering technique gives some quality indicators, such as overall entropy or the inter- and intra-cluster distances. The smaller the intra-cluster distance and the bigger the inter-cluster distance, the better the clustering will be. In the Weka implementation of k-means, the sum of squares error is given, which measures the distance to the centroid, or mean value, of each cluster, the cluster centroid (or prototype/mean) being given for each cluster. As the objective is to minimize this error, it can be considered equivalent to the intra-cluster distance mentioned earlier.

In order to evaluate and analyze the clustering result, one can plot the frequencies of categorical labels and the distributions of the numerical variables for each cluster, and evaluate and compare the different profiles for each cluster.

OTHER METHODS AND TECHNIQUES FOR CREATING PREDICTIVE MODELS

So far, the chapter has described neural networks, rule induction, and regression as three of the most widely used techniques for creating predictive models in data mining. These are methods that tend to be present, with their specific variations, in almost all general data mining systems. However, it must be emphasized that other methods do exist, and the more advanced data miners may wish to experiment with alternative methods in order to find one that works particularly well for their data and business objectives. Other systems recommended for predictive modeling include the Naïve Bayes probabilistic classifier, the IBk instance-based learner, and the SMO Support Vector Machine. These three methods are now briefly described in the following part of this section.

The SMO (sequential minimal optimization) Support Vector Machine (SVM) is a non-probabilistic, binary linear classifier. That is, it processes a set of input variables and predicts, for each record, which of two possible classes will be produced as the output. The model created by an SVM represents the input records as points in a geometric space, which are mapped so that the records in each category are divided by a gap that is as wide as possible. SVMs can also perform non-linear classification by using a "kernel function" to map the inputs into a higher-dimension feature space.

For example, consider two classes of records: profitable customers and non-profitable customers. Each record is comprised of, say, 10 descriptive variables. The SVM is trained with a sample dataset of these records and finds a "hyperplane," which divides the two classes (profitable clients and non-profitable clients) into two regions in the classification space, such that the distance (the space) between the two regions is maximized. The records that lie on the margins of the hyperplane are called the support vectors. (For more information about support vector methods, refer to Wikipedia: http://en.wikipedia.org/wiki/Support_vector_machine.)

A Naïve Bayes classifier is a simple probabilistic classifier based on applying Bayes theorem with strong (naïve) independence assumptions. This method assumes that input variables are independent from each other with respect to the output (class) variable. For example, a given vehicle might be classified as a motorcycle if it has two wheels, an engine, and weighs about 400 pounds. A naïve Bayes classifier would consider that the number of wheels, the power source, and the weight contribute independently to the probability that this object is a motorcycle, uninfluenced by the presence or absence of other characteristics.

Finally, IBk is the Weka system (see Chapter 19) implementation of the k-nearest neighbor classifier, which is an instance-based learning algorithm. Instance-based learning, as the name suggests, compares new instances with instances used for training. This contrasts with other methods, which are based on explicit generalization. An instance is analogous to a customer record with its corresponding variables. Consider again that there are two classes of records: profitable customers and non-profitable customers. A new instance is evaluated by first calculating its distance to each of the existing instances, made up of profitable and non-profitable customers. Then a value for k is assigned, where k is the number of nearest records used for comparison. Typical values are 1, 3, and 5. If $k = 3$, then the algorithm will find the three records closest to the new record, based on a distance metric. (For numerical values, it is usually the Euclidean distance.) Consider the case where the algorithm finds the three ($k = 3$) records closest to the new record, of which two are profitable and one is non-profitable. Hence, by simple majority, the new record will be assigned to the "profitable" class. The same process is followed for other values of k. In this way, the value of k can be found that best predicts the class, which, in some versions of the algorithm, is an automated process.

For more information about IBk and k-nearest neighbor, refer to:

Abernethy, Michael. June 2010. "Data Mining with WEKA, Part 3: Nearest Neighbor and Server-Side Library." Available at: http://www.ibm.com/developerworks/library/os-weka3/.

Wikipedia: http://en.wikipedia.org/wiki/K-nearest_neighbors_algorithm.

The methods described in this section are included in the top ten algorithms in data mining as determined by the authoritative paper by Wu et al. in 2007:

Xindong Wu, Vipin Kumar, J. Ross Quinlan, Joydeep Ghosh, Qiang Yang, Hiroshi Motoda, Geoffrey J. McLachlan, Angus Ng, Bing Liu, Philip S. Yu, Zhi-Hua Zhou, Michael Steinbach, David J. Hand, Dan Steinberg. 2007. "Top 10 Algorithms in Data Mining." *Knowledge Information Syst.*, 14, pp. 1–37.

APPLYING THE MODELS TO THE DATA

Once a reliable, precise model that works well for all the test dataset samples has been obtained, then it can be tried out with the complete customer dataset. For example, consider a model of likelihood of purchase of a product that a business is going to offer to current customers who don't have that product. This is called cross-selling. The marketing department has elaborated a nice but generic publicity leaflet, which explains to the client the benefits of the given product. There are currently about two million clients, of which about one million do not actually have the product. (For readers who don't have so many customers, reduce the following amounts proportionately.) The business thinks that 7 percent of them (about 70,000) are likely to buy the product. So, does the company have to send a million leaflets to hit on the 70,000? The answer is no. The marketing department typically selects a sample of the total, based on the available data about the client, such as marital status, solvency, gender, zip code, other products the client has, and how long the client has been a customer. Let's say the company does a mailing of 200,000 and they have a positive response from 7 percent, that is, 14,000 customers, who purchase the product. However, the company calculated at the beginning that there were 70,000 clients who were likely to buy; therefore, there are 56,000 clients who the company didn't reach.

Now the marketing department tries again, but first it runs a data model, created using the processing and know-how seen in this book, against the database of one million clients. The model makes a ranking of all the clients, ordered by likelihood of purchase. The marketing department selects the first 200,000 clients from the ranking and sends them the leaflet. From these 200,000, there is a response of 95,000 and, of them, 40,000 contract the product. What a success! The business has gone from 14,000 to 40,000 sales, with the same mailing volume—an increment of nearly 200 percent! This is possible through a precise selection of the target group of clients.

Figure 9.6 summarizes this example. When the company applies the likelihood of purchase model to the current customer database, the objective is to maximize the number of likely customers found while evaluating the minimum number of customers. The figure illustrates that the model found all the most likely clients (100 percent) by evaluating only 20 percent of the total number of clients (curve on the left). The marketing department's traditional methods (segmentation by standard business criteria: zip code, age, etc.) must evaluate between 38 percent and 75 percent of all the clients (central curves). Lastly, a random selection (like throwing a coin) needs to evaluate 100 percent of the client database in order to find 100 percent of the most likely clients.

SIMULATION MODELS – "WHAT IF?"

Any one of the modeling methods in this chapter can be used to create simulations. A simulation allows for varying one or more of the model's input variables in order to see its effect on the output. For example, recall the example of Mr. Strong's factory in Chapter 2, in which the objective was to model part of the customer call center data processing to attend to customer reclamations more efficiently.

In the sales area, a simulator could be applied to observe, in X percent, the effect on a company's net profit of increasing the number of branch offices, taking into account the investment and fixed costs implied. The company can vary the percentage of offices (input variable), trying different percentages (15, 20, 25 percent, etc.), and observe the output value (global net profit) produced in each case. Another variable could be macro-economic in nature, such as the base lending rate of the US Treasury, inflation rate, and so on. The company

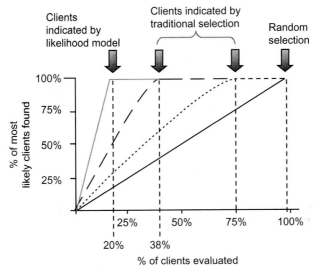

FIGURE 9.6   Three methods for identifying clients who are likely to buy, and their respective efficiency rates for finding those clients

could also try experiments with their customer profiles: what would happen if 80 percent of clients were aged between 18 and 30 years, instead of the current 50 percent? What would happen with net profit if the product lines were diversified in 40 percent instead of the current 25 percent?

To create simulation models, they must be calibrated by using historical (test) data and trying different permutations and values for the inputs until the closest result is obtained for the historical data. Obtaining a good simulator can be a time-consuming process. For this reason, when a business is developing its first simulator, one of the simplest approaches is to define a model in terms of IF–THEN–ELSE rules.

Stochastic Models

Inflection Points

More sophisticated stochastic models try to find inflection points on a curve: at an inflection point, a given factor (such as profit or debt level) may have a tipping point, at which the tendency/gradient starts to rise or fall more quickly. A stochastic (or non-deterministic) system is one that contains a random element, which means that its output or its state cannot always be predicted completely. Many real-world systems are stochastic in nature. (For more information, refer to Wikipedia: http://en .wikipedia.org/wiki/Stochastic.)

SUMMARY OF MODELING

Modeling is a cyclic process, given that failure in this phase can mean that a company must go back and select new samples or variables, or even redefine the business objectives. Figure 9.7 shows the general scheme for this process. However, if it has conscientiously carried out the previous phases, the company will have created a solid basis for the modeling task. Inevitably, in practice, typical errors are committed, such as defining a variable containing "zip code" as a numerical variable (it's categorical), or giving the client address as an input to the model. If it isn't right the first time, other modeling techniques, such as neural, induction, and regression, can be tried with the same data to see which one gives the best results. The technique used also depends on whether the priority is to create profiles (for which the most adequate technique is rule induction), or if predictive precision is the most critical aspect (in which case a neural network would be used). Another consideration is the data type: some techniques work better for variables that are mainly categorical, and others work better with numerical variables.

In terms of advice for model construction, one trick is the age-old "divide and conquer." That is, first segment the data (by customer type, product type, etc.), and then create distinct models for each of the most important segments.

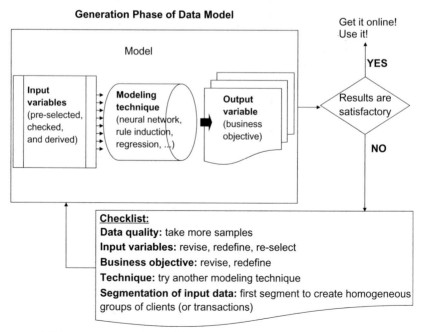

FIGURE 9.7   How to create a data model

Another piece of time-proven advice is Occam's razor: if there are several possible explanations of why the results are not good, first investigate the simplest explanation, followed by the second simplest, and so on.

For further reading on data modeling and predictive analytics:

Morelli, T., Shearer, C., Buecker, A., 2010. *IBM SPSS Predictive Analytics: Optimizing Decisions at the Point of Impact*. IBM Redguide.

Witten, I., Frank, E., Hall, M., 2011. *Data Mining: Practical Machine Learning Tools and Techniques*. Burlington, MA: Morgan Kaufmann. ISBN: 978-0123748560.

Deployment Systems: From Query Reporting to EIS and Expert Systems

INTRODUCTION

This chapter reviews the various ways that the results of data mining, such as predictive models, rules, and analysis results, can be presented in a way that allows a business to feed those results directly in its decision-making and operative processes. First, the chapter addresses simple graphic and reporting formats, followed by more sophisticated executive information system interfaces and a discussion of how the results can be integrated into the business operations, such as CRM systems and call centers. Finally, the chapter looks at more complex applications, such as expert systems and case-based systems.

QUERY AND REPORT GENERATION

This book's approach is the analysis and processing of data for strategic and tactical business objectives. However, there are many businesses that are limited to using simple queries (SQL) and standard reports in order to access and display the information taken from their databases and from their business processes. This information includes summaries of commercial activity together with production and financial figures for the day-to-day functioning of the business.

To summarize the situation, imagine being in a monthly meeting of the Management Committee of Office Stationary, Inc. The meeting is attended by the financial director, the commercial director, the production manager, the accounting manager, the IT director, and the managing director. In this meeting, estimated to last two hours, each director will give a summary of his or her area: results of the previous month, previsions for the forthcoming month, problems solved or expected, and so on.

Note the specific case of the commercial director: he will base his summary on the reports generated for sales by region, commercial outlet, and product. He will present sales totals, differentials, and averages, probably referring to the increase or decrease over a specific period. He will highlight any significant aspect, the region where sales are highest and where they are lowest, actual sales versus the sales objectives for the current year, any problems that need to be solved, and, if necessary, requests for collaboration with other departments. So the commercial director must not only have a mastery of the sales statistics at this level, but must also be supported by reliable, adequate, and coherent data in order to explain his area's current situation in the monthly meetings. On the basis of what is presented, decisions are made on whether or not to make changes to the line of management in these areas.

Now consider how the commercial director (or the financial director, or production manager, etc.) manages to obtain the data he needs each month to present the situation in his area. The commercial director has developed a good working relationship with the IT manager in order to make things more agile with respect to his requests for reports and access to corporate databases. The IT department has developed a set of made-to-measure sales reports, which are delivered to the commercial director one day before each monthly meeting. In Figure 10.1, we see an example of a graph of summarized estimated sales by quarter and region.

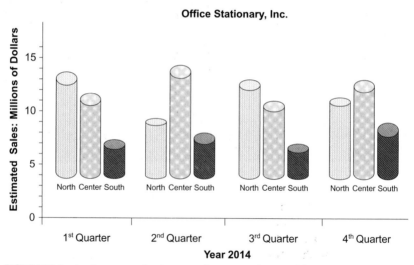

FIGURE 10.1   A sales presentation in terms of quarters and geographic zones

Now let's return to the monthly report that concerns the commercial director. The standard monthly report shows the sales figures first by region, then within region by sales center, and finally for each sales center by type of product. If the commercial director wants to see the statistics in a different form, for example, first by type of product, second by sales center, and third by region, he can change things around in five minutes using his EIS tool. He can also do a drill-down on a given region to see, for example, the disaggregated data that is detailed in the report.

Table 10.1 shows a summary report of sales leads for the month of May for Office Stationary, Inc. It has four levels of detail: region, sales center, CRM

TABLE 10.1 Example of a format for monthly sales lead reporting

OFFICE STATIONARY, INC.
PERIOD: MAY 2014

REGION: NORTH (level 1)
SALES CENTER 1: (level 2)

New Clients (level 3)

Client Name	Sale Est. (K$)	Product Categories	Pipeline Stage	Probability
General Offices, Inc. (level 4)	30.25	Business cards	preprocess	(0.85)
Ecological Products	00.80	Envelopes	preprocess	(0.68)
North-South Poultry	47.10	Writing implements	qualification	(0.75)
Carbide Metallurgy	364.50	Correction instruments	decision-making	0.85
SUBTOTAL: 4 (level 3)				
AVERAGE:	*110.66 (level 3)*			*0.78*

Cross-Sell

Client Name	Sale Est. (K$)	Product Categories	Pipeline Stage	Probability
United Radiators	12.52	Stickers	negotiation	0.75
Fruit Conserves	7.50	Envelopes	negotiation	0.80
Kitchen Refurb, Inc.	15.40	Writing implements	completed	-
MyCar, Inc.	00.50	Business cards	completed	-
SUBTOTAL: 4				
AVERAGE:	*8.98*			*0.77*

WIN-BACK

Client Name	Sale Est. (K$)	Product Categories	Pipeline Stage	Probability
Quality Packaging, Inc.	115.92	Correction instruments	decision-making	0.72
Flywheel Associates	71.33	Business cards	completed	-

Continued

TABLE 10.1　Example of a format for monthly sales lead reporting—Cont'd

OFFICE STATIONARY, INC.

PERIOD: MAY 2014

REGION: NORTH (level 1)

SALES CENTER 1: (level 2)

Makeshift Products (level 4)	74.51	Writing implements	decision-making	0.75
Wind-Solar Solutions	5.51	Stickers	completed	-
SUBTOTAL: 4 (level 3)				
AVERAGE:	66.82 (level 3)			0.73
SUBTOTAL: 12 (level 2)				
AVERAGE:	*62.15 (level 2)*			*0.76*
SALES CENTER 2:				
NEW CLIENTS				
CROSS-SELL				
WIN-BACK				
SALES CENTER 3:				
NEW CLIENTS				
CROSS-SELL				
WIN-BACK				
SUBTOTAL: 134 (level 1)				
AVERAGE:	*80.25 (level 1)*			*0.75*

client type (new, cross-sell, win-back), and client. For levels 1 to 3 there is a summary at the end of each section with the average values for the turnover and (customer acceptance) probability columns. Level 2 aggregates the values for level 3, and level 1 aggregates the values for level 2. The report was designed by the commercial director himself, given that, in the monthly management summary for Office Stationary, Inc., five key data items have to be presented: the number of clients per lead type (new clients, cross-sell, and win-back), the estimated sales in dollars per lead type, the product categories offered to the clients, the pipeline stage (of the sales process), and the probability of acceptance per lead type. Then the variation of these figures can be compared to the same report for the previous month. The way the report is presented allows the commercial director to provide these figures by a regional or sales center level, by lead type, or even by a specific client.

Also, the commercial director can state that in the north region, the billing volume of completed sales has increased by x percent with respect to the previous month, and that the current average probability of acceptable is 75 percent, according to the predictive model estimation. Congratulations to the commercial director! However, the general manager recommends for him to get in touch with the company's representative at sales center number 1, in the north region, to clarify why there are two sales leads whose estimated volumes are less than $1000, and to decide on any corrective actions.

Query and Reporting Systems

This section looks briefly at the specifications of two industry-leading suppliers of query and reporting systems. Recall that standard query and reporting remains an essential requirement of many businesses and organizations, and the state-of-the-art solutions deal with Big Data volumes, distributed systems, and guaranteeing data quality.

The first supplier, Stonefield Query (stonefieldquery.com), describes its product, Stonefield Query SDK, as a user-friendly database report-writing, query, and data mining tool. It enables a business to deliver end-user reporting to customers and/or internal users. It has connectivity to the majority of databases: Microsoft SQL Server, Oracle, Microsoft Access, Visual FoxPro, Pervasive, IBM DB2, MySQL, and so on. It can also create reports from non-database formats such as Microsoft Excel and text files. A second product from the same vendor, Stonefield Query for GoldMine, generates reports by accessing data held in the GoldMine (www.goldmine.com) CRM software database.

The vendor claims its product is a user-friendly database report-writing, query, and data mining tool designed specifically for GoldMine. Its functionality includes a report scheduler, role-based security, report templates, drill downs, exclusion/inclusion filters, emailed reports, customizable SQL select, and advanced report designer. It includes over 60 predefined sample reports, which can be used as is or as the basis to create new reports.

The second supplier, SAP Crystal Reports (www.crystalreports.com), offers a sophisticated solution for multi-vendor systems (not just SAP). According to the supplier, its software can be used to design formatted reports with Flash integration and interactive charts, and has flexible export options. It can deliver reports via the Web, email, Microsoft Office, or embedded in applications, empowering end users to explore reports with on-report sorting and parameters. In terms of connectivity, the vendor states that it can connect to the majority of data sources and structures, including relational, online analytical processing

(OLAP), XML data, OLAP cubes, spreadsheets, and log files. Other functionality includes wizards and experts for report creation and custom templates. A comprehensive formatting and design tool allows for the definition of sub-report objects; charts based on subtotals, group details, and formulas can be created; graphic image support for BMP, TIFF, JPEG, PNG, PCX, TGA, and PICT formats is built in, as are geographic maps with smart navigation (group tree, drill down, and search); and a .NET WinForm viewer is available.

Other characteristics of data access and processing include exporting to Microsoft Excel/Word, processing heterogeneous data sources, sorting data on SQL database servers, supporting multi-value parameters for SQL commands, and accessing OLAP data.

EXECUTIVE INFORMATION SYSTEMS

Some months after the management meeting described in the previous section, the commercial director decides to create an Access database on his desktop computer, which allows him to generate his own graphics and statistics in MS Excel, reports in MS Word, and presentations in MS PowerPoint. This data mart in MS Access is updated by periodically exporting data from the Oracle database in the company's central computer.

Also, in order to be able to play with the data and see the business from different perspectives, the commercial director has installed an EIS tool on his PC, which uses his Access database as the data source.

Query, Reporting, and EIS

Deploying Data Mining Results

Standard query, reporting, and EIS tools manipulate and show existing information in diverse and ingenious ways, but do not create new information per se. Hence, in the deployment of data mining results, the output data of the predictive models and analysis must be prepared, and in a form that can then be displayed and manipulated by the query, reporting, and EIS tools. This may be as simple as indicating which table to read the data from, or it may require some additional customizing of the tool. Also, note that the EIS system could be integrated into a CRM (Customer Relationship Management) application. (Chapter 13 looks in detail at CRM applications.)

EIS Interface for a "What If" Scenario Modeler

Figure 10.2 shows a typical presentation of part of an EIS system (executive information system) with a GIS (graphical information system) interface. It is able to show a ranking of the different regions (level one) using multiple criteria. Clicking on a state performs a drill-down to the next level of detail and generates a ranking by county, city, and so on. It is important that the user can define the selection criteria, thus obtaining a customized version of the menu, shown on the lower right.

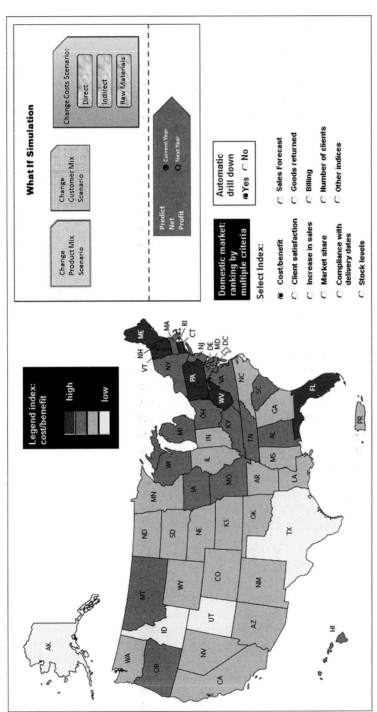

FIGURE 10.2   The first level of data access and functionality of an EIS (executive information system) tool

The EIS in the figure has a legend index, which uses four shades of gray to indicate which of four possible levels (from high to low) correspond to each state. The domestic market can be ranked by multiple criteria, which can be combined on the graphic: cost/benefit, client satisfaction, increase in sales, market share, compliance with delivery dates, stock levels, sales forecast, goods returned, billing, and number of clients.

Finally, the upper right illustrates the functionality of a "what if" scenario generator in which the user can modify different business parameters and see the result on the net profit for the current year or the next year.

EIS Interface

Net Profit Predictive Variable

For the net profit 'what if' simulation (top right of Figure 10.2), the output variable could be defined as a continuous value that represents the real net profit of the business in dollars. Alternatively, it could be a relative value that indicates the percent increase or decrease with respect to a net profit baseline.

In the figure, the modifiable business parameters are divided into three categories: product mix, customer mix, and costs. The product mix allows the business to evaluate the effect of, for example, selling more of one type of product and less of another; the customer mix evaluates the effect of, say, having more customers from type A and less from type B; and the costs modifier allows the business to evaluate repercussion of, for example, a rise in interest rates, energy costs, having to pay more for the basic materials used in the products, transport costs, and so on. In terms of implementation, achieving a simulator with this capacity might be quite a challenge; hence a business would probably have to conform to a subset of the functionality shown. Each scenario (product mix, customer mix, and costs) could have a separate predictive model, or there could be just one—more complex—model whose inputs come from all three scenarios.

Executive Information Systems (EIS)

This section looks briefly at the specifications of an industry-leading supplier of query and reporting systems, IBM Cognos Express (http://www-01.ibm.com/software/analytics/cognos/express/). The supplier states that its solution is designed for midsize companies and includes basic reporting; analysis; interactive dashboards; scorecard; planning; budgeting; and forecasting capabilities for departments, business units, and midsize organizations. It states that this system is a preconfigured solution that is easy to install and use.

The vendor has two specific software products: the IBM Cognos Express Advisor uses an embedded in-memory analytics server to connect to operational data sources and create a multidimensional view of a business. The user can analyze key areas, such as products or channels, and compare them with respect to other key factors, such as regions, customers, and time. The vendor states that the Cognos Express Advisor also facilitates queries such as "Which are our most profitable products and what makes them profitable?" or "Who are my best customers?" However, one would have to ascertain whether these queries are answered by basic SQL or whether they use embedded data mining models or functions. Secondly, the IBM Cognos Express Xcelerator is an extension for spreadsheet data processing and incorporates functionality for analysis and SQL query optimization. It is designed for users who are accustomed to manipulating data in an Excel environment; it allows users to define their own "what if" business scenarios. It manages the data to guarantee consistency and integrity and has an in-memory analytics engine to deliver high-performance, multidimensional analysis.

Excel also has its own "what if" analysis function (in previous versions it was called the solver), which comes as an add-in with Excel itself. (Refer to http://office.microsoft.com for details.) Chapter 19 will run through the basics of how to use this tool.

EXPERT SYSTEMS

John, the IT manager of a pharmaceutical company, attends a seminar on business information systems. The seminar deals with "expert systems." John is surprised at seeing this technology, which had its heyday in the 1980s, at which time it represented the cutting edge of intelligent approaches to information systems.

This technology was the forerunner of data mining as well as business intelligence; the area is now known as corporate knowledge management, among other things. Companies spent fortunes developing massive expert systems for their businesses. However, currently, the term "expert system" has almost disappeared. So what happened?

Expert systems, or rule-based systems, started at the opposite end of the spectrum from that of data analysis. That is, instead of supposing that "the truth is in the data," they assumed that the truth resided in the experience of people. Thus the proposal was to embody the knowledge of people (the experts in a given area) in rules of the form if–then–else. For example, a consultant could, through a series of interviews with the director of the credit department, extract the rules and key procedures for the credit scoring of customer loans: IF amount greater than $5,000 THEN request authorization from head office; IF time as client less than 6 months AND monthly income less than X, THEN REJECT credit application, etc.

Expert Systems

Difficulties in Building Expert Systems

One of the difficulties of the traditional approach, that of building expert systems by depending on human experts to define the expert rules, is that the people who know the most about a given area are not necessarily the best at explaining or transmitting this information to other people. It often happens that experts make correct decisions intuitively but are not able to explain in detail how they do it. Another difficulty is that people who know a lot about something may be reticent in sharing this information with others, often for irrational reasons associated with a perceived loss of power or usefulness for the organization or company they work for. This could well be one of the main reasons why many computer software systems are so badly documented. One of the ways to obtain good expert rules is to ask for the same information from two or more people in the company and compare the results for consistency.

As if these two difficulties were not enough (the difficulty of being able to explain what one knows, and the reticence to explain it), a third problem with expert systems is that humans don't think only in terms of if–then–else rules. The way people think and store information is more complex than just linear reasoning: it is also associative, connectionist, and non-linear. In order to solve this problem, expert systems incorporated multiple levels of rules, forming a hierarchy made of base rules, meta rules, and control rules, together with a powerful inference engine that allowed a probabilistic execution of the rules.

Over time, expert systems were merged into new concepts such as knowledge management, business intelligence, data mining, and CRM/ERP systems. Within the field of data mining, there were two powerful technologies—neural networks and rule induction—that, at the beginning of the 1990s, reached maturity and came within reach of the general public and the business world in the form of commercial, easy-to-use systems.

Even so, expert systems have left their mark, given that today many large databases, data warehouses, and CRM/ERP systems include triggers that are deployed as expert rules for a diversity of things, such as credit scoring, alerts, and business indicators.

The approach of analyzing data to extract knowledge, instead of interviewing people, has been possible due to the large investment made by businesses in data storage system infrastructures (transactional systems, databases, data warehouses, data marts, server farms, etc.) over the last decades. Now these businesses need to get a return on their investments by exploiting the mountains of data they now have available. This has also gone hand in hand with a greater level of sophistication of marketing techniques for capturing client data through client cards, all kinds of online forms and questionnaires, and the meticulous capture of feedback from front office employees and websites.

Hence, instead of the original proposal in the 1980s, that of building an expert system from rules uniquely defined by human experts, one can imagine that twenty-first century expert systems will contain rules and functionality primarily derived from data mining processes, such as rule induction techniques. Also, trained predictive models, for example, neural networks, can be embedded in the expert system to provide online decision support. However, this does not discount the participation of human expert knowledge and knowledge repositories in the design and content of a contemporary expert system.

> **Expert Systems**
>
> *Deployment*
>
> From a deployment point of view, an expert system would be an adequate option for a call center (refer to the example in Chapter 2), in which non-expert support staff could access rule-based expert knowledge and predictive models as support for decision-making processes (for example, evaluating the credit-worthiness of a client or of a possibly fraudulent request), online and in real time. As mentioned earlier, data models can also be embedded as SQL trigger functions in complex database relational definitions to create alerts and flags.

CASE-BASED SYSTEMS

This section considers a way of representing information and modeling data that is related to the rule-based approach of expert systems and the rule induction- and supervised learning-based approaches. Case-based reasoning, as the name suggests, is based on a database of historical cases used to match and classify new cases. As part of the system, it is necessary to correctly define the cases in terms of their most characteristic attributes and to have a way of measuring the distance between a historical case in the database and a new case.

Case-based reasoning follows a processing cycle of four major steps:

- First, it retrieves the most similar case or cases in order to solve a new problem.
- Next, it reuses the information and knowledge in the retrieved case or cases to solve the problem. This initial solution is often called a ballpark solution because it is approximate.
- Then, the CBR system revises the ballpark solution and adapts or customizes it, if necessary.
- Finally, the CBR system may store the solution in its database if it decides that the solution represents new knowledge that can be used to solve future problems.

The concept of how a CBR system operates has a strong analogy with how problems are solved in some important domains such as law and medicine. A lawyer or a doctor would look for historical cases similar to the case of a new client or patient. A commercial example is defining a new type of product by adapting products known to have given good results in the past for a similar set of circumstances and customer profiles.

SUMMARY

This chapter has given a brief introduction to how the results of data mining projects (analysis and modeling) can be deployed in the business environment. Simple but effective options such as query/reporting and EIS have been discussed, as have more complex options such as expert systems and case-based systems. The option chosen depends on the type of business, how it is run, and the specific data needs for decision-making. If a simple report of sales leads, each with an associated probability of acceptance, does the job, then installing a complex expert system doesn't have to feel obligatory. However, even query/reporting and EIS are not necessarily plug and play applications and usually need customizing and some technical support to get them to do what the user wants.

Finally, the following is a brief explanation of a recent news story that serves as a cautionary tale about the preparation of statistical summaries and their usage. In April 2013, world economists were surprised and perplexed by the news that two prestigious Harvard academics had made a basic error when using an Excel spreadsheet to summarize their findings and publish an influential economic model. This model has been used in recent years (circa 2013) by economists around the world to support the economic arguments that countries should cut spending to promote economic growth.

The elemental error was in the definition of an average function cell that was based on the range of values in a given column of data. Each row showed the GDP growth for a given country when the country's debt-to-GDP ratio was 90 percent or more. The conclusion from the data (which included the error) was that, were a country's debt-to-GDP ratio to go over 90 percent (the critical threshold), economic growth would drop off sharply. However, the range defined in the average function missed out the last five cells. (These cells included data from the countries of Denmark, Canada, Belgium, Austria, and Australia). If these countries had been included, the average GDP growth would be 2.2 percent instead of −0.1 percent! The evaluations of the findings and of this error are still being debated.

Apart from the error itself, another criticism is the lack of control of how such an error can pass unchecked and become common wisdom. However, aside from the implications of this Excel error on world economic policy, in the context of presenting key business information derived from data mining (which is the theme of this chapter), we can learn the lesson that a report and the data it is based on should be doubled-checked—not by the same person, but by a peer, colleague, manager, or subordinate who is able to independently debug any possible faulty calculations or fundamental assumptions.

Chapter 11

Text Analysis

BASIC ANALYSIS OF TEXTUAL INFORMATION

This chapter discusses simple and advanced text processing and text analysis: the basic processing considers format-checking based on pattern identification; the advanced techniques consider named entity recognition, concept identification based on synonyms and hyponyms, and information retrieval concepts.

Text Processing

Relation with Data Quality

Recall that Chapter 5 discusses the data quality of textual information, describing a basic validation analysis of data formats for names, addresses, and telephone numbers. Recall also the examples of surveys, questionnaires, and registration forms seen in Chapter 3, which includes textual information fields. If text-based analysis can be used to correct errors or fill out incomplete records when processing text, the data quality will be subsequently boosted.

The analysis of textual information has similarities with data analysis, although there are some considerations specific to the nature of textual information. Human beings have a facility for analyzing and synthesizing textual information by, for example, reading a book and writing a summary of it. In contrast, a page full of numerical data is, in general, less intelligible and interpretable to the human eye.

Textual analysis can be carried out manually, as in the case of the traditional editing and correction (proofreading) of book manuscripts. Another way to analyze text is through the use of semiautomatic reviewers. An automated reviewer generates a lexical ranking (ordering) based on affinities, using a search based on specific criteria or using free text. It can also create a ranking by relevance for the detection of orthographic errors of words not in its dictionary, such as commercial brand names, new technical terms, and so on. For example, in the analysis of a text document, one part of the text has the spelling of Mississippi as Misissipi. If a later search is conducted for the text "Misissipi," Mississippi will also be found, given that it will have been automatically added to the dictionary. The next section follows an analysis of textual information to identify different formats for the names of people.

Table 11.1 shows a diversity of different formats for first and last names, name prefixes, and so on, which are then used to identify these structures in the text. The most common name format found is "L L F" (e.g., J. M. Jackson), with 23,700 names. The least common format is "T C C" (e.g., Att.: Marketing Dtor.), with only 714 cases. By using techniques based on pattern recognition and lexical analysis, it is possible to identify structures without the need to have *a priori* knowledge about the data. For example, interrelated information can be discovered inside of observation or comments fields. This type of field is often (incorrectly) used to include important additional details about clients and other relevant business information hidden in free format text.

TABLE 11.1 Example of frequency counters for different name formats

Format	Frequency	Name
L L F	23,700	J. M. Jackson
F L F	18,630	Kenneth L. Wheelock
R F F	14,450	Mr. Mark Shapiro
R F F F	11,951	Mrs. Sarah Jane Roberts
F F O	8297	Earl Franklin, Jr.
F L P	4782	Edward D. Elkins-Carter
R F L F	1085	Dr. James T. Levy
T C C	714	Att.: Marketing Dtor.

Legend: F=alphanumeric, R=name prefix, O=name suffix, P=joint surname, L=initials, T=Att., C=commercial terms

Examples of useful information found in free text fields include: names of people, organizations, and locations; dates and monetary quantities; hyphenated terms made of multiple words; and abbreviations. For example, when analyzing a group of financial news articles, one could recognize insurance policy, insurance cover, Direct Insurance, and New York Insurers as four distinct entities. But by using a canonical form for each entity, Senator Johnson, Mr. Johnson, and Michael Johnson are recognized as the same person.

ADVANCED ANALYSIS OF TEXTUAL INFORMATION

This section describes a semiautomatic process for analyzing free text. Consider a customer comment feedback log related to call center customer service. The process has four main steps: (i) define keyword sets of interest to find in the text,

(ii) execute the queries on a document corpus (information retrieval step) to obtain a reduced document set, (iii) identify specific names and data in the retrieved documents, and (iv) preform a concept generalization based on categories derived from the WordNet online application (wordnet.princeton.edu) to identify blocks of text related to the keywords of interest. Finally, the text is manually revised from a contextual point of view to choose the most relevant and interesting complete sentences, paragraphs, and sections. Figure 11.1 illustrates a simplified schematic representation of the text processing steps.

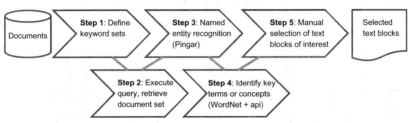

FIGURE 11.1   Scheme for text document processing

Text Processing

WordNet – Online Synonym Repository

WordNet is a large online lexical repository for the English language. Nouns, verbs, adjectives, and adverbs are grouped into sets of synonyms (synsets), each representing a different concept. Hence it can be used to look up synonyms for a given word.
  For further reading on WordNet, see:
  G. A. Miller, R. Beckwith, C. D. Fellbaum, D. Gross, and K. Miller. 1990. "WordNet: An Online Lexical Database." *Int. J. Lexicograph.* 3 (4): pp. 235–244.

Keyword Definition and Information Retrieval

Table 11.2 defines four keyword sets to find in the text. Plurals and other grammatical versions of the keywords also need to be matched. Hence the text must be preprocessed to obtain root versions of the words by using a process called stemming. Once the queries have been defined, they are launched on a document corpus (in the table, imagine that each text block is a separate document), and the information retrieval system (search engine) returns the top-ranked document for each query.

Identification of Names and Personal Information of Individuals

One way to identify names and personal information is to use the Pingar online application (http://www.pingar.com) and API to process the text of interest, which identifies the following: people, organizations, addresses, emails, ages,

TABLE 11.2 Queries and documents used to mine text

ID Keyword Set	Keyword Sets (utility queries)	Example Text Blocks Found
q₁	{wait, time, long}	"After initially connecting by telephone with the call center, I had to **wait** for a **long time** to be attended."
q₂	{quality, problem}	"There is a **problem** with the **quality** of the service."
q₃	{complicated, option selection}	"When I initially connected to the call center, I was asked to respond to a lot of **options** that I found **complicated** and I didn't make the right **selection**."
q₄	{quality, good}	"Having navigated through the options, I found the **quality** of service was **great** and the person who helped me was polite and knowledgeable."

phone numbers, URLs, dates, times, money, and amounts. This allows the information to be extracted and used. If the concepts (keywords), and not specific personal data, are of interest, the personal data can be eliminated, which may also be a necessary step in order to comply with any data privacy requirements. The elimination process simply substitutes the information with {Pers1, Pers2, ...}, {Loc1, Loc2, ...}, {Date1, Date2, ...}, and so on. The names of states and cities are unchanged in this process. (To access Pingar, see: Pingar – Entity Extraction Software. http://www.pingar.com.)

Identifying Blocks of Interesting Text

As seen in the table, text blocks are identified by the presence of one or more primary keywords. However, there may be other words in the text that are not in the primary keyword list. The online WordNet ontology database (http://wordnetweb.princeton.edu/perl/webwn) is then used to find the synonyms and hyponyms for each term in the list, taking into account the specific or closer sense to the original term. (Note that this word sense disambiguation can be performed manually.) A hyponym refers to the lower part of the ontology tree, starting from the given keyword. For example, the keyword "quality" gives the following result when searched in WordNet:

S: (n) quality (an essential and distinguishing attribute of something or someone) direct hyponym/full hyponym
S: (n) appearance, visual aspect (outward or visible aspect of a person or thing)
S: (n) clearness, clarity, uncloudedness (the quality of clear water): "With the new spectacles she could see with more clarity."

S: (n) opacity, opaqueness (the quality of being opaque to a degree; the degree to which something makes understanding difficult)

S: (n) divisibility (the quality of being divisible; the capacity to be divided into parts or divided among a number of persons)

S: (n) ease, easiness, simplicity, simpleness (freedom from difficulty or hardship or effort): "He found it fairly easy to obtain the information he wanted"; "They put the information online for ease of consultation."

S: (n) difficulty, difficultness (the quality of being difficult): "They agreed about the difficulty of choosing the right option."

Then the documents are processed and an output file is generated, in which all the keywords and their hyponyms (found using WordNet) are signaled thus: "****Keyword****(20)"; this output file also indicates the relative distance of each keyword found from the start of the file (in this case, 20). These distances can be clustered for each file and the information used to signal documents with text areas that have a high density of keywords, which would then be candidates for selection from the file. A stemming process is first applied (using the Porter Stemming algorithm, version 3) to the keyword list and the words in the documents in order to match as many variants of the root term as possible. Finally, the labeled files are manually revised using the clustered distance information for support and the paragraphs are selected that have the highest clustering of terms of interest.

For further reading about the stemming algorithm, see:

M. F. Porter. 1980. "An Algorithm for Suffix Stripping." *Program: Electronic Library and Information Systems.* 4 (3): pp. 130–137.

Information Retrieval Concepts

Information retrieval concepts can be used when a business wants to automatically find documents relevant to a given set of keywords. Two of the most used concepts in the retrieval of textual information are term frequency and inverse document frequency. Term frequency refers to the number of times that a term t occurs in document d. The inverse document frequency is a measure of whether a term is common or rare in a given document corpus. It is obtained by dividing the total number of documents by the number of documents containing the term in the corpus. Once these two metrics have been calculated, they can be combined (multiplied) to get a new measure: the term frequency $\times$ the inverse document frequency. This value reflects how important a word is with respect to a given document in a corpus of documents. These metrics are often used by online search engines in order to retrieve the most relevant documents for a user query.

For further reading about information retrieval, see:

Baeza-Yates, R. and Ribeiro-Neto, B. 2011. *Modern Information Retrieval: The Concepts and Technology behind Search*, 2nd ed. New York: ACM Press Books. ISBN: 0321416910.

Assessing Sentiment on Social Media

Many businesses now have corporate pages on social media websites, such as Facebook, where they publish content about their products and services. This allows customers (fans) to be followers and to give feedback to the business, and the company can respond to questions from its followers. There is typically a "like" button for users to express positive responses (endorsements), as well as the functionality to write a comment or share an item with friends.

Figure 11.2 shows an example of a comments forum associated with the social media corporate page of a beauty products company. The free-form text comments store a wealth of potentially useful information in order to carry out a sentiment analysis of specific product launches. However, as the text volumes may be large and the text is unstructured, data processing represents a challenge. A simple approach is to export all the text comments to a .txt file and process the file using techniques described in the previous sections. For example, queries could be executed based on selected keywords and then a frequency count performed on the keywords of interest.

Beauty products forum

Company announcement 1: new hair shampoo ABC (photo and description).

    User 1: is that the same color for hair and lipstick?

    User 2: I love the new colors, but I would also like to know that the products made by this company are *not tested on animals*. I know that this is prohibited in US and Europe, but not in other countries.

Company announcement 2: Famous music star XYZ uses our products (photo and description).

    User 1: I love this shade.

    User 2: *Red shades* are always so *dramatic*.

    User 3: *Lovely shade.*

    User 4: You have such *amazing products*. You should do an end of season *giveaway* for your *fans*.

Company reply 1: Thank you!

    User 2: Do you have products *especially for* people with *skin allergies*?

    Company reply 2: We have a special line of *products for delicate skin*, maybe you can check them out!

FIGURE 11.2 Fan page forum for beauty products company

Figure 11.3 illustrates a semantic network, which has been extracted from the text comments shown in Figure 11.2. Recall from Chapter 4 that a semantic network shows the relations (indicated on the links) between entities (indicated in the ovals). In general, relations tend to be verbs or adverbs, whereas entities tend to be nouns or adjectives. It can be seen in Figure 11.3 that additional

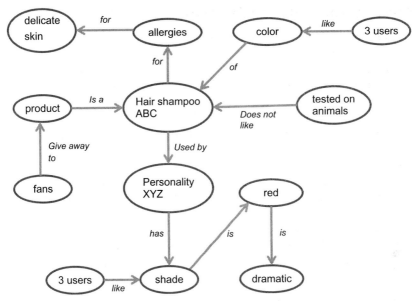

FIGURE 11.3   Semantic network extracted from comments in forum

information is included in the semantic network, such as frequency counts. For example, the lower left of the semantic network shows that three users expressed their liking for the hair shade of personality XYZ.

In order to create a semantic network like that in the figure, the comments could be manually inspected and the entities and relations determined. However, automating the process to some extent would probably be considered for large volumes of text. Extracting entities and relations separately from free text, and the calculating frequencies, can be done without too much difficulty. However, a significantly greater challenge is presented if this information is to be unified into a semantic network. For example, when looking back at the comments in Figure 11.2, it may not be clear which verbs or adverbs relate to which nouns.

One system that automates the extraction process is called TEXTRUNNER. The system performs a single data-driven pass over a text corpus and extracts a large set of relational tuples without requiring human input. The tuples are then assigned a probability and indexed to support efficient extraction and exploration via user queries. TEXTRUNNER has been used as an unsupervised approach to extracting semantic networks from large volumes of text. The approach uses the system to extract the tuples then induce general concepts and relations from them by jointly clustering the objects and relational strings in the tuples. This approach is defined using basic rules to extract meaningful semantic networks. However, be warned that natural language text processing is difficult to implement and is still considered more useful as a research topic than it is for mainstream commercial systems.

For further reading on the TEXTRUNNER system and its use for unsupervised learning, see:

Banko, M., M. J. Cafarella, S. Soderland, M. Broadhead, and O. Etzioni. 2007. "Open Information Extraction from the Web." In: Proceedings of the International Joint Conference on Artificial Intelligence, 2007, Hyderabad, India. AAAI Press.

For further reading on the unsupervised approach, see:

Kok, S. and P. Domingos. 2008. "Extracting Semantic Networks from Text Via Relational Clustering." ECML PKDD '08 Proceedings of the 2008 European Conference on Machine Learning and Knowledge Discovery in Databases – Part I, pp. 624–639.

COMMERCIAL TEXT MINING PRODUCTS

This section briefly comments on two commercial systems for text mining: the IBM SPSS Modeler Text Analytics 15 and the SAS Text Miner. The IBM SPSS Modeler Text Analytics 15 is a user-friendly system for capturing the knowledge of business domain experts into dictionaries and semantic rules for re-use. It allows for customizable information extraction for logical reasoning to draw inferences from natural, unstructured textual information. It also offers entity and relationship recognition to classify words or phrases into categories that can be analyzed for business meaning. It can be interfaced with other applications such as email and instant messaging systems.

For further reading, see:

IBM SPSS Modeler Text Analytics 15 User's Guide 2012. Available at: ftp://public.dhe.ibm.com/software/analytics/spss/documentation/modeler/15.0/en/Users_Guide_For_Text_Analytics.pdf.

"SPSS Text Analytics for Surveys." IBM. http://www-03.ibm.com/software/products/es/es/spss-text-analytics-surveys/.

"Discover the Hidden Value in Unstructured Information." IBM. http://www-01.ibm.com/software/ebusiness/jstart/textanalytics/.

The second system, the SAS Text Miner, has different modules for content categorization, ontology management, and sentiment analysis. The content categorization module performs business information retrieval and automatic content categorization with functionality for prebuilt taxonomies, text summarizations, file system and Web crawling, faceted search and indexing, and duplicate document identification. The ontology management module defines semantic relationships to consistently and systematically link text repositories together within a managed environment. The sentiment analysis module automatically locates and analyzes the sentiment of electronic text in real time from websites, internal files, reports, surveys, forms, emails, and communication centers to spot trends and identify customer priorities.

For further reading, see:

SAS Text Analytics, http://www.sas.com/text-analytics/.

SAS Text Miner, http://support.sas.com/software/products/txtminer/.

Halper, F., Kaufman, M., Kirsh, D., 2013. Text Analytics: The Hurwitz Victory Index Report. Hurwitz and Associates. Available at: http://www.sas.com/news/analysts/Hurwitz_Victory_Index-TextAnalytics_SAS.PDF.

Chapter 12

Data Mining from Relationally Structured Data, Marts, and Warehouses

INTRODUCTION

Data storage is one of the fundamental uses of information technology. The simplest way to store data is in the form of a flat file, text file, spreadsheet, or table. However, many businesses have more complex relational database systems based on data structures that reflect the relations between the key data entities, using primary indexes/keys, secondary indexes, normalized data structures, and so on. This chapter discusses the concepts of data mart (DM) and data warehouse (DW) and comments on how the informational data is separated from the operational data. Then the chapter follows an example of extracting data from an operational environment into a data mart and finally into a unique file that can be used as the starting point for data mining.

Consider a unique customer data file consisting of several data columns, such as client ID, first name, last name, and volume of purchases in the last month, and which is ordered by last name in ascending alphabetical order. This file format is often the type used as input to a data analysis process. It is typically extracted from several different sources, such as a client database table, a product database table, and a sales transactions database table. In order to define the data analysis file, one or more business or operative objectives must first be established. For example, the business objective could be "to obtain a better understanding of the purchase tendencies and preferences of our customers in order to sell them more products and offer them a better service."

Hence, in practice, the business commences with several files or tables, each one containing a specific type of information. For example, file (or table) A could contain the basic customer data and file (or table) B could contain the purchase transactions made by the customers. The files must have a common index, for example, customer ID, so that they can be mutually related.

The data tends to be divided into two types: the first type represents the static data, that is, data such as name, address, telephone number, age, gender, marital status, and so on; the second data type represents the dynamic data, that is, transactional data such as date of last purchase, number of purchases in last month, products and services bought, amount spent per purchase, purchase location/channel, and so on. Thus, the company can envision that it will need some tables or files for the static data and several tables for the dynamic data. It can then interrelate all the tables using the customer ID. The process of database normalization (a series of steps taken to organize the fields and tables of a relational database to minimize redundancy and dependency and to guarantee consistency) is out of the scope of this book.

For further reading on relational database construction, see:
Devlin, Barry. 1997. *Data Warehouse: From Architecture to Implementation.* Boston, MA: Addison-Wesley Professional. ISBN-10: 0201964252.
Westerman, Paul. 2000. *Data Warehousing.* Burlington, MA: Morgan Kaufmann. ISBN-10: 155860684X.

DATA WAREHOUSE AND DATA MARTS

A data warehouse is a complete, unique, and consistent storehouse of data obtained from a variety of sources. These sources are made available to data users in a comprehensible form and in such a way as to be usable in the business context. The data in a data warehouse is different from the data in the operational environment, given that the first tends to consist of summarized data (reports, aggregations, etc.) and the second contains data that is updated on a daily basis (account transactions, customer records, etc.). A data mart can be considered as a specific type of data warehouse for a given department or business area. For example, a data warehouse could store the aggregated data of all the departments of a company (purchasing, commercial, accounting, production, logistics, human resources, etc.). But a data mart would only store the aggregated data of, for example, the commercial department, for the specific business objective of publicity campaigns and its costs and sales data.

Data Marts and Warehouses

Tools for Data Analysis

The analysis and exploitation of the data in the DW and DM use sophisticated tools, which allows for processing and visualizing multiple visions, as well as searching for complex interrelations in the data. In addition to presenting and manipulating known information in the data warehouse, new information can also be discovered. Data mining is essentially characterized by the discovery of new knowledge. Therefore, it must be distinguished from methods such as simple querying (SQL, query, and reporting), and data manipulation (OLAP, EIS), which do not add value to the data.

Figure 12.1 depicts various data sources and examples of how they can be processed to extract data files that can be used for data mining. On the upper left are the most simple data sources, consisting of spreadsheet files, flat text files, and so on. At center left is a relational database, which could be MS Access or MySQL. This relational database could contain informational data and/or operational data. On the lower left is the most sophisticated data repository, which is a data warehouse. To its right is an intermediate, more specialized data repository, or a data mart. On the right side are the forms of extraction, depending on the level of sophistication of the data source. For non-relational sources, data extraction could simply imply manual selection. For a relational database, SQL queries and/or a reporting type interface could be used. For a data mart, more sophisticated front-end tools can be assumed, such as an EIS (executive information system), OLAP (online analytical processing), and SQL queries.

Commercial EIS (Executive Information System) Tools

Functionality

Commercial EIS tools, such as Business Objects or MicroStrategy, create a level on top of the relational structure, which allows the user to create new relations, aggregations, objects, and structures in terms of the basic variables and tables. This allows a multidimensional vision of the data, displaying it in the most convenient form for the business objectives and for data extraction.

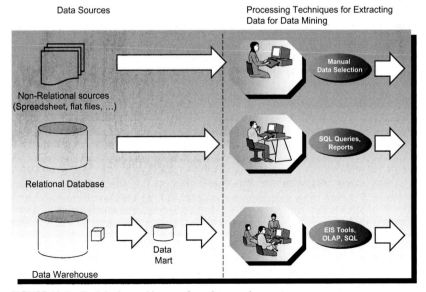

FIGURE 12.1   Exploitation architecture for a data warehouse

One of the most powerful aspects of EIS is the SQL analytical engine, which lets the user formulate complex database queries through a simple interface that manipulates business objects. The analytical engine makes this complexity transparent, eliminating the need to write SQL and executing the query in a very efficient form, which results in a high processing speed that uses the smallest amount of computer resources. Currently, EIS has become standard information technology for many businesses; however, there are many companies who still rely on simple query/reporting.

Consider the following example: the marketing department requests a new report from the IT development department. The report is complex, containing aggregates and sub-aggregates for different time periods, groups of products, departments, regions, and other criteria. The IT department says that, due to the report's complexity, they will need two weeks to prepare the report. After two weeks, the IT department informs the marketing department that the option to execute the report is now available on its screen menu. However, IT adds that it will be necessary to plan the report's execution for two o'clock in the morning, it will take two hours to run, and it will use 90 percent of the company's central computer resources.

Now consider a scenario in which the marketing department has its own EIS that is used to launch informational queries. In one afternoon, the department defines its own complex query/report with support from the IT department. The query is launched at 5:30 pm and at 5:45 it has finished. The IT department (systems) registers that the query used 5 percent of the server cluster's assigned CPUs' resources. (Some merit must also be given to improvements in hardware!)

Executive Information Systems (EIS)

Characteristics

An important characteristic of EIS and data mart is the option of defining alerts in the database that warn the user when a given set of conditions becomes true. For example, during a marketing campaign, users can automatically receive alerts relating to sales volumes, clients who are most likely to buy a given product, clients with a risk of cancelling an account, and so on. For the discussion in Chapter 10, the EIS is considered a deployment tool.

A key utility of a data warehouse/data mart is the ability to separate the informational data from the operational data. This is very important because the operational data, as the name suggests, is involved with the online real-time business operations. Hence, one must avoid making these processes go more slowly by launching heavy informational queries and/or running the risk of perturbing the content of data values that are being constantly updated. So the operational data is periodically loaded and updated into the data warehouse, and all informational processing is performed on the data warehouse. This process also has its cost overheads, due to the complexity of transforming and cleaning the data in a format that is adequate for informational needs.

The present chapter briefly considers this transfer process from the transactional or elemental files into the data warehouse/data mart. This data transfer process is often called "populating."

Data Warehouse

Data Population from the Operational Processes

Figure 12.2 outlines the data population process, from the operational data on the left to the informational system on the right. The process typically consists of three main phases: extraction, transformation, and load, which are together known as ETL. The first phase involves extracting the data from the source systems; the transformation phase then applies a series of rules or functions to the extracted data to prepare it for loading into the target system; finally, the load phase loads the data into the target system, which is typically a data warehouse or data mart. Some issues involved in the ETL processing include correcting invalid data, reassigning data values, and maintaining data integrity (primary keys, enforcing column constraints, not null constraints, and foreign key constraints).

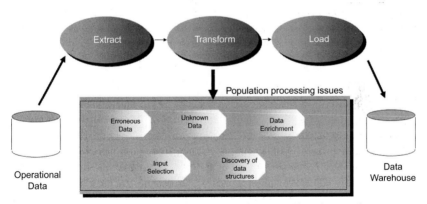

FIGURE 12.2   Schematic representation of the population process for a data warehouse

Statistical data analysis is used for the transformation phase in Figure 12.2, which has some parallels with the data mining analysis, although it is of a more elemental nature, with the standard SQL-type data processing rather than data mining processing. The objective is to guarantee the data quality and to put the data in the most adequate form for the end users who will access the business data in the data warehouse.

CREATING A FILE OR TABLE FOR DATA MINING

This section follows the steps for creating a file with a format and content adequate for data analysis, using as a basis the operational (transactions) and informational data (data warehouse or data mart). The following figures and tables illustrate this process: Tables 12.1 to 12.4 correspond to Figure 12.3, Tables 12.5 to 12.7 correspond to Figure 12.4, and Table 12.8 corresponds to Figure 12.5.

Example of the use of a relational data model as the basis for constructing a data file appropriate for analysis (1) – Operational Data

Customer Table

Customer Code	alphanumeric (10)
Company Name	alphanumerical (20)
Address	alphanumerical (64)
City	alphanumerical (20)
County	alphanumerical (20)
State	alphanumerical (20)
ZIP	alphanumerical (5)
Telephone	alphanumerical (10)
Email	alphanumerical (25)
Date Created	date (mm/dd/yyyy)
Observations	alphanumerical (255)

Sales Transactions Table

Sale Code	alphanumerical (10)
Date of Sale	date (mm/dd/yyyy)
Customer Code	alphanumerical (10)
Product Code	alphanumerical (10)
No of Units	alphanumerical (10)
Unit Price (Dollars)	numerical (10)
Total Sale Price	alphanumerical (64)
In stock (Y/N)	alphabetical (1)
Delivery Date	date (mm/dd/yyyy)
Payment Date	date (mm/dd/yyyy)

Product Category Table

Product Category	alphanumerical (10)
Description	alphanumerical (64)

Product Table

Product Code	alphanumerical (10)
Product Category	alphanumerical (10)
Name	alphanumerical (25)
Description	alphanumerical (64)
Retail Unit Price (Dollars)	numerical(10)
Observations	alphanumerical (64)

FIGURE 12.3 Operational tables of clients, products, and sales

Figure 12.3 shows the basic data and information about clients, products, and sales. The three corresponding tables are interrelated by some common IDs, such as client ID for the sales and product tables. Thus there is an indirect relationship between the client and product tables that allows them to be interrelated. The primary key of the customer table is customer code, for the product category table it is product category, for the sales transaction table it is sales code, and for the product table it is product code. The sales transaction table has two foreign keys—customer code and product code—and the product table has one foreign key, product category. Recall that a foreign key is so called because it is a primary key in another table.

Tables 12.1A and 12.1B show many basic fields that are needed for administrative purposes, such as the billing address. With respect to fields of potential data mining utility, the state, zip, and county could be used for classification (supervised) and clustering (non-supervised) purposes; in Table 12.1B, the date created tells how long this company has been a client, and the free text observations field could be processed for key words and unstructured information. Table 12.2 shows one record for each un-aggregated sales transaction, per customer and product, and Table 12.4 again shows unstructured information stored in the free text observations field.

TABLE 12.1A Customer table

Customer Code	Company Name	Address	City	County	State	ZIP
C0299202L	Metri Tech Engineering Inc	85 S Beachview Dr	Jekyll Island	Glynn	GA	31527
C0301834M	Guaranty Chevrolet Geo	500 SW Loop #-820	Fort Worth	Tarrant	TX	76115
C0187321B	Consolidated Mechanical Inc	1515 Wyoming St	Missoula	Missoula	MT	59801
C0002908X	Crain Industries	45 Church St	Stamford	Fairfield	CT	6906
C0091345L	Finkelstein, Bernard A CPA	827 E 10th Ave	Anchorage	Anchorage	AK	99501

TABLE 12.1B Customer table

Telephone	Email	Date Created	Observations
912-635-3866	emery@reek.com	03/21/2008	Payment at 30 days, deliveries to 131, Riverview Avenue
817-921-5560	bert@schadle.com	01/01/1997	VIP customer
406-728-0501	marietta@bjornberg.com	04/12/2010	New customer
203-359-2824	brent@vaidya.com	05/12/2009	Urgent delivery
907-277-9294	rich@gleave.com	11/21/2009	

TABLE 12.2 Sales transaction table

Sale Code	Date of Sale	Customer Code	Product Code	Number of Units	Unit Price (Dollars)	Total Sale Price (Dollars)	In Stock (Y/N)	Delivery Date	Payment Date
V003125/12	04/18/2014	C0299202L	P2510	5	35.5	177.5	Y	04/20/2014	05/18/2014
V003125/13	04/18/2014	C0299202L	P2520	10	22.70	227	Y	04/20/2014	05/18/2014
V003125/14	04/18/2014	C0299202L	P2530	10	33.85	338.5	Y	04/20/2014	05/18/2014
V003125/15	04/18/2014	C0299202L	P2550	2	122.35	244.7	Y	04/20/2014	05/18/2014
V003091/62	04/18/2014	C0301834M	P2510	10	35.5	355	Y	04/20/2014	05/18/2014

TABLE 12.3 Product category table

Product Category	Description
AUTOMOBILE	Automobile Accessories
MOTORCYCLE	Motorcycle Accessories
TRUCK	Truck Components
AGRICULTURE	Agricultural Vehicle Components
WIND	Wind Turbine Components

TABLE 12.4 Product table

Product Code	Product Category	Name	Description	Retail Unit Price (Dollars)	Observations
P2510	AUTOMOBILE	Goodyear Tires Eagle GT	Goodyear Tires Eagle GT	35.50	Offer of 10% discount for preferred clients until 10/31
P2510	TRUCK	Tail Lamp	Tail Lamp	22.70	Supplier also sells indicators, markers, license lamps, & warning triangles
P2510	TRUCK	Head Lamp	Head Lamp	33.85	
P2510	MOTORCYCLE	Leather Seat Covers	Leather Seat Covers	150.20	High grade leather upholstery
P2510	AUTOMOBILE	Exhaust Silencer	Exhaust Silencer	122.35	

Figure 12.4 shows the informational version of the data shown in Figure 12.3, and whose differences are that it contains aggregated data about the number of products, units, sales, and aggregates for different periods (year, quarter, and month). Given that the calculations are already made in terms of the reports that the company's management requires, it is much easier and faster to produce these

Example of the use of a relational data model as the basis for constructing a data file appropriate for analysis (2) –Informational Data

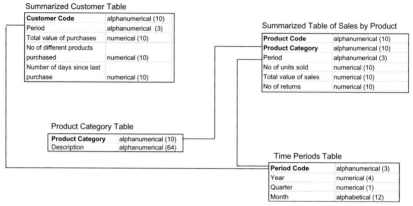

FIGURE 12.4   Informational tables of client purchases, product sales aggregated by different time periods and product categories

reports. Also, this reduces the possibility of errors, given that the reports are derived from data consolidated and filtered from the operational tables. The primary key of the summarized customer table is customer code, for the product category table it is product category, for the summarized table of sales by product it is product code, and for the time periods table it is period code. Also, the summarized customer table has one foreign key (period), and the summarized table of sales by product has two foreign keys (product category and period).

Table 12.5 shows aggregated data for each customer and time period (which is assumed to be the second quarter of the year in Table 12.7). Table 12.5 contains CRM metrics, such as number of different products purchased and number of days since last purchase, which give indicators of diversity and latency, respectively. Likewise, in Table 12.6 product data is aggregated for each product and period (second quarter). One CRM indicator included is number of returns, which gives information about quality relative to units sold.

TABLE 12.5 Summarized customer table

Customer Code	Period	Total Value of Purchases	Number of Different Products Purchased	Number of Days Since Last Purchase
C0299202L	2	3500.12	4	5
C0301834M	2	7214.90	35	10
C0187321B	2	650.45	1	25
C0002908X	2	22,456.22	125	0
C0091345L	2	31,791.78	7	1

TABLE 12.6 Summarized table of sales by product

Product Code	Product Category	Period	Number of Units Sold	Total Value of Sales	Number of Returns
P2510	AUTOMOBILE	002	450	15,975	18
P2520	TRUCK	002	2250	51,075	5
P2530	TRUCK	002	1500	50,775	150
P2540	MOTORCYCLE	002	100	15,020	102
P2550	AUTOMOBILE	002	500	61,175	30

TABLE 12.7 Time periods table

Period Code	Year	Quarter	Month
002	2014	1	March
002	2014	2	April
002	2014	2	May
002	2014	2	June
002	2014	3	July

Example of the use of a relational data model as the basis for constructing a data file appropriate for analysis (3) -File extracted for analysis

Historical Table of Clients and Products

Customer Code	alphanumerical (10)
Period	numerical (10)
Total value of purchases	numerical (10)
No of different products purchased	numerical (10)
Number of days since last purchase	numerical (10)
Product Code	alphanumerical (10)
Product Category	alphanumerical (10)
No of units sold	numerical (10)
Total value of sales	numerical (10)
No of returns	numerical (10)

FIGURE 12.5   Unique historical table prepared for data analysis and modeling

TABLE 12.8 Historical table of clients and products

Customer Code	Period	Total Value of Purchases	Number of Different Products Purchased	Number of Days Since Last Purchase	Product Code	Product Category	Number of Units Sold	Total Value of Sales	Number of Returns
C0299202L	2	3500.12	4	5	P2510	AUTOMOBILE	450	15,975	18
C0299202L	2	3500.12	4	5	P2520	TRUCK	2250	51,075	5
C0299202L	2	3500.12	4	5	P2530	TRUCK	1500	50,775	150
C0299202L	2	3500.12	4	5	P2550	AUTOMOBILE	500	61,175	30
C0301834M	2	7214.90	35	10	P2510	AUTOMOBILE	450	15,975	18

Lastly, Figure 12.5 shows the data format that can be used for analysis and modeling. It represents one unique data file/table with the variables preselected for their relevance to the business objectives and for their reliability. There are also derived variables, such as number of days since last purchase, and others that are the same as the ones in the operational tables, such as customer code and product code. However, this file is just the starting point for deriving new factors with a greater descriptive capacity, and some of the variables will later be eliminated in preference to others of greater relevance. Also, depending on the defined business objectives, distinct operational and derived variables could be chosen for inclusion in the data mart in Figure 12.5.

Extracting a File for Data Mining

End Product of Data Transformation Process

Table 12.8 is the end product of the data transformation process; the first seven columns refer to the customer, whereas the last three refer to the product. In this way the customer data can be related with the product data and possible interrelations analyzed. The combination in Table 12.8 could respond to a business objective such as a customer retention model: customers with a high value for number of days since last purchase and for number of returns could be at risk of not renewing their orders. However, this is not the only possible combination of variables, and others could be chosen depending on the business objective.

In conclusion, observe that the steps followed in this chapter do not necessarily require a large computer infrastructure and could be performed on a laptop using an Access or a MySQL database to define the relational tables and a spreadsheet to process the data.

Chapter 13

CRM – Customer Relationship Management and Analysis

INTRODUCTION

The area of CRM (Customer Relationship Management) has attracted a lot of attention, and many businesses who are end users of IT solutions have spent considerable amounts of money on implementing CRM systems integrated to a greater or lesser extent with their operational and business processes. However, what should be kept in mind is that CRM is a basic, commonsense idea that can be put into practice with nothing more than a spreadsheet and a modest database.

This chapter introduces the reader to CRM in terms of recency, frequency, and latency of customer activity, and in terms of the client life cycle: capturing new clients, potentiating and retaining existing clients, and winning back ex-clients. The chapter then discusses the relation of data analysis to each of the CRM phases and considers customer satisfaction and integrated CRM systems. Next, it briefly describes the characteristics of commercial CRM software products, and finally, the chapter examines example screens and functionality from a simple CRM application.

CRM METRICS AND DATA COLLECTION

Any street-smart small businessperson has always kept a tally of two or three key statistics about the business's customers. For example, "Who comes most often to my shop?" and "Who came most recently?" These are the concepts that are the essence of CRM or KYC (know your customers): frequency and recency. A third key concept is latency, that is, the time period between purchases. Latency takes into account the sales cycle, which, of course, depends on what the business sells. The customer of a shoe store may buy one pair of shoes every 12 months, whereas the customer of a candy store may go in to buy candy every other day. However, consider the following: a shoe store client buys one pair of shoes from the same store every year for five years running; then two years pass when the customer doesn't come to buy any new shoes. What can be concluded? Well, it may be that the (ex) customer has gone and bought shoes from another store. In the case of the candy store, maybe after a period of two weeks without a visit, the store owner could start to get worried.

From an information technology point of view, historical data can be accumulated about customers, which relates the number of clients with the product or service bought, quantity, date of purchase, and (if desired), hour of purchase. This historical data can then be assembled into a unique file or table. On the other hand, it is assumed that the business already has a customer table (client ID, client name, etc.) and a table of products and services (product ID, product name, price, etc.).

The business then has three tables/files that contain, respectively, (i) historical data of commercial activity, (ii) customer data, and (iii) data about the products and services. Thus, the business already has a small data mart with the minimum necessary information to be able to analyze its customers. Using these three tables, the company can extract into a flat file/table or spreadsheet the data that it is interested in — such as all the purchases made in March — which can then be analyzed.

CUSTOMER LIFE CYCLE

Following on from recency, frequency, and latency, another key concept of CRM is the customer life cycle. This can be defined as simply as: new client, current client, and ex-client. This idea can be made use of by maximizing the acquisition of new clients, potentiating the sales to actual clients, minimizing the loss of clients, and trying to recover ex-clients. All of this is carried out while keeping in mind customer profitability. Therefore, there needs to be a way of measuring the profitability of clients in order to select new clients based on this criteria (most profitable) and avoid wasting resources on the least profitable ones.

Related to the customer life cycle is the concept of customer loyalty. A customer is loyal to a company or brand if purchases are always bought from this company and not from another. It is clear that there can be different grades of loyalty, given that an individual may buy some products or services from company A and buy other products from companies B and C who are A's competitors in the same sector. The grade of loyalty tends to be relative to the sector and the type of product or service. For example, in general, television viewers don't tend to be very loyal to a given channel, because in general they follow specific programs rather than the channel itself. And it's very easy to change channels! (Pay channels are a different matter.) On the other hand, bank customers who have a mortgage find it more difficult to change banks and tend to acquire other products from the same entity. The objective of data analysis in this context is to detect tendencies that indicate possible changes in a customer's loyalty and take *a priori* preventive actions to avoid losing the customer to the competition. Such actions could be, for example, to personally contact the client by telephone, email, or post, and give notice of some special offer, discount, etc. The grade of loyalty could also be quantified with an index, calculated for each client.

One aspect that leads into the field of analytical CRM is that of customer segmentation. The idea of segmentation is essentially simple, and it existed long before computers came onto the scene: depending on one or more criteria, the totality of customers is divided into groups in which the customers are similar. For example, one criterion could be profitability, which could be defined in three ranges: high (75–100), medium (25–75), and low (0–25). The profitability can be calculated for each customer, using whatever formula is most adequate, and which gives as the result an index between 0 and 100, where 100 indicates maximum profitability. Then, depending on the calculated value, each client is placed in one of the three groups, high, medium or low, and *voilà*!

Customer Relationship Management

Selection Criteria for Campaign Targets

Modern marketing methods use multiple criteria to group clients, target campaigns, and publicity messages for products and services. For example, age is a criterion that is often used. This is an important criterion, and the message can vary greatly depending on whether the target individual is an adolescent, a middle-aged mother with kids, or a retired person. Other key criteria are gender and area of residence (large city, medium-sized town, etc.) and, within the city, the zip code, which can identify an area as affluent, poor, residential, and so on. These criteria are relatively easy to obtain if clients complete a simple registration form when they acquire a product or service. Other types of criteria exist that are specific to what is sold, which may be useful, but which also may be more difficult to obtain, such as information about occupation, income level, number of kids, and so on. For companies that sell insurance or bank products, this kind of data about its customers is easier to obtain.

Figure 13.1 shows a general vision of the phases in the life of a business's clients. There are two major groups: new clients and clients/ex-clients. The company should focus on new clients who are most desirable for its line of business. This means defining these clients in terms of their profiles, and then designing and executing campaigns to capture them via different communication channels. Moving right across the figure, it can be seen that, once a client is obtained (he or she bought something), then that client must be developed, meaning products and services should be offered that are complementary with what the client has already bought and/or what is most recommendable for that customer's profile. Finally, on the right of the figure is the ex-client category. This category might represent a dynamic environment, given that customer loyalty can be won back by appropriate actions, such as understanding why a customer has gone to the competition. It is often said that it is cheaper, in terms of time and effort, to win back an ex-client than to find a new one. However, the best tactic is to avoid losing clients in the first place; this is done by keeping

Phases in the life of clients

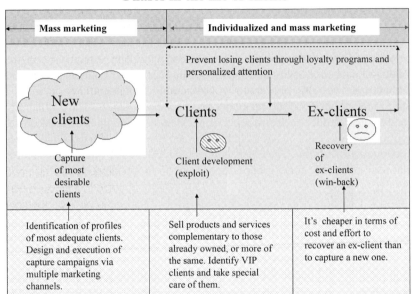

FIGURE 13.1 Phases in the client life cycle and appropriate actions for each phase

them satisfied with competitive pricing and quality and keeping in touch with them via loyalty programs and personalized attention.

Another type of data that can be used to segment customers is in terms of the products and services that each client has bought, that is, their business transactions. Typical variables are type of product/service acquired, value, date/day/ hour of purchase, frequency of purchase, time since last purchase (recency), time between purchases (latency), and so on.

But how can a business make use of all these variables and segments? By returning to the customer life cycle, a company can determine which products and services are most adequate for which customer profile, and when the most opportune moment is to offer them.

EXAMPLE: RETAIL BANK

Consider an example from the banking sector, although the idea can be generalized to almost any sector. The bank has a new customer (defined as having been a client for less than three months) who is a single female between 18 and 30 years of age, lives in Manhattan, and has opened an account where she will deposit her salary. Perhaps the first product the bank can offer her is a credit card (Visa, etc.), if she doesn't have one already. Why? Because people in this age group tend to spend a lot on things like clothes and going out to bars, restaurants, cinemas, theater, and so on. Also, this client lives in an affluent part of the city (Manhattan). Once she becomes more established (depending on her age, or whether she gets married), the bank could offer her products such as a general savings account, a savings account for purchasing a property, a mortgage, a loan to buy an automobile, and so on. Products that the bank would probably not offer this client, at least initially, include a pension plan, life or medical insurance, and stock investment products, although this last product would also depend on the client's wealth and solvency more than just on her age.

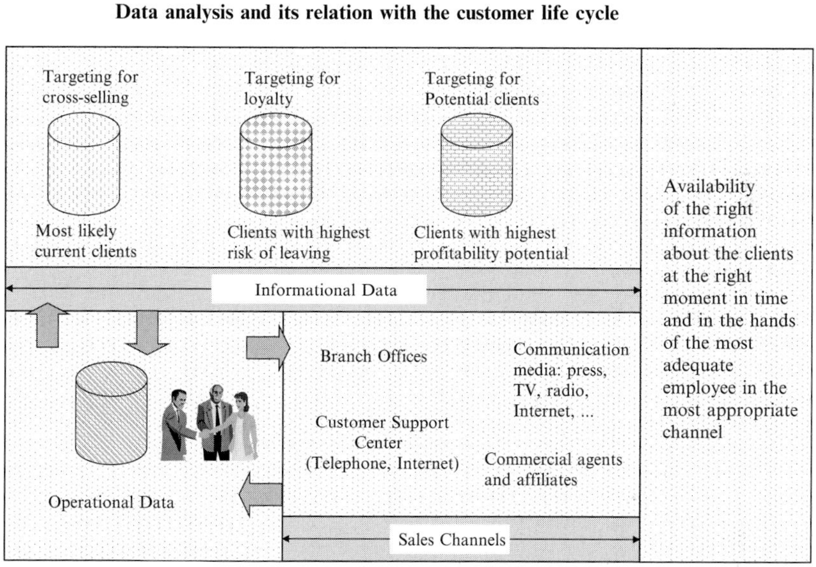

Data analysis and its relation with the customer life cycle

FIGURE 13.2   Data analysis and its relation with the customer life cycle

Figure 13.2 shows a general scheme of various data analysis business objectives with the customer life cycle seen in Figure 13.1 and the data marts from Chapter 12. Each of the targeting data bases can be considered as functions of a data mart that accesses the informational data layer in the center of Figure 13.2. Recall that, for each campaign, a subset (a target group) has been selected so as to optimize effort and focus only on the top category of clients in each case: those most likely to become clients, those with most risk of leaving, and those with most potential for earning more revenue. Below the informational layer of data is seen the operational database on the lower left and sources of incoming data and information from business activities on the lower right. Of course, a key requirement for analytical CRM is that the right data and information from the business processes are captured and fed into the IT system in a timely way.

INTEGRATED CRM SYSTEMS

In recent years, companies have invested in CRM systems that become integrated with many of the other business processes in their organizations. The development and installation of this kind of system, for example, unifying a telephone/Internet call center with a data capture system that feeds into a large client database, can be expensive and complex. But the system can retrieve client data from the database and make it available to the sales and customer service staff, which will give them greater success in their commercial dealings with clients. Commercial systems such as Siebel, PeopleSoft, and Genesys are parametrizable standard systems that integrate databases such as Oracle and DB2 with customer service centers, sales force, telemarketing, telesales, and so on. The systems tend to be modular, consisting of a base module with optional modules for report design and generation, wireless communications, and campaign management, among others.

> **Customer Relationship Management**
>
> *Call Centers*
>
> Some customer service centers offer service twenty-four hours a day, seven days a week, with human operators with agreeable voices and empathy toward clients. Some systems have been completely or partially automated as an alternative to the human operator. Using a voice recognition system based on keywords ("please state your ID number," "please state your city of residence," etc.), the interlocutor is guided with easy-to-reply-to questions.

CRM Application Software

There are many different CRM application software systems currently available, from low-cost personal computer programs to corporate solutions, such as Salesforce (http://www.salesforce.com/assets/pdf/misc/BP_SalesManagers .pdf). There are also "cloud" service solutions, such as Microsoft CRM (http://www.microsoft.com/en-us/dynamics/default.aspx). However, in general, these systems do not contain true data mining functions by default (as do the data mining models presented in this book), and probably require significant customization in order to integrate more advanced capabilities.

The following section briefly runs through the functionality of the Salesforce CRM. According to the vendor, this application has the following main capabilities: decision support (prioritizing customer issues, training for new sales people, forecasting, providing on-demand reports), dashboards (EIS-style interfaces to key indicators with emphasis on use of color codes), trending analysis and benchmarking (using reports and dashboards to show long-term business goals and key performance indicators), lead/opportunity management analysis (classification and qualification of leads), and activity management analysis (ensuring that biggest deals and highest priority customers receive the most attention). According to the vendor, the forecasting capability includes algorithmic modeling and uses probabilities; however, forecasting is dependent on sales people correctly assigning the commercial lead pipeline categories. The sales pipeline has nine major categories: prospecting, qualification, needs analysis, value proposition, identify decision makers, perception analysis, proposal/price quote, negotiation/review, and closed/won. Each category is assigned a default probability of success for the sale. For example, prospecting is assigned 10 percent; identify decision makers, 60 percent; negotiation, 90 percent; and closed/won, 100 percent. Hence, as the pipeline stages progress, the probability of sale success increases.

The overall mission of the application is to provide a system that shows key information at a glance for sales personnel and commercial management. (See http://www.salesforce.com for more details, screenshots, and so on.)

CUSTOMER SATISFACTION

To complete this chapter, a key aspect that affects the business must be mentioned: customer satisfaction. This can be a very influential factor in a customer's loyalty and can be a source of new customers via favorable references. In order to obtain information and data about customers' degree of satisfaction, the easiest way is to ask them—directly, if they are accessible, or via feedback questionnaires sent by post or from the business's website. The customer service department itself can be a mine of information, as well. This department is the company's interface for returned goods, complaints, and occasionally, letters of gratitude. IT systems play a key role in attending to customer problems and queries (as well as the interpersonal skills of employees) by giving informational support for a rapid solution. It is important to avoid delays when attending to customers, be it due to inefficiency in the administrative circuits, or due to a lack of resources.

Again, it is evident that a business can accumulate statistics about products, services, sales channels, and regions in terms of the number of complaints, returned goods, and so on. In order to capture feedback data about the quality of service or about products, the business can design a questionnaire and send it to customers, with some incentive for them to return it duly completed. In this way, the business can identify which of its regional offices are excellent and which are in need of attention. Of course, the company also needs to have previously defined what is meant by an acceptable level of service or product quality. For example, the best level for returned goods is, of course, zero percent. Feedback about defects identified by clients is a valuable source of information for the production and research and development departments and can be used to make corrections to the product or service.

EXAMPLE CRM APPLICATION

The following section runs through the basic functionality of a simple CRM application: its overall structure, customer record definition, campaign definition, action definition, campaign management, client action history, commercial activity indicators, and graphics. This system allows a business to capture and process essential customer prospection activity and combines data about customers with the day-to-day activities of the company's commercial infrastructure. More advanced features relating to data mining techniques, such as customer segmentation and predictive models for ranking customers by purchase likelihood, will also be discussed. (These advanced features would probably not be included as standard in a CRM system and would require customization.)

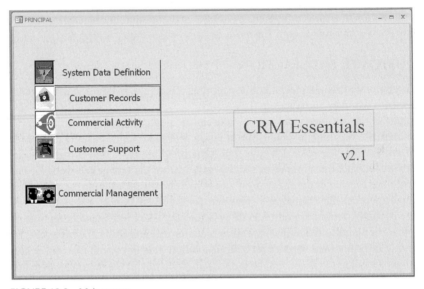

FIGURE 13.3   Main screen

Figure 13.3 shows the main screen, which gives access to the five principal modules of the application: system data definition, customer records, commercial activity, customer support, and commercial management.

Figure 13.4 shows the customer record management screen. The data fields on the left define the client company data and those on the right are for contacts for the company. In addition to basic data such as address, telephone, fax, email, and so on, there is specific CRM information such as the origin of the contact and the type of client. Knowing where the contact came from enables the business to accumulate statistics about which contact channels, media, and marketing campaigns are giving the best results. The classification for client type can be given in terms of the CRM life cycle: new client, cross-sell, win-back, and so on. There is a risk checkbox that detects clients at risk of going to the competition or cancelling their contracts; it could be assigned by a data mining process.

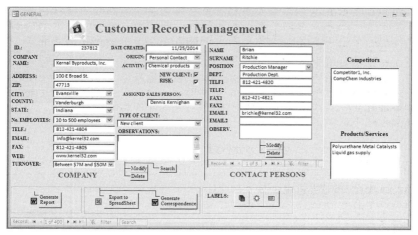

FIGURE 13.4   General customer record

Unstructured information about the company and/or the contact people can be added in the free-text observation fields. For example, it could be noted that one of the contact people plays golf at such-and-such a club and has a scratch handicap or studied for an MBA at a given business school. Potentially useful pieces of information that are not included in this screen are the recency, frequency, and latency factors discussed earlier in the chapter: that is, time since the last purchase, number of purchases by the client over a given time period, and the average time between purchases. This information could be included in the customer record screen, or it could be derived from the client historical actions data. Finally, along the bottom of Figure 13.4 are displayed auxiliary functions that facilitate data processing and communication with the client: a report generator, an Excel/Outlook interface, a FAX/letter generator, and labels for postal campaigns.

Customer Relationship Management

Personalized Treatment

One thing a customer likes is personalized treatment — to be treated as if that person were the only customer. Personalized treatment requires knowing about customers: remembering things about them, their preferences, likes, dislikes, how much money they are prepared to spend, and so on. All this information can be stored in a CRM and accessed by a sales person before seeing the customer again or accessed dynamically online when a call center agent has a customer on the phone.

Figure 13.5 shows the screen that allows the user to define a target group of clients for a marketing campaign. The target group can be selected

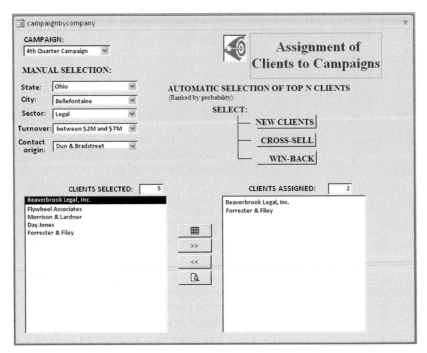

FIGURE 13.5 Assigning clients to campaigns

automatically, manually, or by a combination of the two. Clients are manually filtered and selected from the complete client base using the criteria on the top left of the figure, which causes the data to appear in the "clients selected" area on the lower left. The clients can then be manually assigned to the "assigned clients" area on the lower right. For the 4th Quarter Campaign, the sales person is interested in selecting clients from Bellefontaine, Ohio, who are in the legal sector, have a turnover of between $2 million and $7 million, and for whom the origin of the contact was the Dun & Bradstreet commercial database. Applying these criteria as filters has produced a list of five companies, seen on the lower left. The user has, for the moment, assigned two of those contacts to the campaign, as seen on the lower right.

Alternatively, the salesperson can click on one of the three buttons on the top right to generate a list of the top N (assigned by the user) clients ranked by a probability generated by a predictive model (for example, a neural network). Clicking on the topmost button, "new clients," will generate a list of the top N new clients ranked by probability. This list will then appear in the "clients selected" area on the lower left. Finally, the user can pass all of these clients directly over to the "clients assigned" area or select manually from the list by, for example, choosing a subset based on geographical area.

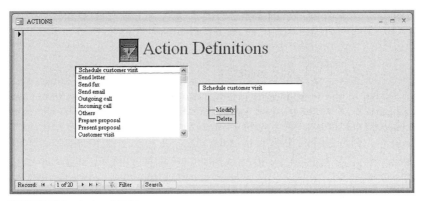

FIGURE 13.6   Action definitions

Figure 13.6 shows the basic screen for defining all the possible actions that a commercial agent or call center agent can perform with respect to a client. These are the action labels that will be assigned in the commercial activity data. It is recommended that this list be carefully defined so as to correctly reflect the most habitual actions carried out by the sales force, and with names everybody recognizes and understands.

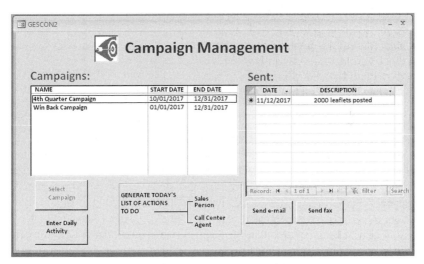

FIGURE 13.7   Campaign management

Figure 13.7 shows the campaign management screen. Once the target has been defined (using the screen seen in Figure 13.5), global actions can be performed with the assigned customer list, such as a mass mailing of a publicity leaflet, a systematic telephone campaign, an email campaign, and so on. On the right of the screen the date of a global action and its description can be entered. This screen also has important functionality for individual commercial agents to document and keep track of their activity. Clicking on the Enter Daily Activity button allows a sales rep or call center agent to enter the daily activity. Also, the rep or agent can generate a list of "to-do" actions using the icons at the bottom center.

Once a significant amount of commercial activity data has been accumulated, the data can be consulted using the screens shown in Figures 13.8, 13.9, and 13.10. Note that the "client historical actions" information shown in Figure 13.8 could be used by an individual salesperson or by the sales manager; the statistics and graphics screens in Figures 13.9 and 13.10 would probably be accessible only by the sales manager. Figure 13.10 shows a typical dashboard display for key business information: pipeline of sales leads (top right), indicator of objectives completed (bottom right), "slice & dice" of pipeline by business sector (bottom left), and client segmentation in terms of profitability (top left). The term 'slice & dice' refers to a systematic reduction

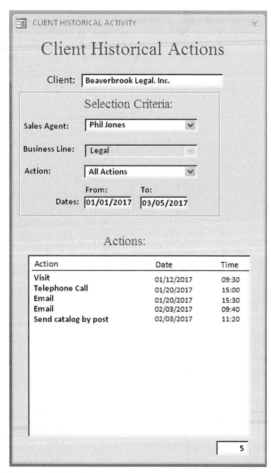

FIGURE 13.8 Client historical actions

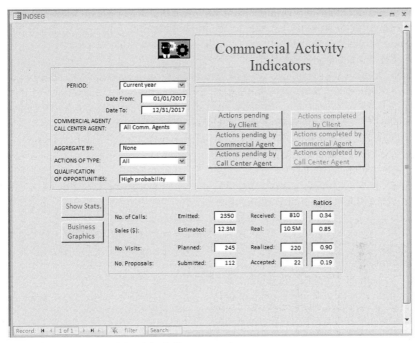

FIGURE 13.9   Commercial activity indicators

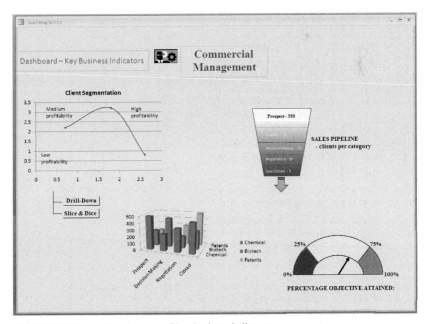

FIGURE 13.10   Dashboard screen of key business indicators

of a body of data into smaller parts or views that will provide more specific information. It also refers to the presentation of information in a variety of different ways.

For further reading, see:

Dyché, J., 2001. *The CRM Handbook: A Business Guide to Customer Relationship Management.* Addison-Wesley: Boston, MA, ISBN: 0201730626.

Novo, J., 2004. *Drilling Down – Turning Customer Data into Profits with a Spreadsheet*, third ed. Jim Novo, St. Petersburg, FL, ISBN: 1591135192. www.jimnovo.com.

Chapter 14

Analysis of Data on the Internet I – Website Analysis and Internet Search

Note: This chapter is available on the companion website: http://booksite. elsevier.com/9780124166028.

ABSTRACT

This is the first of four chapters that deal with the analysis of data on the Internet and in an online environment. This chapter gives an introduction to website analysis and Internet search using two contrasting case studies: first, the chapter discusses how to analyze the transactional data from customer visits to a business's website, and second, it explores how Internet search can be used as a market research tool. The examples serve to illustrate how the Internet can be used as a tool for individual marketing, mass marketing, and marketing sentiment surveys. The examples also illustrate the following two business objectives: (i) analyzing activity on a website to adapt the website's commercial offering at both the general and individual levels, and (ii) gathering commercial information on the Internet from a diversity of sources in order to analyze and understand the marketplace. From a data mining perspective (and recalling the data sources in Chapter 3), throughout this chapter the Internet could be considered as a meta data source born from a company's Internet presence. Following each case study, details are given of which technical techniques are relevant and which software applications could be used for the examples.

CHAPTER OUTLINE

Chapter 15

Analysis of Data on the Internet II – Search Experience Analysis

Note: This chapter is available on the companion website: http://booksite. elsevier.com/9780124166028.

ABSTRACT

This is the second of four chapters dealing with the analysis of data on the Internet and the online environment. This chapter gives an in-depth insight into the Internet's structure and how users search the web. The first section considers basic ideas about the Internet and Internet search categories. The second section follows an example of processing, analyzing, and modeling a user search log in order to evaluate the search experience quality of a business's users (customers, employees, etc.).

CHAPTER OUTLINE

Chapter 16

Analysis of Data on the Internet III – Online Social Network Analysis

Note: This chapter is available on the companion website: http://booksite. elsevier.com/9780124166028.

ABSTRACT

This is the third of four chapters dealing with the analysis of data on the Internet and the online environment. This chapter gives an insight into the analysis of online social networks (OSNs). Throughout the chapter the exploitation of information for commercial use is addressed and a selection of references for OSN analysis application tools is given.

CHAPTER OUTLINE

Chapter 17

Analysis of Data on the Internet IV – Search Trend Analysis over Time

Note: This chapter is available on the companion website: http://booksite. elsevier.com/9780124166028.

ABSTRACT

This is the fourth and final chapter dealing with the analysis of data on the Internet and the online environment. This chapter gives an insight into how to analyze search keyword tendencies over time using the Google Trends application. The chapter is divided into two main sections. The first section examines practical examples from Google Trends, showing the changing frequencies of Internet search terms over time. Then a classification of four major trend types is defined, using real-world examples of search terms for each tendency type. The second section follows the processing of the trend data, defining a set of descriptive factors for the time series, and then applying a clustering technique and a predictive modeling technique to classify the example query trends into one of the four categories defined in the first section. There are comments throughout the chapter on how the information can be exploited for commercial uses, such as Internet marketing and brand and sentiment analysis.

CHAPTER OUTLINE

Chapter 18

Data Privacy and Privacy-Preserving Data Publishing

INTRODUCTION

This chapter discusses "the other side of the coin" to data mining—which is not often dealt with in data mining books—namely, data privacy and privacy-preserving data publishing. The chapter first considers how some popular Internet applications deal with data privacy, followed by a brief look at some of the legal aspects. Then it looks at "privacy-preserving data publishing," which is perhaps the area of most concern for data miners: concepts, anonymization techniques, and document sanitization.

Data mining is performed on collected data, so first, the dataset obtained for analysis must be verified as being legal; that is, having being obtained within the law. For example, consider that an analyst has a dataset of records with details of user search histories on the Internet or user profiles and activity from an online social network. If the analyst works for a search engine company and the records belong to that search engine company, or if the analyst works for an OSN provider and the records are of the users of that OSN, then one might think that no wrong would be done by using those records. But if the analyst works for another company, that is, a third party, and has obtained the same dataset, what would one now think? Disclosure control to third parties is a key issue in Internet usage privacy.

Another aspect of privacy is the tracking of activity by application providers, for example, by using cookies to obtain personal information and tendencies about individual users, such as specific websites they visit and things they search for.

> **Data Privacy**
>
> *Financial and Medical Data*
>
> Two key domains that are considered especially private relate to financial and medical data. For financial data, the unauthorized access to personal account details, credit card numbers, asset details, debts, and so on, can open the door to identity theft, fraud, or theft of money from an account. Medical data can reveal undesired personal information such as specific illnesses and medical or psychological conditions.

By using mobile phones and devices that incorporate geolocation function-ality, OSN users can know exactly where their friends are at a given moment. However, users may be unaware that an application is tracking their move-ments. Also, analyzing the historical data of OSN users' movements may reveal undesirable or personal information that the user does not want in the public domain.

Table 18.1 shows an example of what may be considered non-confidential data, such as age and zip code, and what may be considered confidential data, such as salary and illness details.

TABLE 18.1 Example of confidential and non-confidential data

Non-Confidential		Confidential	
Age	*Zip*	*Salary*	*Illnesses*
25	ABC	$25,250	Diabetes
35	ABC	$40,938	AIDS
70	QE2	$0	Deafness
50	QE1	$75,400	None

One of the dangers in data mining is inadvertently cross-linking datasets from different ambits that may disclose private information about individuals. Also, public and private organizations, such as the tax office, police department, local government, central government, insurance companies, and medical orga-nizations, among others, have the potential for cross-referencing an individual's data records, which, as a consequence, form an unnecessarily complete picture of that individual. The result could constitute a legal infraction of civil rights and/or be potentially dangerous if the information falls into the wrong hands.

POPULAR APPLICATIONS AND DATA PRIVACY

In recent years, major application providers, such as Google and Facebook, have put a privacy policy in place for their users. This policy includes incor-porating functionality into the application that allows users to control which of their data is in the public domain.

On Google's main search page, the lower part of the screen may display a declaration similar to: "Cookies allow us to offer our services. If you use our services, you accept how we use the cookies. <Accept> <More information>." Some of the services cited include: remembering preferences for SafeSearch, augmenting the relevance of the publicity you are shown, counting the number of visits received to access a given web page, and helping in registration for services and data protection. However, identifiers such as IP addresses, mobile device IDs, and details about a user's computer may also be captured during user sessions.

Google states that it does not share a user's personal data with companies or organizations outside of Google, but there are detailed exceptions, such as: when a user gives specific consent, or when Google considers there is a reasonable need to access the data by a company, organization, or specific person who doesn't work for Google. An exceptional or reasonable need would be, for example, a legal reason, in light of suspected fraud or crime. For more detailed information about privacy on Google, see www.google.com/policies/privacy.

Facebook's official privacy information page covers the following topics: the information Facebook receives and how it is used; how content is shared; how people find one another; privacy configurations that allow users to control their information; social plug-ins and information-sharing in games, applications, and websites that users and their friends may use outside of Facebook; how publicity announcements and sponsored content work; how publicity works without sharing user information with sponsors; and how publicity is matched with a user's social context, cookies, and pixels.

When a user registers on Facebook, the basic information gathered to create the account is the user's email, date of birth, and gender. Facebook states that the date of birth (and therefore the age) is a key piece of data used to offer the right services, publicity, and so on, to each user. Again, the IP address, mobile device, and computer details can also be captured during user sessions. Once a user starts creating content, uploading photos, and so on, the user can specify who can see this information, choosing between public, friends, and custom. The custom option allows a user to specify which individuals or groups of individuals can see which content. This can also be specified when a user writes something on his or her wall. A user can deactivate or delete the account. If an account is deleted, Facebook claims that some information may remain in the application for a maximum of 90 days after deletion; however, it is usually completely deleted within a month. For more detailed information about privacy on Facebook, see: https://www.facebook.com/about/privacy.

Searching on the Internet is usually performed using a web browser, such as Mozilla Firefox or Microsoft's Internet Explorer. Figure 18.1 shows Mozilla Firefox's information page referring to privacy and security. Options are included that allow the user to specify privacy settings for such things as managing search history, storing cookies for tracking, controlling pop-up publicity banners and windows, and so on. The user can define the configuration by choosing the Tools option from the main menu, then Options, then selecting the Privacy and Security tabs.

Under the Privacy tab, the tracking setting allows the user to prevent tracking and to not allow preferences to be stored by websites. The user can also block the recording of forms and download, search, and navigation information. Cookies can be completely blocked, but many applications will not work

FIGURE 18.1   Mozilla Firefox privacy and security information

properly if this is done, so the normal option is to allow cookies until Firefox closes and then Firefox will delete them. A user can also specify that Firefox automatically delete the history each time it closes.

Under the security tab, options are available to notify the user when a website tries to install components, to allow the user to block websites reported as hostile or fake, and to set password storage options. The simplest security measure is to specify that Firefox delete everything every time the user closes the browser. Then, if the user completes a transaction that involves filling in personal details in a form, or performs a transaction on a bank's website, the information will not remain on the user's computer for other applications to pick up.

Internet Explorer has similar options accessed by the Tools, Internet Options page of the upper menu. Internet Options has two tabs, Privacy and Security. Internet Explorer takes a slightly different approach to its Security options from that of Firefox. IE allows the user to specify default levels, defined as low, medium, high, and so on, which offer progressively stricter security levels. Also, an InPrivate session can be established, where the privacy options are predefined. The Content tab allows the user to filter out explicit content (e.g., parental controls), defines the use of the secure sockets layer (SSL) identification certificates for secure transactions (such as online purchases, bank transactions, and so on), and activates/deactivates the auto-complete option for web page forms. Finally, a user's home modem can occasionally be reset (switched off, turned on) so that the IP address is dynamically reassigned, which can throw off the "scent" any "sniffers" who may be interested in the user's IP address.

LEGAL ASPECTS – RESPONSIBILITY AND LIMITS

About 80 countries have some form of data protection legislation, which varies greatly from one country to another. The major legal points are as follows: for all data collected there should be a stated purpose; information collected about a person cannot be disclosed to other organizations or individuals (third parties) without legal authorization or that person's consent; the data kept about a person should be accurate and up to date; mechanisms should exist to allow people to access and check the accuracy of the data stored about them; data should be deleted when it is no longer required for the original purpose it was captured for; the transmission of personal data to third party organizations with inferior data protection to the current organization is prohibited; and the collection of sensitive data such as sexual orientation or religious beliefs is prohibited unless there exists an exceptional reason to do so.

Additional sources of information on the legal aspects of data privacy are as follows:

- Unesco Chair in Data Privacy: http://unescoprivacychair.urv.cat/
- European Commission – Justice – Personal Protection of Data: http://ec.europa.eu/justice/data-protection/index_en.htm
- Electronic Privacy Information Center – Privacy Laws by State (US): http://epic.org/privacy/consumer/states.html
- Wikipedia – Information Privacy Law: http://en.wikipedia.org/wiki/Information_ privacy_law
- Wikipedia – Information Privacy (general): http://en.wikipedia.org/wiki/Information_privacy

PRIVACY-PRESERVING DATA PUBLISHING

Privacy-preserving data publishing considers the processing necessary to make a dataset safe enough to publish it in the public domain or distribute it to third parties. Some basic concepts of data privacy will first be discussed, followed by a look at some of the most common techniques used to anonymize various types of data. Finally, the associated topic of document sanitization is addressed.

Privacy Concepts

This section examines the key concepts of privacy-preserving data publishing, namely anonymity, information loss, and risk of disclosure.

Anonymity

The most general concept of anonymity in data privacy is called k-anonymity; that is, for a given dataset, an individual is indistinguishable from k other individuals. This is also known as the privacy level. It is possible that, in a dataset considered to contain anonymous individuals, the analyst is able to pinpoint a specific person. For example, consider a dataset containing one record per person with three variables: town, illness, and age group. Now consider a person defined as living in a (named) town with 300 inhabitants, whose age is between 30 and 50 years, and who has a (named) rare illness. Someone who lives in that town will probably be able to easily identify the person, given that, in a population of 300 people, only some will be between 30 and 50 years old, and it is likely that just one of them has the named rare illness. Hence, without giving any specific details, the person can be uniquely identified.

In order to avoid inadvertently identifying individuals in this way, one solution is to generalize one or more of the descriptive variables. In the previous example, the first consideration would be to generalize the geographical location, so that instead of naming the town, the district or county would be identified. This would significantly increase the number of possible candidates with the same profile and reduce the risk of associating a specific individual with the profile.

Data Anonymization

Quasi-Identifiers

One of the difficulties in data anonymization is that, even if each descriptive variable is anonymized separately, a unique identifier may be formed by joining together several distinct variables. Hence, in order to determine that a dataset is anonymized correctly, permutations and combinations of the descriptive variables must also be checked. These types of identifiers are often called quasi-identifiers, and include variable combinations such as zip code + date of birth + gender.

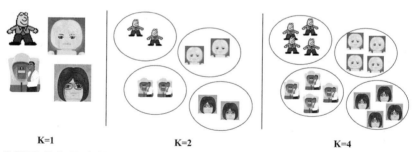

K=1   K=2   K=4

FIGURE 18.2   Basic idea of *k*-anonymity

Figure 18.2 illustrates a simple depiction of *k*-anonymity. On the left, each person is uniquely identifiable with respect to the others, so $k=1$. In the middle, each person has at least one other person who is indistinguishable from him or her, so $k=2$. On the right, each person has at least three others who are indistinguishable from him or her, so $k=4$. What is really depicted is the profile of each person, and for each increasing value of *k*, selected individual profiles are altered to make them the same. Therefore, the four ladies with blonde hair grouped on the right would originally have had slight differences; they have been modified so that they are identical.

Information Loss

In the previous example, the town variable was generalized by substituting it with county. However, this anonymization process incurs what is known as information loss. That is, the information value of knowing the town is greater than that of knowing the county, because the former is more specific. But it may be that more information would be lost if the illness category were changed by substituting it with a more general category. This depends on how the utility of the information is measured, which in turn depends on what the analyst wants to analyze. If medical data is being analyzed, one could assume that illness is a key factor, and the geographic location is less important.

Information loss can be measured in various ways, such as by correlating the data (each variable) before and after anonymization and then calculating the difference. The assumption is made that the correlation of the data with itself is perfect (equal to 1.0), so if, after anonymization, the correlation of the age attribute went down to 0.8, the information loss would be calculated as being $1.0 - 0.8 = 0.2$, or 20 percent.

Another way of measuring information loss is by having a series of utility queries. These could be SQL-type queries on a table, such as "select * from table where age between 30 and 40 and city = Chicago." A comparison would then be made of the number of records returned from the original dataset using this query with the number of records returned from the anonymized dataset.

Risk of Disclosure

The risk of disclosure is typically evaluated from the point of view of an adversary who wants to identify individuals in a set of records. The percentage of records that are uniquely identified by an adversary can be used as a measure of risk of disclosure. The adversary can use exact matching or approximate matching to identify individuals.

If k-anonymity has been applied, then the risk of disclosure will be directly related to the level of k; that is, the higher the value of k, the lower the risk.

Another way of evaluating risk of disclosure is to define a set of adversary queries. The degree of success by the adversary queries should be lower on the anonymized dataset, with respect to the degree of success when applied to the original dataset. For example, the adversary query "select * from table where illness = Alzheimer and age = 75" may return five records in the original dataset and none in the anonymized dataset, given that the term "Alzheimer" has been generalized to "dementia," and age has been generalized into the range of 65 to 85 years.

Anonymization Techniques

The anonymization technique depends on the type of data to be anonymized, such as categorical, numerical, or mixed. Micro-aggregation is a common technique and can be performed using partitioning or aggregation. Partitioning involves dividing the records into several distinct groups or clusters, each of which contains at least k records that are indistinguishable. Aggregation involves first performing a clustering, during which the centroid of each cluster is calculated. Then the original records in each cluster are substituted by the prototype record of the cluster, that is, the record closest to the centroid. Micro-aggregation can be applied to numerical and categorical (nominal or ordinal) data.

TABLE 18.2 Example of micro-aggregation based on clustering and average/modal values

	Before			After	
	Age	*Zip*		*Age*	*Zip*
	25	ABC		29	ABC
Cluster 1	35	ABC	$\longrightarrow$	29	ABC
	28	DEF		29	ABC
	70	QE2		58	QE2
Cluster 2	50	QE1	$\longrightarrow$	58	QE2
	55	QE2		58	QE2

Table 18.2 shows a simple example of micro-aggregation that first clusters the data into small groups and then substitutes the values in each record for the prototype for each cluster. The prototype in the example has been defined as being the average for numerical attributes and the mode for attributes that are categories. In this way, new records are obtained that are close to the original values but are indistinguishable within each cluster.

Generalization can be used to replace quasi-identifier components with more general values, for example, city → state → country. For a numerical value, such as age, the values are aggregated into more general ranges; for example, for three people whose ages are 45, 49, and 55, ranges such as "45 to 50" and "51 to 55" would be used.

The transformation of data is referred to as recoding and can be performed locally or globally. Local recoding means that a given specific value (such as zip code) is generalized using the various values in its local group of data, clustered from the complete dataset. Global recoding means that a given specific value is substituted with a more general value that can be selected from anywhere in the whole dataset. For example, if the dataset has first been clustered by gender, then for local recoding the zip code would be generalized differently, depending on the gender. If global recoding is performed, the zip code would be generalized in the same manner, irrespective of the gender or of any other descriptive variable. The recoding process can also be single-dimensional or multi-dimensional. In the former, each attribute is individually mapped (e.g., zip code), and in the latter, the mapping can be performed on a function of several attributes together, such as in quasi-identifiers (e.g., zip code + date of birth + gender).

After micro-aggregation, rank swapping is the second major technique used to anonymize data and avoid individual identification. Rank swapping involves switching around attribute values in a dataset so that each record is anonymized, while maintaining the statistical properties of the distribution of each attribute. The attribute values being swapped are randomly and uniformly selected from the list of values available in the dataset from the other records. This normally involves first sorting (ranking) the records on a given attribute, and then performing the swaps. The range of values permitted to perform a swap can be increased or decreased using a parameter based on the rank positions. If the allowed range is wider, there is more information loss but less risk of disclosure; if the allowed range is narrower, there is less information loss but more risk of disclosure. For example, given a dataset of records with an attribute of age, substituting age values between records within a range of plus or minus three rank positions could be defined. First, the data is ordered based on the age attribute. Then, for example, the ages are switched between a person with a record in rank position 12 and a person with a record in rank position 14. The distance between 12 and 14 is less or equal to a range limit of 3. However, if their respective ranks were 12 and 16, then they could not be switched because their rank distance would be four, which is one more than the defined limit.

Table 18.3 shows a simple example of rank swapping, which first orders the records on a given variable (age, on the left) and then swaps the values around in a random, uniform fashion and within a specified rank range limit of two. In the

TABLE 18.3 Example of rank swapping with a rank limit of two positions

Record	Before Age	Before Zip	After Age	After Zip
1	25	ABC	28	ABC
2	28	DEF	25	DEF
3	35	ABC	50	ABC
4	50	QE1	35	QE1
5	55	QE2	70	QE2
6	70	QE2	55	QE2

example, the allowed substitution range for age is plus or minus two rank positions. Table 18.3 shows that the age values of records 1 and 2 have been swapped, as well as those of 3 and 4, and 5 and 6. The zip code attribute is left unchanged, as would be the rest of the record.

Document Sanitization

Document sanitization deals with the process of eliminating sensitive or restricted information from a document so that it can be made available to a wider audience. It is often referred to in the context of government agencies that declassify official documents before releasing them publicly. When documents were in paper format, sanitization involved blacking out terms, phrases, sections, or whole blocks of text.

Other contexts where document sanitization could be applied are, for example, legal summary documents of a court case that are to be made available to the press, or documents containing medical or personal data.

> **Document Sanitization**
>
> *Utility versus Risk*
>
> A key aspect of the document sanitization process is that the sanitized document should still maintain information utility while not disclosing the sensitive information.

In order to formalize the sanitization process, general official guidelines have been defined, such as those of Executive Order 13526 (2009) of the United States Government. Other cases of sensitive information are content and domain dependent and require an evaluation by experts of what is considered publishable and what is not.

When the number of documents and volume of text is considerable, manual sanitization can become impracticable. Semi-automatic document sanitization systems have been developed, such as ERASE (Efficient RedAction for Securing Entities) and the algorithms SIMPLEREDACTOR and K-REDACTOR. ERASE is a system for the automatic sanitization of unstructured text documents, which prevents disclosure of protected entities by removing certain terms from the document. The terms are selected in such a way that no protected entity can be inferred as being mentioned in the document by matching the remaining terms with the entity database. SIMPLEREDACTOR and K-REDACTOR are algorithms for protecting sensitive information in text data while preserving known utility information. The detection of a sensitive concept is considered a multiclass classification problem, applied in a similar manner to feature selection techniques, and the algorithm allows the definition of different levels of sanitization.

For further reading on ERASE, see:

Chakaravarthy, V. T., H. Gupta, P. Roy, and M. K. Mohania. 2008. "Efficient Techniques for Document Sanitization." In: Proceedings of the 17th ACM Conference on Information and Knowledge Management. CIKM'08, October 26–30, 2008, Napa Valley, California, pp. 843–852. New York, NY: ACM.

For further reading on SIMPLEREDACTOR and K-REDACTOR, see:

Cumby, C. and R. A. Ghani. 2011. "Machine Learning Based System for Semi-Automatically Redacting Documents." Innovative Applications of Artificial Intelligence, North America. Available at: http://www.aaai.org/ocs/index.php/IAAI/IAAI-11/paper/view/3528/4031.

The following section discusses a simple example of the sanitization of a block of text using two applications, Pingar and WordNet. (See Further Reading at the end of the chapter.) Pingar performs named entity recognition and substitutes the entities in the text with anonymous values. The following entities are anonymized: people, organizations, addresses, emails, ages, phone numbers, URLs, dates, times, money, and amounts. This process simply substitutes the information with {Pers1, Pers2, ...}, {Loc1, Loc2, ...}, {Date1, Date2, ...}, {Org1, Org2, ...}, and so on.

WordNet is an ontology database that can be used to find the synonyms and hyponyms of an initial list of risk terms. For example, the noun "account" would give the following:

account, accounting, account statement (a statement of recent transactions and the resulting balance) "they send me an accounting every month" hyponyms: capital account, profit and loss account, suspense account, expense account, and so on.

By using the initial list of risk terms together with the hyponyms for the given content (account in the monetary sense), the document would then be processed and all the instances of these terms labeled. As a final step, the texts would be manually checked with the labeled terms to select the parts of the texts for deletion.

As a simple example, consider the following text. It will first be processed with Pingar to eliminate the named entities and then with WordNet to eliminate blocks of text containing the risk terms and their hyponyms.

Mr. Smith told Mr. Jones that XYZ, Inc. had a debt of $10 million dollars, which was ten times their revenue over the past three years. Mr. Smith also told Mr. Jones that XYZ, Inc. had lost the majority shareholding in their subsidiary, ABC, Inc., in San Paolo, Brazil and would soon be taken over. The share price on the NYSE had gone down from $15.20 to $7.10 over the past financial year and was expected to go down even more. The price of raw materials had gone up 50 percent over the last year, having an impact on overheads and profit margins.

After processing with Pingar, the result is:

PERSON1 told PERSON2 that ORGANIZATION1 had a debt of MONEY1, which was ten times their revenue over the past three years. PERSON1 also told PERSON2 that ORGANIZATION1 had lost the majority share holding in their subsidiary,

ORGANIZATION2, in San Paolo, Brazil and would soon be taken over. The share price on the NYSE had gone down from MONEY2 to MONEY3 over the past financial year and was expected to go down even more. The price of raw materials had gone up PERCENTAGE1 over the last year, having an impact on overheads and profit margins.

After processing with WordNet using the risk base terms revenue, share, price, and accounts, the result is:

PERSON1 told PERSON2 that ORGANIZATION1 had a debt *of MONEY1, which was ten times their* revenue *over the past three years. PERSON1 also told PERSON2 that ORGANIZATION1 had lost the majority* share *holding in their subsidiary, ORGANIZA-TION2, in San Paolo, Brazil and would soon be taken over. The* share price *on the NYSE had gone down from MONEY2 to MONEY3 over the past financial year and was expected to go down even more. The* price *of raw materials had gone up PERCENTAGE1 over the last year, having an impact on overheads and* profit margins.

In this text area, the individual risk terms have been identified, together with compound terms and one term, debt, which is related to accounts. The latter would be from the WordNet hyponym list for accounts.

As a last step, a semi-automated process could identify areas of the text with a high concentration of risk terms and eliminate complete phrases that contain them. The process would be semi-automated given that, before deleting a text area, the system would ask for confirmation from a human supervisor. For example, in the last text segment, the system would ask confirmation to delete the first sentence and the last two sentences, leaving just the second sentence.

Alternatively, instead of deleting text, the system could substitute the risk terms with a more general concept. For example, using a concept hierarchy tree, the term "financial" could be chosen to substitute all the risk terms found in the text. A third option is to use a mixture of both methods: first performing substitution and then using deletion as a final resort.

For more information on Pingar, see:

Pingar – Entity Extraction Software: http://www.pingar.com

For further reading about WordNet, see:

Fellbaum, C., (Ed.) 1998. WordNet: An Electronic Lexical Database. MIT Press, Cambridge, MA.

Princeton University, 2010. About WordNet. WordNet. Princeton University. http://wordnet.
    princeton.edu.

Chapter 19

Creating an Environment for Commercial Data Analysis

INTRODUCTION

This chapter discusses two approaches to using computer software programs for commercial data analysis. There are the powerful, integrated tools with higher price tags, which tend to be used by multinational companies, banks, insurance companies, large retail stores, large online application providers, and so on. These tools often require the assistance of consultants or manufacturers as support for utilizing them and are best for high data volumes and data base integration. The low-cost, artisanal approach consists of acquiring ad hoc, or open source, software tools, which tend to be more technique-specific, but which can offer greater independence for analyzing commercial data.

INTEGRATED COMMERCIAL DATA ANALYSIS TOOLS

There is a diverse offering of general commercial data analysis tools. The principal systems, in terms of sales, are: Intelligent Miner for Data (IBM), SAS Enterprise Miner, IBM SPSS Modeler (previously SPSS Clementine), and the Oracle Data Mining Suite. Descriptions of the main features for each of these data mining systems are as follows:

All of the systems contain a basic repertory of statistical functions for data preparation, exploration, and modeling. They also offer one or more techniques for classification and segmentation (clustering). For prediction, they normally include techniques such as neural networks and linear or logistic regression; for classification, rule induction (C5.0, ID3, or similar); for grouping data, k-means or Kohonen SOM neural network.

IBM's Intelligent Miner for Data has the Radial Basis Function (RBF) for prediction, and for segmentation there is a technique based on the Condorcet Criteria, which is used to create demographic models. Condorcet offers an improvement for data with many categorical values. There are also techniques for association analysis, time series, and sequential patterns, which are based on frequency analysis and sequential pattern recognition. (What a person does manually by visual recognition, the system can do automatically and faster.)

Intelligent Miner for Data is characterized by the quality of its algorithms and its capacity to work with large data volumes. With respect to the user interface, one of the most powerful features, in the hands of an expert user, is the way of displaying the data for exploration and results viewing. It can show all the variables (or as many as fit in the display window) together with their distributions (histograms for numerical variables and pie charts for variables that are categories). This allows for scrutinizing the tendencies of each variable, making comparisons between variables, and using different processing techniques (neural network, RBF, etc.) and datasets (training set, only clients from New York, only clients between 18 and 30 years of age, and so on).

SAS Enterprise Miner embodies a data analysis methodology called SEMMA (Sample, Explore, Modify, Model, and Assess). It has a canvas-style user interface based on the use of distinctive icons representing the available techniques and processes. The icons are manipulated by a drag-and-drop method. The interface itself is designed to guide the user through the SEMMA methodology. It offers specific techniques for associations, sequential patterns, decision trees (CHAID/CART/C5.0), neural networks, logistic regression, segmentation (k-means), RBF, and a wide selection of statistical techniques. The strong points of this tool are its statistical inheritance (SAS started as a company specializing in statistical tools) and the good practices imposed on the user by the SEMMA methodology. It also has a tool called the SAS Rapid Predictive Modeler, which is designed for use by non-experts to allow them to create predictive data models.

IBM's SPSS Modeler was originally called Clementine and was created by a UK company called ISL, which was then bought by SPSS and most recently has been acquired by IBM. It includes techniques such as neural networks, regression, and rule induction, with Kohonen networks for segmentation and C5.0 for decision trees. Other techniques included in the latest version are: support vector machines, Bayesian-based modeling, sequence analysis, and time series analysis.

The IBM SPSS Modeler makes extensive use of visual techniques, which provides the user with a great agility for data manipulation and processing. The data and results can be visualized by a variety of graphical representations such as plots, scatter charts, histograms, and distribution tables (aligned horizontally), and "spider's web" diagrams to reveal relationships among the data. Data modeling includes prediction, prognosis, estimation, and classification, and the models can be exported as C language, which can then be used in other programs. It has a canvas-type interface, similar to the Enterprise Miner. The strong point of this tool is its agility for data manipulation: the user can generate a graph plot, select a region of it, and perform a "drill-down" on the data, as well as connect the modeling processes with those for preprocessing with a certain ease.

Figure 19.1 shows an example screen of the IBM SPSS Modeler. In the left-hand window is the canvas on which the user creates a work flow by dragging

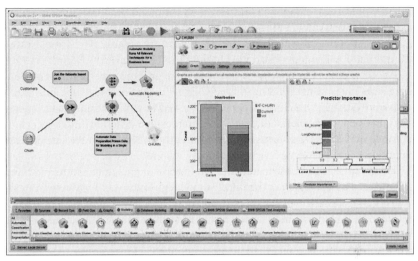

FIGURE 19.1   Screenshot from the IBM SPSS Modeler. *By permission from: Morelli, Theresa, Colin, Shearer, and Axel Buecker. 2010. "IBM SPSS Predictive Analytics: Optimizing Decisions at the Point of Impact." IBM Redbook (REDP-4710-00, 2010). Available at: http://www .redbooks.ibm.com/abstracts/redp4710.html.*

and dropping the functionality icons (bottom of the screen) and then connecting them. Within this window a workflow consists of, from left to right, two data input icons (for the input datasets or tables), which feed into a merge process to create just one data stream. One dataset consists of loyal customers, and the other consists of unloyal (or churn) customers. After the merge, the data flow goes into a "type" processing icon, which assigns the correct types to all the variables (integer, data, category, and so on). The type process then feeds in a downward direction into an "automatic data preparation" process icon, which performs outlier and skew analysis and identifies erroneous or missing data values. The two arrows going to the right from the type process icon feed into two modeling processes. (One is the training model and the other, the diamond, is the test model.) In the right-hand windows are informational data about the predictive model that has been created. In the distribution histogram the model has classified the customers into two categories, "current" and "vol." Each vertical bar shows the proportion of customers who are correctly classified. The "predictor importance" bar chart shows the relative importance of the inputs with respect to the output (classifier label). In the row at the bottom, the user has clicked on the modeling tab, and the icons show the data modeling techniques that are available.

Finally, the Oracle Data Mining Suite provides methods for classification, regression, attribute importance, anomaly detection, clustering, association, and feature extraction. The classification methods include logistic regression, Naïve Bayes, support vector machines, and decision trees. These techniques can be used for predicting categorical outputs such as yes/no, high/medium/low, and so on. The regression methods include multiple regression and support vector machines, which can be used to predict numerical outputs. The Oracle Data Mining Suite is integrated into the Oracle 11 g database.

Another alternative for more basic statistical analysis together with modeling capability is IBM SPSS Statistics. This software represents the old SPSS statistics package, which was acquired by IBM, with some enhancements and improved connectivity to external databases and functionality.

How are commercial analysis tools currently evolving? In the last decade there has been a tendency to offer, for an additional cost, specific modules for sectors such as banking, insurance, and telecommunications. These modules incorporate an added value of sectorial knowledge and a set of variables, ratios, and functions preselected for specific business objectives. Manufacturers have developed ready-made models for business objectives, such as cross-selling, loyalty, and fraud detection (especially for the insurance industry). The tendency has been to incorporate these tools into the CRM (customer relationship management) cycle. In this way, the outputs from data models (for example, the list of clients who are most likely to buy product X) feed directly into the marketing processes (such as promotional campaigns, customer support, loyalty campaigns, etc.). Data captured by the sales force and customer support can be input directly into the data mart, which is then analyzed by the data analysis processes, thus closing the CRM cycle. The objective is to enrich the available client information in order to give maximum leverage to analysts and decision-makers.

Data analysis tools have gotten closer to databases, not only via data access interfaces (ODBC), but also as embedded functions in the database server (as in DB2). Vendors are including in their general data mining tools other analytical capabilities that were previously in separate tools. For example, the IBM SPSS Modeler Premium has reincorporated text mining tools and incorporated entity analytics and social network analysis. Ensemble modeling is another trend that allows the user to combine various techniques in a transparent manner. Solutions for Big Data are now being included in database/data mining repertories such as Oracle's, which integrates Apache Hadoop to process large amounts of unstructured data on multiple computers that are clustered together.

How much do these tools cost? Each manufacturer has its own pricing scheme based on the various versions (professional, premium, etc.) and the dependence on a proprietary database (DB2, Oracle, etc.). Companies who currently have proprietary databases may obtain the data mining software in the bundle without additional cost. The cost of training courses and/or external consulting must be added to a project budget, given that the first project is often carried out with a consultant or manufacturer. For example, the IBM SPSS Modeler comes in two versions: professional (basic) and premium (extended functionality). Each version can have the concurrent option (high speed database access) or not, and there are several license options. The professional non-concurrent version currently costs $11,300 and the premium concurrent version costs $45,300, although the manufacturer's website should be checked for updated prices.

What platforms are best? Currently manufacturers tend to offer their products across a complete range of platforms from mainframe/server to workstation and desktop PCs and laptops in client/server configuration. The operating systems include: AIX, UNIX, Linux, Sun Solaris, and Windows, in addition to others. Some limited-functionality cloud computing solutions are also appearing.

For further reading on this topic, see:

Earls, Alan R. n.d. "Data Mining with Cloud Computing." Cyber Security and Information Systems, Information Analysis Center. Available at: https://sw.thecsiac.com/databases/url/key/222/8693#.UadYwq47NlI.

Internet addresses for the referenced products are as follows:

(Note that Internet addresses change frequently, so if a referenced link is not found, use a search engine to find the latest link using the product name as keywords.)

- IBM SPSS Modeler (previously Clementine): http://www-01.ibm.com/software/analytics/spss/products/modeler
- IBM SPSS Statistics: http://www-01.ibm.com/software/analytics/spss/products/statistics
- IBM Intelligent Miner for Data: http://publib.boulder.ibm.com/infocenter/db2luw/v8/index.jsp?topic=/com.ibm.db2.udb.doc/wareh/getsta06im.htm
- SAS Enterprise Miner: http://www.sas.com/technologies/analytics/datamining/miner/
- Oracle Data Mining: http://www.oracle.com/technetwork/database/enterprise-edition/odm-techniques-algorithms-097163.html

CREATING AN AD HOC/LOW-COST ENVIRONMENT FOR COMMERCIAL DATA ANALYSIS

How can a company set up a commercial data analysis laboratory without having to go overboard with its budget? Which ad hoc tools are available for specific data mining techniques? This section presents some solutions for these questions. These may be good options for small- and medium-sized businesses (SMBs) and for larger companies who want something different from the integrated systems offerings seen in the first section of the chapter.

Remember that a data mining project will not be successful just because of the tools used, but also by a well-planned and executed project. For this reason, a review of the essential requirements of a data mining project is warranted. A project requires: (i) people prepared to participate in the project, with a minimum commitment from the company's management; (ii) agreement on business objectives that are useful for the business and are clearly defined (e.g., analyze the last two years' worth of data and apply the results to the next quarter of the current year), including defining starting and ending dates for the analysis and deployment phases; (iii) availability of the identified variables (with sufficient quality, coverage, and volume) in the business's current data sources; (iv) a definition of the preprocess that will be performed on the data in order to guarantee its quality, and enriching the data with derived business variables, if necessary; (v) exploration tools; (vi) modeling tools; and (vii) a clear idea of how to exploit the results (for example, as a list/report of the 100 clients with the highest risk of canceling their contract) and deploy the information to the marketing, customer service, and production departments, and so on, so the results can be incorporated into their operational processes.

Point (iii), availability of data, is emphasized because more than one project has met with the problem that, after having spent several weeks defining a project, the necessary data is not currently available. In this case, after having evaluated that the cost/benefit values are favorable, operative processes can be defined to capture the data for the variables needed.

Now consider (v) exploration tools and (vi) modeling tools. Weka, an integrated data mining software, is free software available under the GNU General Public License. Weka's popularity has grown significantly over the past decade mainly due to its widespread use in universities and by researchers. Generally, it is not a system for beginners; it requires some knowledge of statistics to interpret the results and the ability to delve into the options and formats that the different algorithms and functions offer. Weka initially reads data from a .csv format file, although an API can be programmed in Java to connect to databases via Java Database Connectivity (JDBC). MySQL could be used for the database, which is also freeware under a GNU License. A possible inconvenience is that, whereas the proprietary systems seen in the beginning of the chapter are guaranteed with respect to their functionality, Weka and MySQL are used on an as-is basis. Another disadvantage is the restricted scalability of the algorithms to process large data volumes. However, as the source code is available, a Java programmer could execute the algorithms as stand-alone, with a direct database connection. Weka 3.6, which is the current version (circa 2013), has three main modules: Explorer, Experimenter, and Knowledge Flow. The Explorer is the main user interface, which gives access to the data preprocessing, analysis, and modeling functions. The Experimenter provides functionality for the systematic comparison of the predictive performance of Weka's machine learning algorithms on a collection of datasets. This is useful when, for example, the user wants to perform a large number of tests of separate folds of the data (n-fold cross-validation). Finally, the Knowledge Flow interface offers the same functionality as the Explorer, but in a canvas-style, component-based interface (similar to the IBM SPSS Modeler data flow interface).

Figure 19.2 shows a screenshot of the Weka Explorer. In the menu at the top are the general menu tabs: data processing, clustering, classification, attribute selection, and data visualization. The clustering functions include k-means and hierarchical clustering; the classification functions include Bayesian, rule/tree based (M4, J48 [C4.5], ID3, etc.), and function based (neural networks, RBF, SVM, etc.). In the figure, the user has chosen the J48 classification function with default options. The dataset is from the "labor.arff" demonstration data, which comes with the Weka system. Notice that the labor conditions class is defined as the output variable and there are a series of input variables, such as pension, vacations, contribution to health plan, and so on, which are used to classify the labor conditions of the person as "good" or "bad" (the two possible values of the output class). In the window on the right, part of the modeling result is shown with the pruned model tree and the precision. In the sub-window to the right, the user has selected the option to show the tree with a graphical representation.

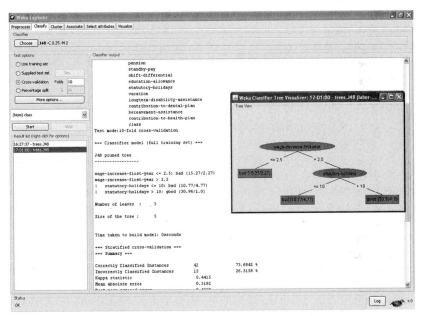

FIGURE 19.2   Weka main screen. *Reproduced with permission from: Weka: http://www.cs.wai kato.ac.nz/ml/weka/.*

When importing the data as a .csv file (which can be generated from a spreadsheet), it is important to check the imported data for things such as columns that have disappeared, a column that has become mixed with another, truncated fields, date formats, and so on.

Weka's visualization is generally limited to plots and distributions. It has functions for correlation and covariance to identify relationships between the variables. The "standard deviation" and "mode" indicate the quality of the numerical and categorical data, respectively. Derived variables can be created using "principal components." Predictive models can also be created using linear regression (for data with a linear relation between the input and output variables), non-linear regression (for data where the relationship between the inputs and the outputs is described by a curve) and logistic regression (when the output variable is binary, e.g., yes/no). For segmentation, Weka offers k-means, and for modeling it includes C4.5 (called J48) and a simple neural network, among other techniques.

A spreadsheet (e.g., Excel) is an alternative general tool and is good for visualizing data in table format; preprocessing; ordering; creating ratios through its extensive library of functions; and generating graphics such as plots, histograms, and pie charts.

Consider Excel's Solver function, which can be installed as an add-on and which then appears as an option on the Data tab (see Microsoft Office help for details). Excel's Solver is designed to solve optimization and "what-if"-type problems. It calculates an optimal value for a formula in a target cell on the spreadsheet based on other cells related to the formula in the target cell. The user specifies a set of cells that can be modified by the optimization process to give a result specified by the target formula. The user can also specify a set of constraints to limit the ranges of values to be modified. According to the information on the MS Office website, the Excel Solver uses the Generalized Reduced Gradient (GRG2) nonlinear optimization method, and for linear and integer problems it uses the simplex method with bounds on the variables, and the branch-and-bound method.

Figure 19.3 shows Solver as used for an optimization problem. The data in the spreadsheet refers to a production scenario of supply (units produced), demand (orders), and costs of materials, personnel, and profit margins. The idea is to optimize the profit over the given six month period, for the given supply, demand, and resource data. The dataset is based on the prodmix.xls demo data file that comes with the Excel Solver add-on.

The target cell (B11) contains a formula that multiplies the units produced (row 2) by the unit sale net profits (row 8); that is, it gives the overall profit to be maximized by the solver. This is done by changing (optimizing) the data values in row 2. The constraint cells refer to the materials and personnel, which are defined in rows 13 and 14, and states that the personnel and materials used (2,000 and 8,000, respectively) cannot exceed the personnel and materials available (also 2,000 and 8,000, respectively). The user presses the "Solve" button and the optimum production plan appears in row 2 with the values for all the other cells related to the profit function. The figure shows that the solver has found an optimum profit of $1,742.86 by producing 50 units from January to March, followed by 100 units in April, 78 units in May, and no units in June (vacations!).

RuleQuest's C5.0 is software specifically for rule induction and is one of the most accepted and referenced of the rule induction algorithms, and which the manufacturers of large commercial tools tend to incorporate as-is. RuleQuest is the company created by the original author of the C4.5 and ID3 algorithms, Ross Quinlan, and buying it directly from his website will cost about $1,050. (Check the latest price at RuleQuest's website, www.rulequest.com.)

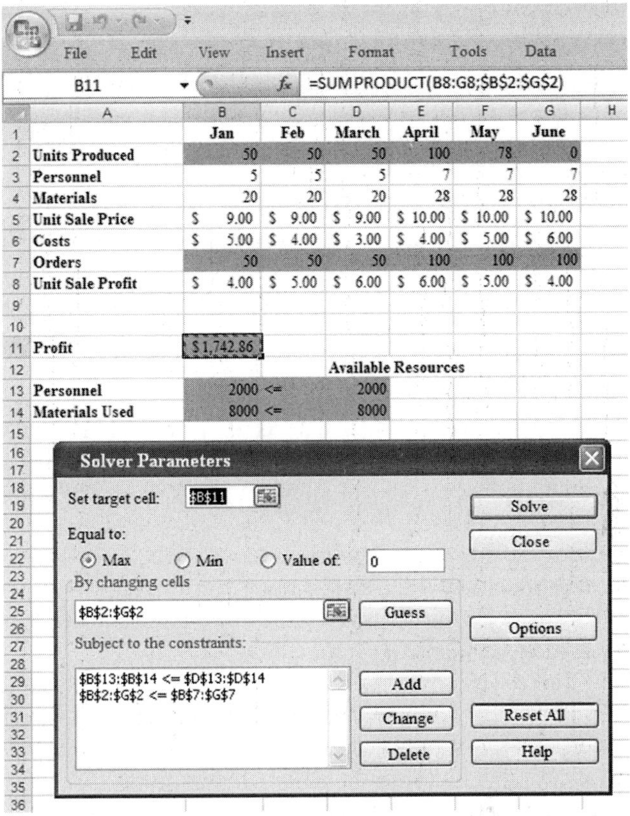

FIGURE 19.3   Example configuration of the Excel Solver add-on for optimization problems

For neural networks, the NeuroShell software from Ward Systems offers multiple types of neural networks, including Kohonen for segmentation, automatic identification of relevant variables, and modes for novice, average, and expert users. It has a spreadsheet-type interface and an extensive section of user help and tutorials with practical examples for novice users. NeuroShell currently costs about $870.

The products mentioned in this section, especially those offered by Rule-Quest, NeuroShell, and the Excel Solver, are relatively easy for beginners to use.

Figure 19.4 shows a summary of the tools discussed in this low-cost/ad hoc section. On the left the data can be read from a flat file, a .csv-type format, or directly from a relational database. As seen in the upper row, the Weka and Excel tools are applicable for data preprocessing, basic statistics, exploration, modeling, and optimization problems (Excel Solver). The middle row shows that RuleQuest's C5.0 is specialized in rule induction, and in the lower row Ward Systems' NeuroShell performs modeling using neural networks.

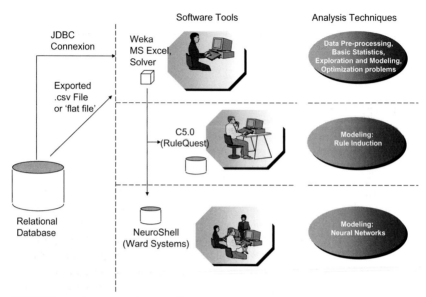

FIGURE 19.4   Low-cost environment for data analysis

To learn more about the products in this chapter, see:

- C5.0 software for rule induction and decision trees by Ross Quinlan: http://www.rulequest.com
- Microsoft Excel: http://office.microsoft.com/en-us/excel/
- Microsoft Excel Solver: http://office.microsoft.com/en-us/excel-help/determine-optimal-product-mix-with-solver-HA001124596.aspx
- NeuroShell from Ward Systems: http://www.wardsystems.com
- Weka Data Mining Software: http://www.cs.waikato.ac.nz/ml/weka/

Chapter 20

Summary

This book has described the basic elements and some of the more advanced aspects of commercial data analysis. Clearly, a significant amount of time has to be dedicated to the definition phase and the adequate preparation of the data in order to guarantee the quality of the analysis and modeling phases.

A key aspect is choosing a deployment method for the data mining results that corresponds to business needs, with the simplest being Query and Reporting, followed by Executive Information Systems (EIS), integrated Customer Relationship Management Systems (CRMs) and the more sophisticated option of Expert Systems incorporating data mining models. However, all the methods covered in this book are within reach of small- and medium-sized businesses and freelance professionals, if their needs justify such processes.

The book has followed a methodology consisting of a series of steps for data analysis corresponding to Chapters 2 through 10. A series of topical aspects related to the analysis and exploitation of commercial data were discussed in Chapters 11 to 19.

Since the early 1990s, data mining has evolved from processes that analyzed data accumulated by applications in large, stand-alone computer systems, through the advent of the Internet, to the analysis of data generated on the web. The designers of some of the tools described in the book had the vision to make data mining easy for users with an average expertise level, via canvas-type user interfaces that showed the workflow in a way that was easy to understand. The algorithms and techniques are still basically the same as they were in the 1990s, since the application developers' efforts went into optimizing systems for speed, memory usage, and reliability. Now, with online weblogs, online social networks, cloud computing, Big Data, and more and more content online, one still must consider the basic aspects of data quality, variable selection, and deriving new factors.

The key objective of data mining, which differentiates it from data processing in general, is the discovery of new knowledge. Thus, even though customer analytics is now an established mainstream activity for many companies, the pioneer spirit still exists in mining out a golden nugget of useful commercial insight from data that no one else has yet noticed, or in creating a predictive data model that "beats the street."

Lastly, I hope that you enjoy your commercial data analysis projects and that they are profitable.

Case Studies

This appendix details three real-world examples of commercial data analysis projects using the techniques and methods described in the book, especially Chapters 2 through 10, and how they apply in actual situations. All names and identifying information have been changed and the data modified to maintain the anonymity of clients and companies.

The first case study deals with an insurance company's client loyalty, that is, how to identify the clients most at risk of leaving. The second case study is about cross-selling a pension plan for retail bank clients, and the third considers audience prediction for a television channel.

CASE STUDY 1: CUSTOMER LOYALTY AT AN INSURANCE COMPANY

This case study considers the generic business objective of reducing customer loss. The first two sections follow the steps explained in Chapter 12 by first defining the operational and informational data and then extracting the data of interest and creating one or more files for analysis. Next, the data is explored using methods described in Chapters 6 and 8. Finally, data modeling is performed using the rule induction and neural network techniques discussed in Chapter 9.

Introduction

For this project, the first business objective was to improve the targeting accuracy in customer loyalty campaigns using a smaller mailing volume than earlier campaigns. A second objective was to be able to conduct a priori actions to prevent customer losses while improving the quality of customer service.

With these objectives in mind, two data analysis approaches were defined. The first approach was to identify, by using historical data, the characteristics of clients who had canceled their accounts, and those who had not. The second approach was to create a data model to identify current clients who had the highest risk of canceling their accounts.

To obtain the characteristics of the records corresponding to the "canceled" and "not canceled" labels, rules and decision trees were generated and defined from the available customer data. The tendencies and characteristics associated with the most loyal clients and the clients with the highest risk of canceling, together with intermediate type profiles, could then be identified.

Predictive models were deployed and applied to the whole current client database, generating a list of clients with the highest risk of cancellation within a given future period of time. This list was given to the marketing and customer service departments so they could contact these clients, by post or a telemarketing campaign, for example, and offer them a personalized special discount.

Definition of the Operational and Informational Data of Interest

Once an agreement had been reached on the project objectives, the next step was to identify the most relevant tables and variables necessary for the project. New variables and categories were then defined using the previously selected ones as starting points.

The first table identified was the "client" table, and after a series of meetings between the data analysis experts and the experts from the customer service department the following variables were selected: office; policy number; policy holder and date of birth; zip code; name, age, and gender of the beneficiary; relationship between policy holder and beneficiary; starting date; termination date; cause of termination; debt indicator; premium at time of termination; previous premium; and form of payment. A new variable was created for the project and named "accident coefficient" to serve as a profitability indicator for this client.

The second table was the "treatment" table, with the following variables selected: policy number, policy holder, beneficiary, date and location of treatment, and treatment identification and name (such as "planned visit to consultant," "major surgical intervention," "diagnostic tests," etc.). Two variables were created for the project: "frequency of treatments," defined as the monthly average during the last twelve months, and "time since last treatment," defined in weeks.

The final table was "channels," which indicates where the client's policy was first registered. The fields "channel code" and "channel sub code" were selected. More specifically, the channel could be "office," "sales representative," "Internet," or "telephone support center"; a sub-channel of "office" would be "urban offices."

Next, a number of restrictions were imposed on the data to be extracted in order to focus the study on the business objective, reduce the volume of data, and define the desired time period. The data was limited to clients in the metropolitan areas of the state of New York, products with valid product codes, and treatments received during the previous 12 months (client profiles could be extrapolated to the next 12 months). Null values were excluded.

Data Extraction and Creation of Files for Analysis

First, the profiles of clients who had canceled were extracted, amounting to about 15,000 records. Only cancellations from the previous 12 months were selected, and only for the regional offices indicated by the business expert in the customer service department. The ages of the beneficiaries were limited to 18 years or older, and the zip codes were limited to New York State. The business expert indicated which clients were to be excluded, using the variables "office code," "sales representative ID," and "cause of cancellation." The variables listed in the client table were then extracted.

Second, a random selection of 15,000 profiles of clients who didn't cancel were extracted. These records included only new contracts registered more than one year prior to the analysis and had the same restrictions and variables as for the clients who canceled, with the exception of date of cancellation and cause of cancellation. Third, treatment records that were registered as "canceled" and "not canceled" were extracted.

The customer service department pointed out that the information related to the last treatments a client received could have influenced whether a client canceled the policy. It could indicate problems related to the quality of service and the frequency of cancellations in terms of type of treatment received and specific treatment centers. The variables extracted are those listed for the treatment table.

Once the "canceled" and "not canceled" cases and treatment records were extracted, they were joined into one file, using "policy number" as the common key. Table A.1 shows the structure of the unified file used for the data analysis and modeling.

Next, a variable called "cancellation flag" was created: clients who canceled were flagged "YES" and clients who had not canceled were flagged "NO." For clients who had not canceled, the variables corresponding to date and cause of cancellation were assigned to "null."

Data Exploration

Once the desired client data had been acquired, the analysis moved into the data exploration phase, when the analyst became familiar with the data by applying various techniques including generating distributions and histograms and calculating statistical values. The analyst also had the task of preparing data for the modeling phase. The data was evaluated from several viewpoints: consistency, noise, coverage, distribution, missing or unknown values, and outliers. Table A.2 shows a summary of the basic statistics of four key variables, the most significant cross-correlation values, and some observations on those correlations.

All the data extracted during the sampling was analyzed—that is, 15,000 cancellations and 15,000 non-cancellations—with the treatment data for each record.

Figure A.1 shows the age distribution of the clients and illustrates a percentage increment of cancellations for clients around 35 years old.

In this first stage of data exploration, decisions about changing, restricting, or augmenting the available data were made by examining what is known. First,

TABLE A.1 Unified file of cases of canceled and not canceled and the corresponding treatments

Variable	Table of Origin	Format
Policy ID	Clients	Alphanumerical (10)
Collective ID	Clients	Alphanumerical (3)
Beneficiary	Clients	Alphanumerical (48)
Office	Clients	Numerical (10)
Gender of beneficiary	Clients	Alphabetical (1)
Age	Clients	Numerical (3)
Relationship between policy holder and beneficiary	Clients	Alphanumerical (3)
Date of birth	Clients	Date
Date of registration	Clients	Date
Cancellation flag	———	Alphabetical (2)
Date of cancellation	Clients	Date
Cause of cancellation*	Clients	Alphanumerical (3)
Current premium	Clients	Numerical (10)
Policy ID	Treatments	Alphanumerical (10)
Beneficiary	Treatments	Alphanumerical (48)
Date of last treatment	Treatments	Date
Location of treatment	Treatments	Alphanumerical (3)
Treatment key	Treatments	Alphanumerical (3)
Concept	Treatments	Alphanumerical (25)

*The cause of cancellation allows for debtors and clients who are deceased to be excluded from the study.

with respect to the variable "channel," approximately 35 percent of the offices had a code value of "0001." The business expert recommended excluding these records, because they correspond to the company's central office. A new field was created, "time since last treatment," and a graph plot generated of "age of client" versus "time since last treatment in weeks," as seen in Figure A.2. After studying Figure A.2, it was concluded that a significant relation existed between "age" and "time since last treatment," so a new variable was created: the *ratio* of "time since last treatment" with "age."

TABLE A.2 Statistics of some of the basic and derived variables

Column	Min.	Max.	Mean	Standard Deviation	Correlation	Observations
Age	18	94	40.57	13.23	Premium: 0.754	Strong correlation
Premium (dollars)	12.35	60.72	27.50	9.32	Age: 0.754	Strong correlation
Time since last treatment (weeks)	0	95	12.84	10.58	Time since last treatment/Freq. of treatments: 0.831	Strong correlation
Frequency of treatments (average month/ year)	0	5.67	1.22	0.21	Age: −0.611	Average negative correlation
Time since last treatment (weeks)/Freq. of treatments	0	16.75	10.52	50.38	Premium: 0.639	Average positive correlation

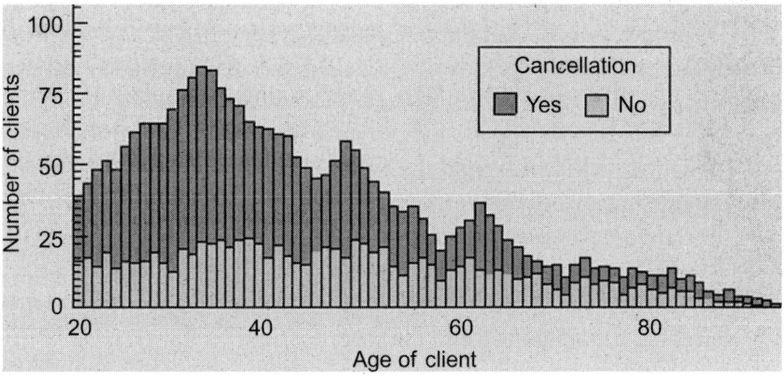

FIGURE A.1 Histogram of the distribution of clients' ages

After a meeting with the business experts, the decision was made to create a new categorical variable indicating the relation between the person who took out the policy (the policy holder) and the person insured by the policy. This variable was called "type of relation," and had 13 categories: PH, signifying that the policy holder and insured are the same person; BR, signifying that the insured is the brother of the policy holder; SI, signifying that the insured is the sister of the policy holder; and so on for husband (HU), wife (WI), son (SO), daughter (DA), mother (MO), father (FA), grandson (GS), granddaughter (GD), grandfather

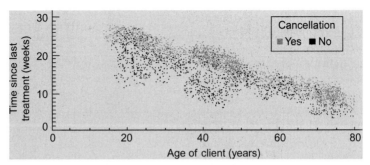

FIGURE A.2 "Age of client" versus "time since last treatment"

(GF), and grandmother (GM). Five categories were also established for the ages of the clients: 18 to 25 years, 26 to 39 years, 40 to 61 years, and 62 to 88 years.

Some variables were derived from the treatment data: time in weeks since the last treatment up to the present; average number of medical attentions per month during the last twelve months; and the claims rate, defined as the sum of the claim amounts paid divided by the sum of the premiums the client has paid since the policy's starting date.

In terms of client gender, 61 percent were male and 39 percent were female. Regarding the relationship between the policy holder and the insured, in 60 percent of the cases the policy holder and the insured are the same person, in 20 percent of the cases the insured was the wife of the policy holder, and in 10 percent the insured was a child of the policy holder. In terms of the age categories, 50 percent of the clients were between 26 and 39 years, 25 percent were between 40 and 61, and 10 percent were between 62 and 88.

The sales channels were grouped into four categories: sales representatives, offices, the client call center, and the Internet website. Currently, the website has the lowest traffic volume with respect to the other sales channels. The percentage distribution of sales channels was: offices, 40 percent; sales representatives, 35 percent; client call center, 15 percent; Internet, 10 percent.

Figure A.3 shows a "spider's web" representation of the relation between the binary variable "cancellation" and the four possible contact channels with the client. A thicker line means that more cases correspond to the relation between the categories the line connects. Conversely, a thinner line indicates a weaker relation. From this, the differences among the channels and the incidence of client cancellations can be observed. From the diagram in Figure A.3 and the supporting data, it is clear that the channel type influences client loyalty.

Figure A.4 shows a histogram of the normalized value for "frequency of treatment." In this figure we see that for a randomly selected sample of clients there is a gradual descent in cancellations as the frequency of treatments increases, the x-axis range going from 0 to 3 for average frequency of treatment.

A study of the cancellations by month indicated that the months with the greatest frequency of cancellation were: April, with 14.27 percent of the

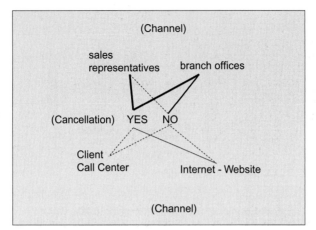

FIGURE A.3 Visualization of the grade of relation between "cancellation" and "channel"

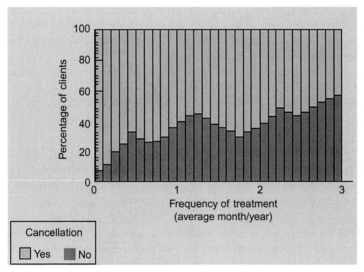

FIGURE A.4 Histogram of "frequency of treatment" (normalized)

cancellations; July, with 13.75 percent; February, with 12.41 percent; and March, with 10.34 percent. The months with fewest cancellations were September, with 5.4 percent; November, with 7.1 percent; and June, with 7.8 percent.

Figure A.5 shows a graph of the amount the clients paid for their policy versus the clients' ages. Figure A.5 illustrates where there is greater incidence of clients who cancel, in terms of the monthly premium in dollars and clients' ages in years. Certain areas of the graph show significant groups of clients with a high incidence of cancellations (greater than 75%).

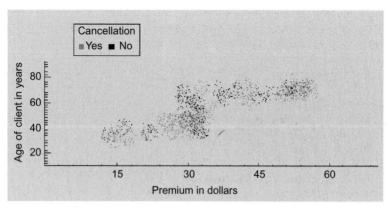

FIGURE A.5   Graph of "premium in dollars" versus "age of client in years"

Modeling Phase

In the modeling phases two types of data models were created: one that extracted descriptive profiles and tendencies from the data in the form of rules and decision trees; and another that was a black box high precision model to indicate which clients were the most likely to cancel. Two distinct types of data samples were used to create the models: one to train the model, and the other to test the precision of the trained model. This sampling process could then be repeated for different (distinct) extractions in order to check that the average results were consistent (this is called n-fold cross validation).

Modeling Phase

Train/Test Datasets – Class Imbalance

With respect to the distribution of the data samples: for training, the distribution of records were balanced out with respect to the output label, given that in the original data the distribution of the cancellations with respect to the non-cancellations in one year was 20 percent and 80 percent, respectively. For training datasets, 50:50, 40:60, and 60:40 balances (for n samples) were tried, testing on distinct datasets whose distribution was equal to the original (real) data (20:80). This was important for the model to be able to predict the "true positives" and "true negatives" with an equally high precision (see Chapter 9, the section "Modeling Concepts and Issues"). Not taking the class imbalance into account could result in poor precision for the training model for the minority class (cancellations) or a splendid precision for the model on the training data but poor precision for the minority category (cancellations) on the test datasets.

For data modeling, after several tests were run with a diversity of variables, those that gave the best result were: age, gender, relation, premium, frequency of treatment, the ratio of time since last treatment with frequency of treatment, age of the client when the policy was first registered, and channel. The output of the model was the cancellation indicator: "yes" or "no."

Data Modeling

Evaluation of Results

Various groups of tests (*n*-fold) were carried out in order to validate the precision and consistency of the data models. To measure the success of the models, they were executed against the totality of the extracted samples (30,000 records). This yielded (i) the number of correct identifications for the cancellations (true positives) and (ii) the number of records that the model said were cancellations (true positives + false positives). For each execution of the model (i) was divided by (ii), giving a percentage, which is the precision. For example, in test 1 the precision was 78 percent, in test 2 it was 75 percent, and in test 3 it reached 81 percent. The true/false negatives could be analyzed in a similar manner, yielding the complete "confusion matrix" (see Chapter 9, "Evaluation of the Results of Data Models").

The definitive test was to execute the models to predict cancellations for a future time period, for example, the next quarter. Thus, at the end of the quarter it would be possible to know which clients really did cancel and, of these, how many had been predicted by the model.

Deployment: Using the Information and the Production Version

The first application of the information derived from the study was for the marketing and customer service departments to identify the client profiles with the highest risk of cancellation. Knowing who these clients were, they could carry out appropriate preventive actions.

The second application of the information was to improve the insurance company's understanding of the causes of cancellation, together with the profiles of the highest-risk clients, and the interrelation among the different factors involved. This information could, for example, motivate the company to re-engineeer the customer service department's operational processes, or to initiate a new plan for capturing data about clients and their tendencies with respect to contracting the company's services and products.

The rules shown below contain information about the client profiles with respect to the loyalty flag. These rules, along with the predictive models, can be used by the customer service department in making decisions, based on documented studies, concerning loyalty campaigns.

One of the most precise rules for clients who cancel is Rule 3, which indicates that if the beneficiary is the wife of the policy holder and the premium is between 24 and 38 dollars, then 250 (training) cases canceled their policy. The precision for this rule is 95 percent.

Among the rules for clients who don't cancel, the most precise is Rule 4, which indicates that if the premium is over 24 dollars, and if the time since the last treatment is between 5 and 30 weeks, and if the ratio of the weeks since the last treatment with the treatment frequency is less than or equal to 0.75, then 1230 cases did not cancel their policy. The precision for this rule is 92 percent.

As we have seen, the ideal rule is precise and also has a lot of corresponding cases. In the example rules, the number of cases in each rule has to be compared with the total number of cases in the sample.

Data Modeling

Evaluation of Rule Precision

The rule induction technique assigns a "train" precision to each rule (in the model) that is fixed relative to the training data. When the test data is run, in order to obtain a "test" precision for each rule, it can be executed as SQL against the test data file loaded into a relational database. Then the output label (Y/N) can be evaluated as a confusion matrix in terms of true/false positives and true/false negatives.

Examples of Rules for Clients Who Cancel

```
RULE 1:
        IF PREMIUM ≤ 36
        AND WEEKS_SINCE_LAST _TREATMENT > 26
        THEN Y (770 cases and 89% precision)
RULE 2:
        IF PREMIUM BETWEEN 24 AND 30
        THEN Y (550 cases and 92% precision)
RULE 3:
        IF RELATION = WI
        AND PREMIUM BETWEEN 24 AND 28
        THEN Y (250 cases and 95% precision)
RULE 4:
        IF GENDER = M
        AND PREMIUM ≤ 50
        AND WEEKS_SINCE_LAST_TREATMENT > 30
        THEN Y (250 cases and 89% precision)
RULE 5:
        IF PREMIUM ≤ 24
        THEN Y (810 cases and 90% precision)
RULE 6:
        IF PREMIUM BETWEEN 48 AND 54
        THEN Y (450 cases and 93% precision)
```

Examples of Rules for the Most Loyal Clients

RULE 1:
    IF AGE > 61
    AND PREMIUM > 44
    AND WEEKS_SINCE_LAST_TREATMENT $\leq$ 30
    AND WEEKS_SINCE_LAST_TREATMENT
                 / TREATMENT_FREQUENCY > 0.15
    THEN N (850 cases and 90% precision)

RULE 2:
    IF AGE $\leq$ 75
    AND PREMIUM > 50
    THEN N (560 cases and 85% precision)

RULE 3:
    IF RELATION = TI
    AND PREMIUM > 50
    THEN N (1180 cases and 78% precision)

RULE 4:
    IF PREMIUM > 24
    AND WEEKS_SINCE_LAST_TREATMENT BETWEEN
             5 AND 30
    AND WEEKS_SINCE_LAST_TREATMENT
                  / TREATMENT_FREQUENCY $\leq$ 0.75
    THEN N (1230 cases and 92% precision)

RULE 5:
    IF PREMIUM BETWEEN 20 AND 28
    AND WEEKS_SINCE_LAST_TREATMENT
                  / TREATMENT_FREQUENCY BETWEEN 0.01 AND 1
    THEN N (350 cases and 92% precision)

RULE 6:
    IF AGE $\leq$ 50
    AND PREMIUM > 36
    THEN N (550 cases and 91% precision)

CASE STUDY 2: CROSS-SELLING A PENSION PLAN AT A RETAIL BANK

This case study examines how a retail bank conducted a data mining project whose objective was to cross-sell a pension plan to current customers who had already contracted other financial products.

The case study follows three generic project steps: definition of the data, data analysis, and model generation. The purpose of the data definition phase is to distinguish between internal and external data, and to define the output of the data model. The data analysis phase is divided into (i) visualization and (ii) definition of new derived variables and filtering of the variables with the lowest relevance. The model generation phase is divided into (i) clustering and profile identification and (ii) predictive modeling. Finally some screen shots of the Weka data mining software used for data processing, analysis, and modeling in this case study are shown.

Introduction

During a monthly meeting of the management team of a medium-sized retail bank, the marketing director, at the managing director's request, presented the cost calculations for the current postal publicity campaigns and the corresponding profitability. The marketing director was already aware of the bank's high expenditure on publicity sent to potential clients whose final conversion rate has been relatively small. Also, because of data quality problems (due to errors and missing data), product publicity material was sent to clients whose profile did not correspond to that of the product. For example, leaflets offering pension plans were sent to recent graduates.

Before the meeting, besides preparing the data relating to the costs and profitability of the campaigns, the marketing director spoke with the IT manager and with an external consultant who was an expert in CRM analytics. They defined a plan to make better use of the considerable repository of data the bank possessed about its clients, the products they had contracted, and the transactional data. They decided to select possible clients for a given publicity campaign and type of product using indicators extracted by data analysis.

The IT manager felt that greater accuracy would achieve an important saving in costs (reducing the number of publicity materials, leaflets, emails, SMSs) and human resources (time and effort involved in preparing the campaign and in follow-up), while increasing the response rate of the clients contacted. The marketing director suggested incorporating time-related information about the customer life cycle into the analysis. This would make it possible to send the appropriate information to the clients most likely to contract at the most opportune moment.

The plan was presented at the management team meeting, and although the managing director was initially skeptical, he finally gave the go-ahead to the initiative. However, he asked the IT manager and marketing director to optimize the time they dedicated to the project and to present the results within six months in order to assess what had been achieved by this approach.

The project was carried out using a diversity of data analysis techniques and tools: "traditional" statistics, "neural networks" and "rule induction," clustering models, and predictive models. After three months of analysis and development, the data model was tested with real clients, using the output variables to target a specific marketing campaign. At the end of the six-month period, the results were used to calculate the precision, cost/benefit, and return on investment (ROI). The IT manager and the marketing director presented the successful results at the management team meeting. The managing director's comment was: "This is all very well, but why didn't we think of this before?"

Data Definition

The project involved two types of data: "internal," meaning data the bank possessed about its clients and their transactions; and "external," meaning macro-economic, demographic, and contextual data. Finally, there was the output of the data model.

Internal Data

The dataset containing information about current clients who had already indicated their interest in the pension plan product represented the historical data. There was also socioeconomic data concerning the clients, as well as data indicating which of the bank's products they had contracted during the last year.

The data included: a sequential code uniquely identifying each client, the client's age, gender, average monthly income (indicating their economic level—salary, passive income, etc.), the type (in terms of population) of the residential area where they live (<10 thousand inhabitants, between 10 and 50 thousand, between 51 and 200 thousand, >200 thousand), their marital status (MA for married; SI for single; DI for divorced; WI for widow), the tax category of their last yearly tax return, their type of employment ("self-employed" or "employee"), vehicle owner (yes or no), and whether they have a savings account with the bank (yes or no), a current account with the bank (yes or no), or a home mortgage with the bank (yes or no).

External Data

The external data was the IRS ranges currently valid in the United States. The IRS ranges determine the percentage rates that taxpayers pay depending on their declared income. These are shown in Table A.3.

TABLE A.3 Marginal tax rates (United States 2011)

Rate Code	Income Base US$	Tax Rate
0	0–8,500	10%
1	8,501–34,500	15%
2	34,501–83,600	25%
3	83,601–174,400	28%
4	174,401–379,150	33%
5	>379,151	35%

Having the tax rate for each client provided some indication of their income level. However, in order to complete the picture we also needed an indicator of their solvency in terms of available cash that could be invested, for example, in a pension plan.

One possible way to do this was to estimate a person's monthly expenses: mortgage, food, energy bills, transport, clothes, children's school fees, car loan repayments, furniture, and so on. If all this information was not directly available, it would also be possible to study the levels of liquidity in the person's accounts (current account, deposit account, etc.) at the bank. The current

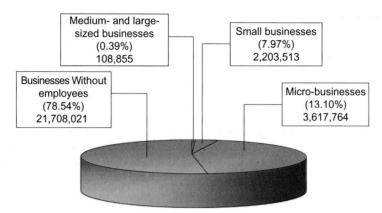

FIGURE A.6 Distribution of businesses in the United States by type (From: www.census.gov/econ/smallbus.html, 2011 data)

account would be especially relevant, being where the salary was transferred each month and where the major monthly expenses were debited. The amount of excess cash in the monthly cycle of income/expenditure would be evident.

Other external data was contextual. Given that the business objective was to offer a pension plan, it was important to know that in the United States there is a significant percentage of self-employed workers and micro-businesses. A different approach would be needed with respect to these people, compared with employees of medium- and large-sized companies.

Workers were classified as: liberal professions (lawyers, doctors, architects, etc.), freelance, micro-businesses with 1–4 employees, small businesses with 5–100 employees, and medium- and large-sized businesses with more than 100 employees on the payroll. In 2011 there were 27,757,676 businesses in the United States (www.census.gov/econ/smallbus.html, 2011 data). Of these, 78 percent were self-employed workers, and 13 percent were micro-businesses. This is summarized in Figure A.6.

Since self-employed workers and the employees of micro-businesses probably have the least financial cover with respect to their retirement (because larger companies often have their own collective or corporate pension plans), it seemed reasonable to focus the campaign on bank clients in these categories.

Output of the Data Model

The output of the model created for the first marketing campaign would be a prediction signaling if the client would acquire the pension plan or not. In the modeling phase two models would be defined: a descriptive, rule-based model that had a binary value (Yes/No) and a likelihood value as output, and a neural network black box model with high predictive precision that would also give a binary Yes/No as output together with a probability value (between 0.0 and 1.0).

Data Analysis

The available client data was analyzed according to: (i) visualization and (ii) definition of new derived variables and filtering of the variables with low relevance.

Visualization

Figure A.7 shows the distribution of the clients in terms of tax rate on their last tax declaration. Tax category "0" corresponds to the lowest tax rate (and therefore the lowest earners), and tax category "3" corresponds to the highest tax rate (and therefore the top earners). The results of this visualization were used later in the analysis.

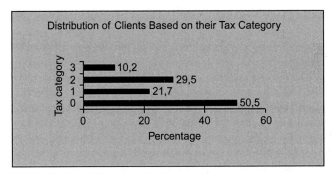

FIGURE A.7   Distribution of clients based on tax rate

Table A.4 shows the first sample of the input data and output flag (Pension Plan, Yes/No) used for the analysis. A quick look at the table reveals the different types of data, the distribution of the different values, and possible problems with respect to errors and missing values. All of the variables are categorical except for age, which is numerical. Of the categorical variables, six are binary (two possible values), and two ("population of district of residence" and "tax category") are ordinal.

Among the variables (or factors) available, three were selected: the tax category, the client's type of employment, and whether the client had contracted a pension plan or not. In Figure A.8, the thicker lines (indicating a stronger relation due to the greater number of corresponding cases) show that the pension plan especially attracted clients whose tax categories were 2 or 3 (that is, those with higher incomes).

Figure A.9 shows how the acceptation index of the pension plan is dependent on estimated available income, which is calculated based on the tax category (IRS) of the client's last tax declaration. In terms of this factor a clear segmentation among clients is evident: whereas the majority of clients with $2,000 or less available cash do not contract the pension plan, above this amount the response is much more positive.

TABLE A.4 Sample of input data, showing example values for input variables and output class (pension plan)

Age	Gender	Population of District of Residence	Marital Status	Tax Category: Income	Type of Employment	Savings Account	Current Account	Mortgage	Pension Plan
48	Female	>200 m	MA	1	SE	NO	YES	YES	NO
40	Male	10-50 m	MA	3	SE	YES	YES	NO	YES
51	Female	>200 m	MA	0	EM	YES	NO	NO	NO
23	Male	10-50 m	SI	3	EM	YES	NO	YES	YES
57	Female	<10 m	MA	0	EM	NO	YES	YES	NO
57	Male	10-50 m	DI	2	SE	NO	YES	YES	NO
22	Male	<10 m	MA	0	SE	YES	YES	NO	NO
58	Male	10-50 m	MA	0	EM	YES	YES	NO	NO
37	Female	>200 m	SI	2	EM	NO	NO	YES	YES
54	Male	>200 m	MA	2	EM	NO	NO	NO	YES

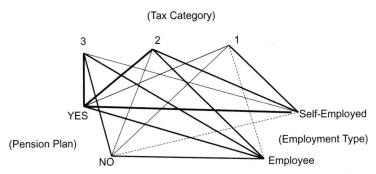

FIGURE A.8 Relation between tax rate, employment type (self-employed or employee), and whether the client is likely to contract a pension plan or not

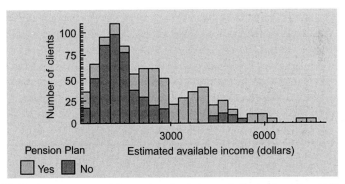

FIGURE A.9 Acceptance rate of the pension plan in terms of client estimated available income

Definition of New Derived variables and Filtering of Variables with Lowest Relevance

The variables were then *ranked* (ordered) in terms of their relevance to the business objective, which was the output flag (Yes/No) for contracting a pension plan. Once the ranking in descending order of the grade of relevance was created, the variables whose grade was less than a given threshold could be discarded.

To assign the threshold, the distribution of the grades of relevance for all the variables had to be studied in order to find a suitable inflexion point. To rank the variables, a model was created using the neural network technique with the Yes/No flag as the output. As a by-product, the neural network performed a correlation analysis of the input variables (based on the strength of connectivity/ activation between the internal neuron links) with respect to the output variable.

Table A.5 shows the ranking that was produced. The most relevant variable is "available income," followed by "tax rate," "type of employment," "marital status," "gender," and "age." The least important attributes are the possession of

TABLE A.5 Correlation analysis between the output variable "contract pension plan" and the input variables

Pension Plan Data Model: Neural Network Technique	
Input variables: 10	
Internal processing units: 3	
Output variables: 1	
Overall model precision: 65%	
Ranking of relevance of the input variables with respect to the output variable	
Available income	0.18039
Tax category	0.12798
Type of employment	0.09897
Marital status	0.09553
Gender	0.07534
Age	0.06630
Size of town of residence	0.04531
Current account	0.03483
Savings account	0.02261

a current account and of a savings account. Notably, this neural network model is not the definitive predictive one. It was used only to identify key variables in the data analysis phase.

The *ranking* of the variables by the neural network was confirmed using other techniques: simple correlation, visualization of graphs of variable pairs ("spider's web" diagram), and the results of a "rule induction" that included variables and attributes in the rules based on a heuristic that measured the value of the information they contributed to the model.

The new factor "available income" was derived by subtracting the client's estimated fixed expenses (mortgage, school fees, car loan, etc.) and other expenses (food, clothes, etc.) from his or her income as indicated by the tax category. This yielded the available income for each client, which, as Table A.5 shows, was more important than the income itself (indicated by the tax category). The model was trained several times on different folds in order to check that the ranking did not vary greatly.

From the distribution of the relevance values seen in Table A.5, an inflexion point (cut-off) was initially defined at 0.075. Later, however, the decision was made to include the variable "age" because other methods (e.g., Pearson cross-correlations) indicated that it had greater relevance.

Model Generation

In the modeling phase, two types of models were created: (i) the first was a *clustering*, in order to obtain profiles that could be interpreted for each *cluster*; (ii) the second was predictive, with the objective of obtaining the maximum precision possible.

Clustering and Profile Identification

A segmentation model (clustering) was created first, using the Kohonen technique. The result can be seen in Figure A.10, where the clusters are conveniently shown in two dimensions. The clustering technique created the majority of groups with a clear distinction between the clients most likely to contract a pension plan (indicated in white), and the least likely (indicated in black). As the next step the *clusters* were analyzed one by one to obtain the profile of the clients corresponding to each group.

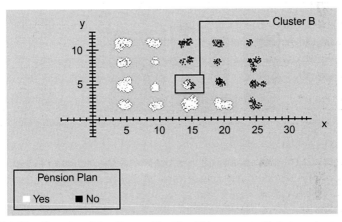

FIGURE A.10 Clustering of the clients to identify which groups are likely to contract a pension plan and which are not

Cluster B in Figure A.10, in the third column from the left and the second row from the bottom, was then chosen. The corresponding records for this cluster were selected and saved in a file. This file was then used as input to train a "rule induction" model, which yielded the decision tree that can be seen in Figure A.11. The first levels of the tree contain the most general variables, in this case, "available income" and "tax category." The lower levels contain the more specific variables, such as "age" and "type of employment." Given that cluster B contains a mixture of clients, some likely to contract and others unlikely to contract (white and black points, respectively in Figure A.10), the profiles in the decision tree describe both the likely clients (indicator after the arrow = YES) and the unlikely ones (indicator after the arrow = NO). The

```
AVAILABLE INCOME > 3021
    TAX CATEGORY ≤ 2
        MARITAL STATUS MARRIED
            TYPE OF EMPLOYMENT = EMPLOYEE → NO
            TYPE OF EMPLOYMENT = SELF EMPLOYED
                AGE < 35 → NO
                AGE ≥ 35 → YES
        MARITAL STATUS NOT MARRIED
            TYPE OF EMPLOYMENT = SELF EMPLOYED → YES
            TYPE OF EMPLOYMENT = EMPLOYEE
                AGE < 40 → NO
                AGE ≥ 40 → YES
    TAX CATEGORY > 2
        ...
AVAILABLE INCOME ≤ 3021
    ...
```

FIGURE A.11   Part of the decision tree showing characteristics of clients who are likely and unlikely to contract a pension plan, generated from the clusters created by the Kohonen technique

cluster contains a mixture of positive and negative cases because the majority of people in this cluster had a tax category of 2 or less, whereas the most affluent (likely) candidates had a tax category of 2 or more.

Predictive Models

To generate predictive models with the maximum possible precision two different techniques were used: a neural network and rule induction. Because they represent distinct methods, using both methods makes it possible to cross-check the consistency of the results.

Figure A.12 shows a set of rules, produced by the induction technique, that indicate the profiles of the clients most likely to contract a pension plan, together with the number of corresponding cases and the training precision. The bank was able to use these profiles to target their campaigns and define publicity. For example, the first rule in Figure A.12 indicates that one profile for likely clients is: available income greater than $3,021, and a tax category equal to 3. The model calculates that the (training) precision of Rule 1 is 92 percent. See the comments made in Case Study 1 about how to calculate the precision of individual rules on the test data.

With the neural network model, the "neural network" molds itself to the input and output data as the model is trained. This model generated two output variables for each client: (i) a predictive indicator Yes/No for contracting the pension plan, and (ii) a probability between 0 and 1 that the predictive indicator is correct. Table A.6 shows a sample of the model's output, with the clients ordered by the probability of contracting in the third column. The average global test precision of the model was 82 percent.

The bank was able to use the list in Table A.6 to target a mailing of information leaflets for the pension plan to the 5,000 clients whose probability of contracting was the greatest.

RULE 1:
  IF AVAILABLE INCOME > 3021
  AND TAX CATEGORY = 3
  THEN YES (850 cases and 92% precision)
RULE 2:
  IF AVAILABLE INCOME BETWEEN
    3021 AND 6496
  AND TAX CATEGORY > 1
  THEN YES (750 cases and 82% precision)
RULE 3:
  IF AGE ≥ 40
  AND AVAILABLE INCOME > 3021
  AND TAX CATEGORY = 2
  THEN YES (450 cases and 89% precision)
RULE 4:
  IF AGE ≥ 35
  AND TYPE OF EMPLOYMENT = SELF EMPLOYED
  AND TAX CATEGORY > 1
  THEN YES (940 cases and 81% precision)
RULE 5:
  IF MARITAL STATUS = MARRIED
  AND TYPE OF EMPLOYMENT = SELF EMPLOYED
  AND TAX CATEGORY = 3
  THEN YES (800 cases and 76% precision)
RULE 6:
  IF AVAILABLE INCOME > 6496
  AND TAX CATEGORY = 2
  THEN YES (1260 cases and 74% precision)

FIGURE A.12 Rules generated for the clients most likely to contract a pension plan

TABLE A.6 Clients with the highest probability of contracting a pension plan

Client ID	Contract Pension Plan?	Probability of Contracting
CI47190	YES	0.84
CI47171	YES	0.84
CI47156	YES	0.84
CI47212	YES	0.82
CI47235	YES	0.82
CI47251	YES	0.82
CI47159	YES	0.80
CI47245	YES	0.79
CI47285	YES	0.78
CI47310	YES	0.78

Data Modeling

Evaluation of Results

For both techniques, rule induction and neural network, it is assumed that an *n*-fold cross validation was performed to obtain an average precision and to check the models as generalized over different datasets. A confusion matrix indicating the true/false positives and true/false negatives was obtained, from which the overall precision and the recall could be calculated. This was explained in Chapter 9.

As mentioned in the previous case study, the rules show the train precision. To obtain the individual test precision for each rule, they could be coded as SQL and executed against the test data, conveniently loaded into a relational database.

Results and Conclusions

In this project, designed to identify a client's likelihood of contracting a pension plan, first the factors and variables for the available data were studied. In the analysis phase, visualization techniques were employed, using tables, histograms, pie charts, and "spider's web" diagrams. A neural network was also used to rank the variables in order of relevance to the business objective: the likelihood of contracting a pension plan.

In the modeling phase, a Kohonen clustering was created to identify groups of likely clients, and a "decision tree" was generated to check these profiles. Then predictive models were created using two distinct approaches: rule induction and neural networks.

The first result was to identify different profiles revealing the behavior and characteristics of the clients most likely to contract a pension plan. This information could then be used in the design of commercial campaigns and publicity messages. The second result, using the neural network and rule induction models, was a list of clients most likely to contract pension plan, ordered by their probability. The bank could use this list to target the mailing of publicity and informational material to the identified clients.

Example Weka Screens: Data Processing, Analysis, and Modeling

The general objective of these case studies is to illustrate data analysis and mining concepts, independent of specific software systems. However, this section contains screenshots of a data mining tool processing the data considered in the second case study. The data mining tool, Weka, was described in Chapter 19. For an in-depth treatment of Weka's practical usage, I recommend the following book:

Ian H. Witten, Eibe Frank, and Mark A. Hall, *Data Mining: Practical Machine Learning Tools and Techniques*, 3rd ed., Morgan Kaufmann, ISBN 978-0-12-374856-0, 2011.

The screenshots in Figures A.13 through A.19 illustrate the following themes: raw data input file (spreadsheet), preprocessing, visualization, attribute selection, clustering, and classification.

Figure A.13 shows the raw data input file, which is in spreadsheet format (outside of Weka). To be inputted into Weka, it has to be exported from the spreadsheet in ".csv" format, that is, a plain text file in which the first row is the column headers separated by commas, and the following rows are the data, each variable/column separated by a comma.

	A	B	C	D	E	F	G	H	I	J	K	L	M	N
1	id	age	gender	region	income	marital_st	tax_cat	type_empl	vehicle	save_acc	current_acc	mortgage	pension_plan	
2	CID0001	51	MALE	<10K	28200	MA	1	SE	NO	YES	YES	YES	YES	
3	CID0032	62	FEMALE	>200K	55250	SI	2	SE	NO	YES	YES	YES	YES	
4	CID0081	31	MALE	>200K	10000	MA	1	EM	NO	NO	YES	YES	YES	
5	CID0112	36	FEMALE	10K->50K	16500	MA	1	EM	NO	NO	YES	NO	NO	
6	CID0351	61	MALE	51K->200K	32500	MA	1	EM	YES	YES	NO	YES	NO	
7	CID0381	27	MALE	>200K	24000	MA	1	EM	NO	NO	NO	NO	YES	
8	CID0873	66	FEMALE	<10K	24500	WI	1	SE	YES	NO	NO	NO	NO	
9	CID0524	47	FEMALE	>200K	17000	WI	1	SE	NO	YES	NO	YES	NO	
10	CID0410	25	MALE	51K->200K	18000	MA	1	SE	NO	YES	YES	YES	YES	
11	CID0411	48	MALE	10K->50K	26000	MA	1	SE	NO	YES	YES	NO	NO	
12	CID0413	22	FEMALE	>200K	18000	MA	1	SE	YES	YES	YES	NO	YES	
13	CID0450	41	FEMALE	>200K	25000	MA	1	SE	YES	NO	NO	NO	YES	
14	CID0455	39	FEMALE	51K->200K	26000	SI	1	SE	YES	NO	NO	NO	NO	
15	CID1012	25	MALE	10K->50K	17000	SI	1	SE	YES	YES	YES	NO	YES	
16	CID1015	29	MALE	<10K	42000	MA	2	EM	NO	YES	NO	YES	YES	
17	CID1024	44	FEMALE	10K->50K	10000	SI	1	EM	NO	NO	NO	NO	NO	
18	CID1234	29	FEMALE	51K->200K	31000	MA	1	EM	YES	NO	NO	YES	YES	
19	CID8736	38	FEMALE	10K->50K	13000	MA	1	EM	NO	YES	YES	YES	NO	
20	CID2344	41	MALE	>200K	15000	MA	1	EM	YES	NO	YES	YES	NO	
21	CID0182	27	MALE	>200K	16000	SI	1	EM	YES	NO	YES	YES	NO	
22	CID8374	34	FEMALE	10K->50K	39000	MA	2	EM	YES	YES	NO	NO	YES	
23	CID3983	32	FEMALE	>200K	18000	SI	1	EM	YES	NO	YES	YES	YES	
24	CID1934	54	MALE	<10K	20000	MA	1	EM	NO	YES	YES	YES	NO	
25	CID1066	23	MALE	>200K	49000	WI	2	EM	YES	YES	YES	YES	YES	
26	CID1714	22	FEMALE	>200K	32000	MA	1	EM	NO	NO	NO	NO	YES	
27	CID1966	28	MALE	10K->50K	12000	SI	1	EM	NO	YES	YES	YES	NO	
28	CID1812	54	FEMALE	<10K	36000	MA	2	EM	NO	YES	YES	NO	NO	
29	CID1989	33	MALE	<10K	49000	WI	2	EM	YES	YES	NO	YES	YES	
30	CID1988	44	FEMALE	<10K	44000	MA	2	EM	YES	YES	YES	YES	YES	
31	CID1898	30	MALE	10K->50K	13000	SI	1	SE	YES	NO	YES	YES	NO	
32	CID1912	50	MALE	>200K	41000	MA	2	EM	YES	YES	YES	YES	YES	
33	CID1969	22	FEMALE	>200K	20000	MA	1	EM	NO	NO	YES	NO	YES	
34	CID2094	30	FEMALE	>200K	21000	MA	1	EM	YES	YES	YES	NO	YES	
35														
36														
37														
38														

BANK DATASET PENPLAN CROSSSELL

FIGURE A.13 Raw data input file in spreadsheet format

Figure A.14 contains the first Weka screenshot, in which the preprocess tab/module is selected, revealing that the data file has been loaded. In this module the variable types can be redefined (for example, changing "tax_cat" from its default numerical type to a categorical type). Also, the values of a numerical variable can be normalized, continuous numerical variables can be discretized, and sampling can be done, all using the filter option on the upper left of the screen. Once the preprocessing is done, the data file can be saved in Weka format, the output file having an "arff" suffix.

In Figure A.14 the "age" variable has been selected; the basic statistics of this variable are shown in the upper right, and its distribution is shown in the lower right. The distribution is overlaid with a selected nominal variable, which in this case is the binary output variable "pension_plan," where the darker gray signifies "Yes" and the lighter gray signifies "No." The customer ID can be retained in the dataset to be able to reference individual records, but it should

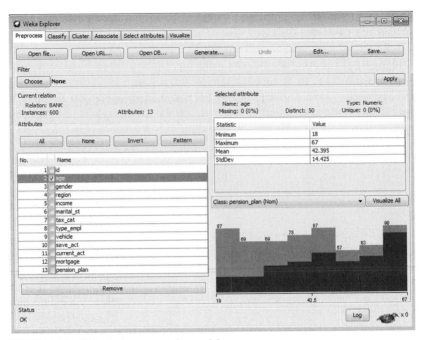

FIGURE A.14   Weka: Data preprocessing module

not be included as input for the data processing itself (clustering, modeling, analysis).

Figure A.15 shows the data visualization screen that by default plots every variable against every other variable and overlays a chosen categorical variable (in this case "pension_plan"). A zoom has been performed by clicking on one of the graphs to show the plot "income" versus "age" with "pension_plan" overlaid.

Figure A.16 displays the select attributes screen, which offers different methods for identifying the most significant variables in a dataset and for generating a reduced number of factors (attributes). In the figure, the principal components method has been used, which has derived 14 factors (attributes) comprised of the original variables weighted by different coefficients. The first column of ranked attributes is a measure of the relative importance of the corresponding factor, which ranges from 0.8151 for the first factor to 0.0284 for the fourteenth factor.

Figure A.17 exhibits the clustering module, in which the Simple K-means clustering method with default values has been chosen. Weka always assigns default values, which usually work reasonably well but can be tweaked by more expert users for a specific dataset and requirements. K-means has generated two clusters from the data (because "-N 2" was specified in the input parameters), and the centroid values of each input variable are shown for each cluster

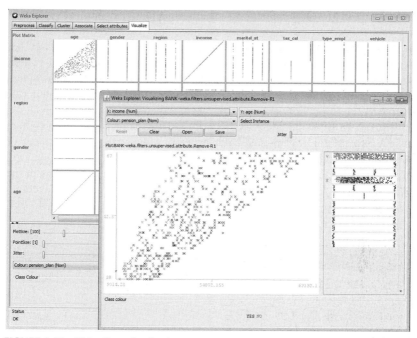

FIGURE A.15 Weka: Data visualization

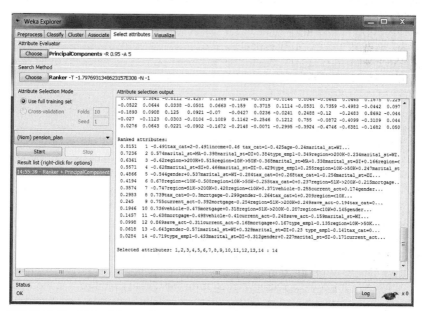

FIGURE A.16 Weka: Select attributes

(mode for categorical variables and mean or median for numerical variables). The input variables are: "age," "income," and "tax_cat." As can be seen from the option chosen on the left (classes to clusters evaluation), "pension_plan" has been assigned as an evaluation variable (not as an input variable, of course, since it would influence the clustering). This makes it possible to see how well the different class values (YES, NO) correspond to the different clusters (the matrix on the lower right shows this).

The results show that the great majority of cases of pension_plan = NO are assigned to cluster 0 (248 cases out of 259). However, the assignment of pension_plan = YES to cluster 1 reveals a more ambiguous distribution (153 cases out of 341). The cases in the clusters can be interpreted in terms of the centroid values for the input variables. For example, the centroid (average) value for "income" for cluster 0 is 20,945, whereas for cluster 1 it is 45,014, which means that the higher earners correspond to cluster 1.

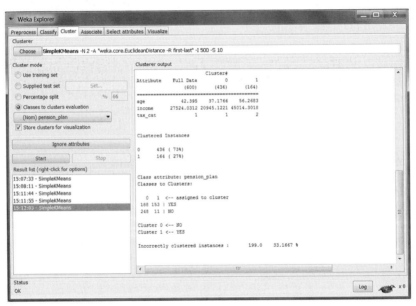

FIGURE A.17   Weka: Cluster

Figure A.18 shows the classify module, in which the classifier option J48 (Quinlan's C4.5 tree induction algorithm) has been chosen. On the upper right is the list of attributes, the output attribute defined on the left as "pension_plan." By default, a 10-fold cross validation is applied to the input data. On the lower right is part of the induced decision tree.

Figure A.19 shows a second screen from the classify module. On the right are results statistics, including the precision, recall, and true/false positive rates, as well as the confusion matrix of the predicted classification versus the real

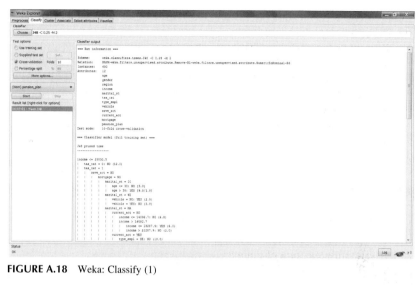

FIGURE A.18   Weka: Classify (1)

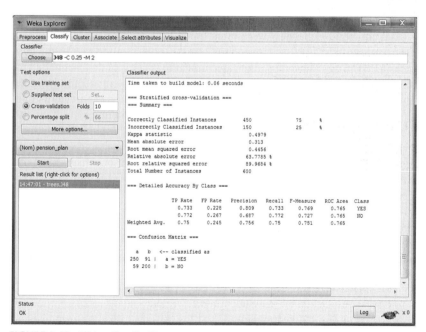

FIGURE A.19   Weka: Classify (2)

classification. (See Chapter 9 for an explanation of these metrics.) There is a reasonable precision for each of the output classes (80.9% for pension_plan = YES and 68.7% for pension_plan = NO), and the false positives do not surpass 27 percent for either output class.

CASE STUDY 3: AUDIENCE PREDICTION FOR A TELEVISION CHANNEL

This case study looks at how to represent historical audience statistical data in order to predict the audience share for a TV program in a given time slot, taking into consideration the programs being shown on competing channels. This case study is somewhat different from the first two, since it involves first determining how to conceptually represent the data so predictions can be made from it, the time window being a critical aspect. The available data is defined, and how to represent the data and the TV emissions environment is formulated. Then the data is analyzed. Finally, modeling approaches for predicting audience share by program and for publicity blocks are considered.

Introduction

During a monthly meeting of the management team the executives of the Audience Research and Measurement Department at the television channel were under pressure because of two business dynamics: other channels who competed for audience share and client companies who contracted advertising space.

The competitor channels were often quick to copy good ideas and design their program offerings to "counteract" the channel's programs, using gimmicks to "steal" its viewers. At the same time, the success of the channel's programs depended on the creativity, innovation, and talent of the program directors and designers, the presenters, the actors, and the content and its relevance to current social trends. The channel was also committed to "quality" television: good reporting and investigative journalism, current affairs, educational programs, theater, quality music, minority sports, and so on.

The scheduling—the planning of which programs to air on which day and in what time slot—was becoming increasingly complex due to the diversity of programs and channels available on television, the actions of the competitors, and fitting the publicity into "blocks" between programs. The audience share of a channel at a given moment depended on various factors: the time of day, the programs airing on other key channels at the same time, the presence of a "star" in a program, and the exclusivity of a broadcast, for example, a specific football or basketball game.

The director of the Audience Research and Measurement Department proposed developing some IT support tools for designing the programming schedule based on the channels criteria and to counteract competitors' programming schedules. The tools could also be used as a support for selling publicity slots, improving the audience share estimates. Also, depending on the characteristics of the publicity, the tools could be used to validate the fit of the programming with the demographic profile for a particular time of day and with respect to the programs being shown, demonstrating that it is a better fit than the programming of the competitor channels for that time slot.

This type of tool is complex and needs constant updating due to the continuous evolution of the television environment. It uses as input the historical data of audience statistics (ratings supplied by the Nielsen Company), demographic data of the viewers, and statistics of the program share by time period (minute by minute). A key factor used for comparison is the time window, together with the variables and indicators derived from it.

Data Definition

Following the management team meeting, the IT director gave his support to the initiative, and work started on the first phase: selecting the most relevant variables. The channel found and contracted a consultant who had worked on several audience prediction projects. The consultant recommended the following initial input variables for the scheduling model: time of day, formatted as hour and minutes; day of the week; month; program genre; and program subgenre. Also, for each competitor channel, the program and subprogram genres were added as input variables.

The initial input file was a "flat" text file, 10 variables (or columns) wide and approximately 5,000 records long. The records corresponded to the programming between 19:00 and 23:00 hours (peak time) for the first six months of the year for the following channels: OBJECTIVE_CHANNEL (the channel doing the study), PBS, ABC, CBS, NBC, Fox, and This TV (cable network). The initial fields used were: channel, day of the week, date, hour of the day, emission, duration, program genre, share, live or prerecorded, and indicator of public holiday.

To generate the audience model, data relating to programs already aired and the (historical) shares they obtained were supplied so the model could detect the tendencies and interrelations existing among the different factors. Then when the model was presented with future programs it would be able to predict their audience share. The modeling techniques used were neural networks and rule induction.

For this project, six months of historical data of the OBJECTIVE_CHANNEL's broadcasts were used. With this data, two initial models were generated and formed the basis for the definitive scheduling simulator model.

As a starting point, the default Nielsen ratings file of "genres" of broadcasts for all channels was used. This file contains one record for each minute of broadcasting, and the columns correspond to the share data and the genre of each broadcast repeated for each channel. From this data a new file was created with just one record for each OBJECTIVE_CHANNEL broadcast. That is, all the records for each minute corresponding to a broadcast were aggregated, and the share of the broadcast was considered the mean value of the individual shares per minute. To each broadcast record in this file were added data of the broadcasts of competitor channels (which had been aggregated in the same way) as additional columns.

The genres file, generated by the process just described, became the input file for the analysis and modeling steps of the project. It contained 5,000 records, each record representing a broadcast and consisting of about 100 columns of data.

Data Analysis

After studying the problem of predicting the audience share in a given moment, the program schedule executives emphasized that audience share had both a strong time aspect and a strong contextual aspect. The time aspect existed because the programming was highly dependent on the time of day. The contextual aspect existed because of the diversity of channels in the United States: one major public educational channel (PBS) and its regional and local affiliates; four major commercial channels (ABC, CBS, NBC, and Fox), Spanish language channels, cable, and satellite (This TV, Create, Disney Channel, Discovery Channel, etc.). Shopping networks and religious television (The Worship Network, TBN, Smile of a Child, etc.) also had a significant presence. This study considered the four major commercial channels, the public channel (PBS), and one cable channel that had recently experienced a significant increase in audience share—in total, six channels. Therefore, at any given moment, there were six different "contexts" competing and mutually interacting.

The first task was to consider the OBJECTIVE_CHANNEL's own environment and predict the audience share of a certain program. This program had its own characteristics: genre, subgenre, duration, start time, star actor/actress, and so on. The program's audience share could also be influenced by the broadcasting that preceded it and that followed it on the same channel. Some derived variables were created to provide this information to the data model in the form of input columns. For convenience, the "target" emission was regarded as existing in a "window" of time together with the preceding program and the following program.

With regard to programs on competiting channels, the first task was to define what was a competitor program. As a criterion, the grade of overlap in time of a program on another channel with a program on this channel was used. If it coincides more than X percent, it was considered a competitor program. Figure A.20 shows a graphical representation of this scheme. Furthermore, we can collect the same information for competitor programs as for this channel's program, that is, genre, subgenre, duration, start hour, star actor/actress, and so on.

The initial variable the model produced as output was the "audience share" as a numerical value with two digits after the decimal point. With this the share of a broadcast could be predicted, given the input data. The historical data of broadcasts and shares were taken from the Nielsen ratings, which rate all the TV companies in America. The shares are divided by age ranges of TV viewers (0 to 4 years, 4 to 12 years, 13 to 24 years, 25 to 44 years, etc.).

At this point there was a data file aggregated by programs of the OBJECTIVE_ CHANNEL with the broadcast, audience share, and other derived fields for the first half of the calendar year during prime time (19:00 to 23:00). This file contains 3,500 records, each record having 100 columns and corresponding to one program.

To train and test the model, the complete dataset was ordered chronologically by date/time stamp. The first 60 percent of the records in the dataset were

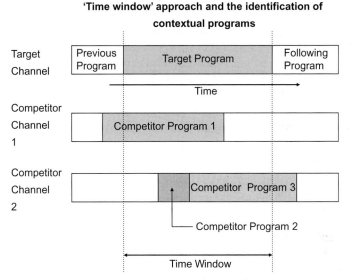

'Time window' approach and the identification of contextual programs

FIGURE A.20   Identification of competitor programs based on time overlap

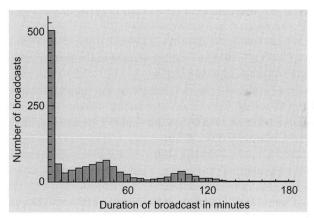

FIGURE A.21   Distribution of the variable "duration of broadcast"

used for training, and the remaining 40 percent for testing. As usual, samples were taken from the train and test datasets to follow an *n*-fold procedure to see if the model extrapolated over time.

Figure A.21 shows that a relatively high percentage of the broadcasts had a duration of between 1 and 5 minutes (first bar from the left of the histogram). This is because "program previews" and "auto-publicity," which the TV channels insert between broadcasts, were also counted as programs.

In Figure A.22, following the groupings of genres used, it is evident that 45 percent of the programs were news (including current affairs), whereas only 4.2 percent of the programs were football (National Football League [NFL] games).

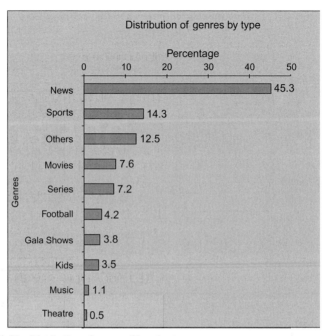

FIGURE A.22   Distribution of genres of broadcasts

The genres of "sports" and "football" contained individual broadcasts with an audience share of more than 40 percent.

The audience shares of the broadcasts in the extracted data file varied between 0 and 45 points. The average value of the shares was 18 points, whereas the standard deviation was 7 points. Among all the broadcasts, there were only 45 which had a share above 40 points.

Figure A.23 shows the audience share on the y-axis, with the broadcast hour/minute (as time of day) on the x-axis. In Figure A.23, the distribution of the share over time shows several differentiating tendencies which are indicated in light gray for the time windows: the first being 19:00 to 20:00 and the second from 20:00 to 21:00.

Audience Prediction by Program

With reference to the distribution of audience share shown in Figure A.23 and what was discussed in the previous section, an individual data model was created for each time window. This is because it was easier to create precise models for each time window than to create one global model for the whole share range and all the broadcast times.

Also, instead of predicting an exact numerical value for the share, a higher precision was obtained using a categorization of the numerical share. Thus the

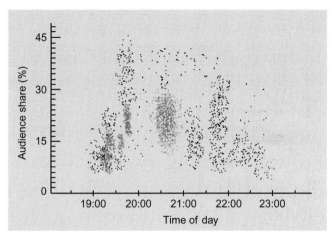

FIGURE A.23 Distribution of the audience share in terms of the hour of broadcast

share category was predicted as an ordinal value, for example, 0–4 percent, 5–8 percent, 9–12 percent, and so on. Finally, greater precision was obtained by predicting specific genres with distinct models rather than all the genres together. For example, distinct predictive data models were trained for the sports genre and the news genre.

The programs that were predicted most successfully included: *The Today Show* (NBC), *Good Morning America* (ABC), *Piers Morgan Tonight* (9 pm show; CNN), *American Idol*, *CBS Evening News*, *The Late Show*, *Celebrity Apprentice*, *Jeopardy*, and *The Big Bang Theory*.

The programs most difficult to predict included: *NFL Championship Game*, *NBA Regular Season* (basketball), *Phoenix Open* (golf), *World Boxing Championships*, *Grey's Anatomy*, *CSI: NY*, *The Voice*, *Undercover Boss*, and *Survivor: One World*.

The programs with the best predictive accuracy were primarily news and variety shows. On the other hand, the programs most difficult to predict were from the sports genre, especially NFL games, given the high corresponding share.

Audience Prediction for Publicity Blocks

This section examines a topic that seems even more of a challenge than predicting the audience share for programs: predicting the audience share and its evolution during the publicity blocks between programs. In terms of data modeling, the publicity space can be simulated using an adequate model, although the share is more difficult to predict than the program share because of the greater fragmentation, shorter duration, and other special characteristics. However, the capacity to model the context of the publicity announcements is useful for justifying the rates charged and for negotiating with the companies who advertise.

Figure A.24 shows that a publicity block can have a structure that is quite complex. It can contain a diversity of spots and announcements, each with a different duration, target program of exit and entrance, and one or more program previews. Also, this structure may vary: for example, sometimes the emission goes directly back into the objective program without showing the entrance title, and the outgoing program may be different from the incoming program.

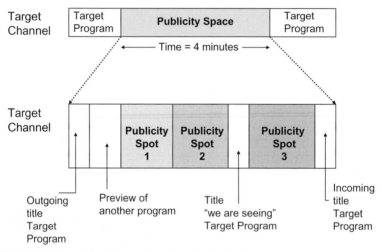

FIGURE A.24   Example of the structure of a publicity block

Figure A.25 shows the evolution of the audience share during the publicity space. There is an initial fall (zone A) that reaches a minimum (zone B) once fully inside the block of announcements. There is a "false alarm" entrance back into the program (zone C) that causes a percentage of the people who were using the non-program time away from the television to come back to the TV screen. And there is a last increment when the viewers anticipate that the program really is going to recommence.

The least expensive publicity would typically be placed in the central part of the publicity space, which is zone B in the figure.

This programming task is actually even more complex, since the programming schedulers can make changes in real time to the publicity blocks. Sitting before a bank of TV screens, a team of programmers simultaneously watch all the key channels. If they observe that a competitor's broadcast goes into a publicity block, they can also cut a program's broadcasting and go into publicity. This is considered an "anti-zapping" measure, that is, if a TV viewer sees that the programming he or she is watching has shifted into a publicity block, a certain percentage will "zap" to see what's showing on other channels. If they see

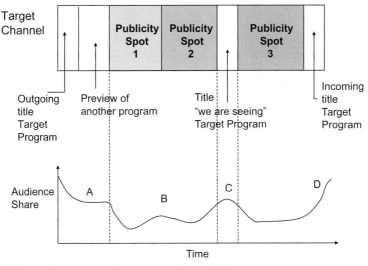

FIGURE A.25   Changes in audience share during a publicity space

that there is also publicity on the other channels, they may return to the original channel. Thus they will not only see the original channel's publicity but also are more likely to stay tuned to its broadcast. Another consideration would be the effect of pay television channels on non-pay channels, and how they mutually compete.

Glossary

Note: This chapter is available on the companion website: http://booksite. elsevier.com/9780124166028.

ABSTRACT

This glossary gives brief descriptions for a selection of specific key terms and phrases that appear throughout the book and are commonly used in the commercial data mining field.

BIBLIOGRAPHY

This section lists a selection of books and information sources that will allow the reader to go into more depth about some of the areas covered in the book. Note that specific references (books, articles, information sources) related to the material in the chapters are included in those chapters. The references are divided into seven sub-topics: books based on specific data mining software applications; statistical books; books that include case studies; web mining; data mining methodology, data warehouse, and CRM; expert systems; and general references to websites dedicated to data analysis.

Data Mining Software

Morelli, T., Shearer, C., Buecker, A., 2010. IBM SPSS Predictive Analytics: Optimizing Decisions at the Point of Impact. IBM Redbook REDP-4710–00, IBM Corporation (IBM SPSS Modeler).

Novo, J., 2004. Drilling Down. Turning Customer Data into Profits with a Spreadsheet. Booklocker .com Inc. ISBN: 978-1591135197 (Spreadsheet).

Parr Rud, O., 2000. Data Mining Cookbook: Modeling Data for Marketing, Risk, and CRM. Wiley, New York, NY (SAS Enterprise Miner).

Witten, I.H., Frank, E., Hall, M.A., 2011. Data Mining: Practical Machine Learning Tools and Techniques, third ed. Morgan Kaufmann, Burlington, MA, ISBN: 978-0-12-374856-0 (Weka).

Statistics

Boslaugh, S., Watters, P.A., 2008. Statistics in a Nutshell: A Desktop Quick Reference. O'Reilly Media, Sebastopol, CA, ISBN: 978-0596510497.

Nisbet, R., John Elder, I.V., Miner, G., 2009. Handbook of Statistical Analysis and Data Mining Applications. Elsevier, Amsterdam, ISBN: 978-0-12-374765-5.

Case Studies

Chakrabarti, S., Cox, E., Frank, E., Güting, R., Han, J., Jiang, X., Kamber, M., Lightstone, S., Nadeau, T., Neapolitan, R.E., Pyle, D., Refaat, M., Schneider, M., Teorey, T., Witten, I., 2008. Data Mining: Know It All. Morgan Kaufmann, Burlington, MA.

Miner, G., John Elder, I.V., Hill, T., Nisbet, R., Delen, D., Fast, A., 2012. Practical Text Mining and Statistical Analysis for Non-structured Text Data Applications. Academic Press, Waltham, MA.

Web Mining

Berry, M.J.A., Linoff, G.S., 2002. Mining the Web: Transforming Customer Data. John Wiley and Sons Ltd., Hoboken, NJ.

Sweeney, S., 2010. 101 Ways to Promote Your Web Site, eighth ed. Maximum Press. ISBN: 978-1931644785.

Data Mining Methodology, Data Warehouse, and CRM

Cabena, P., Hadjinian, P., Stadler, R., Verhees, J., Zanasi, A., 1997. Discovering Data Mining: From Concept to Implementation. Prentice Hall, Upper Saddle River, NJ, ISBN: 978-0137439805.

Devlin, B., 1997. Data Warehouse: From Architecture to Implementation. Addison Wesley, Boston, MA, ISBN: 978-0201964257.

Tsiptsis, K., Chorianopoulos, A., 2010. Data Mining Techniques in CRM: Inside Customer Segmentation. John Wiley and Sons Ltd., Hoboken, NJ, ISBN: 978-0-470-74397-3.

Expert Systems

Beynon-Davies, P., 1991. Expert Data Systems: A Gentle Introduction. McGraw-Hill, New York, NY, ISBN: 978-0077072407.

Hertz, D.B., 1987. The Expert Executive: Using AI and Expert Systems for Financial Management, Marketing, Production and Strategy. Blackie Academic & Professional, London, ISBN: 0-471-89677-2.

Websites Dedicated to Data Analysis

AudienceScience: www.digimine.com. A website dedicated to data mining services applied to marketing.

Drilling Down: www.jimnovo.com. The website of Jim Novo, author of *Drilling Down*, which offers an original spreadsheet approach to analytical CRM.

KDNuggets: www.kdnuggets.com. A website created and maintained by a data mining pioneer, Gregory Piatetsky Shapiro. It has up-to-the-day information about data mining software, jobs, news, datasets, consulting, companies, education and training courses, meetings, seminars, congresses, webcasts, and forums.

Index

Note: Page numbers followed by *b* indicate boxes, *f* indicate figures, *t* indicate tables and '*e*' indicate online chapters, *np* indicate table footnotes and *ge* indicate glossary terms. The numbers indicated in bold signifies key page or range of pages in the book for the given term.

A

Access, 49, 164, 183–184, 193
Address, 9, 27*b*, 28*b*, 29*b*, 52, 69–71, 70*t*, 71*t*, 156, 181–182, e58*ge*
Age of client, 91*f*, 92, 243–244, 248*f*
Analysis
    analysis of text, 171
    data analysis, 1, 2, 2*f*, 3, 4*f*, 5, 6, 6*f*, 7, 8, 13, 15, 17, 18*t*, 20, 59–60, 67, 79, 80, 81–83, 90, 93, 94–95, 98, 103, 105–118, **119–136**, 137, 167–168, 171, 181–194, 191*f*, 195, 196–197, 199, 199*f*, 229–238, 239, 241, 242, 243, 251, 252, 255–258, e27–e42, 262, 270–272, e56*ge*
    text analysis, e8
Associations, 6, 121–122, 230
Atypical values, **58–60**, 73, 150–151
Automobile, 21*b*, 28*b*, 30, 95, 96*t*, 198–199, e3–e5, e6–e8, e8*f*

B

Bank, 5, 22*b*, 25*t*, 43, 46, 47, 47*f*, 52, 65, 83–84, 83*t*, 87–88, 90, 91, 92, 93–97, 93*f*, 96*t*, 98–99, 98*f*, 102, 104, 105, 116–117, 123, 131–133, 135, 196–197, 198–199, 220, 229, 241, **251–267**, e1–e2, 274–275
Behavior, 1, 2, 13, 14, 15, 26–27, 74, 129–130, 262, e6, e21–e23, e24, e28, e43, e44, e45–e46
Beneficiary, 128–129, 242–243, 244*t*, 249
Benefit, 8, **9**, 11, 12–13, 43–44, 234, 252, e55*ge*
Benefits, 9–10, 153–154
Binary, 3, 23, 49, 52, **53–54**, 97, 104, 107, 113–114, 115*f*, 120–121, 145, 149, 150, 151, 152, 235–236, 246, 254, 255, 263–264
Business intelligence, 23, 81, 167–168
Business objective, 2, 6, 7–16, 17, 18*t*, 19, 21–23, 23*b*, 24–26, 27–30, 27*b*, 36–37, 38, 39*b*, 42, 42*b*, 45–46, 49, 67–78, 79, 80, 81–83, 86, 87–90, 92, 95, 98, 99–102, 103, 104, 105, 110–111, 126, 135, 137, 139, 152, 156, 159, 181, 182–183, 192–193, 199, 232, 233–234, **241**, 242, 254, e1, e2, e6, e15–e26, e27, **e55***ge*, e58*ge*, 257, 262

C

C4.5, 99, 146, 147–148, 234–236, 266
C5.0, 99, 146, 148–149, 229, 230, 236, 237, 238
Car, 21*b*, 24, 25*t*, 26*t*, 28*b*, 29*b*, 30, 32, 41, 51, 53–54, 131–132, 136, 253–254, 258, e9
Card
    customer card, 17, **26–38**, 103, 104, 121–122, 129–130
    loyalty card, 18*t*, **26–38**, 49–66, 69, 78
Category, 7, 12–13, 15, 19, 23, 24–26, 27–30, 32, 36, 38, 45, 49, 50–51, 53–54, 54*f*, 55, 60, 64–66, 76*t*, 78, 81, 83*t*, 84, 89–90, 90*t*, 91, 92, 94*t*, 95–97, 96*t*, 101, 107–109, 112, 120–121, 121*f*, 123, 126–128, 134, 138, 140, 141–142, 144, 149, 151, 152, 160–163, 161*t*, 166, 178, 186, 188–190, 189*t*, 190*f*, 191*t*, 192*t*, 197–198, 199, 200–201, 223, 224, 229–231, 242, 245–246, 248, 253, 254, 255, 256*t*, e3, e6, e8, e15, e18–e19, e20, e24, e43, e45, e48, 258, 259–260, 272–273
Categorical, 3, 10, 11, 14, 49–66, 84, 90–92, 101, 104, 107–109, 119, 120, 124, 126, 137–158, 223–224, 229–230, 231–232, 233–234, 235–236, 255, 264–266
    nominal categorical, 53, 60*f*
Classification, 20, 64, 77, 90, 92, 93, 137–138, 144–149, 152, 186–187, 200–201, 202, 226, 229, e7, e8, e21, e43, e50–e51, e52–e53, **e55***ge*, e58*ge*, 230, 231–232, 234–235, 263, 266–267